The Car

Marshall Cavendish
London & New York

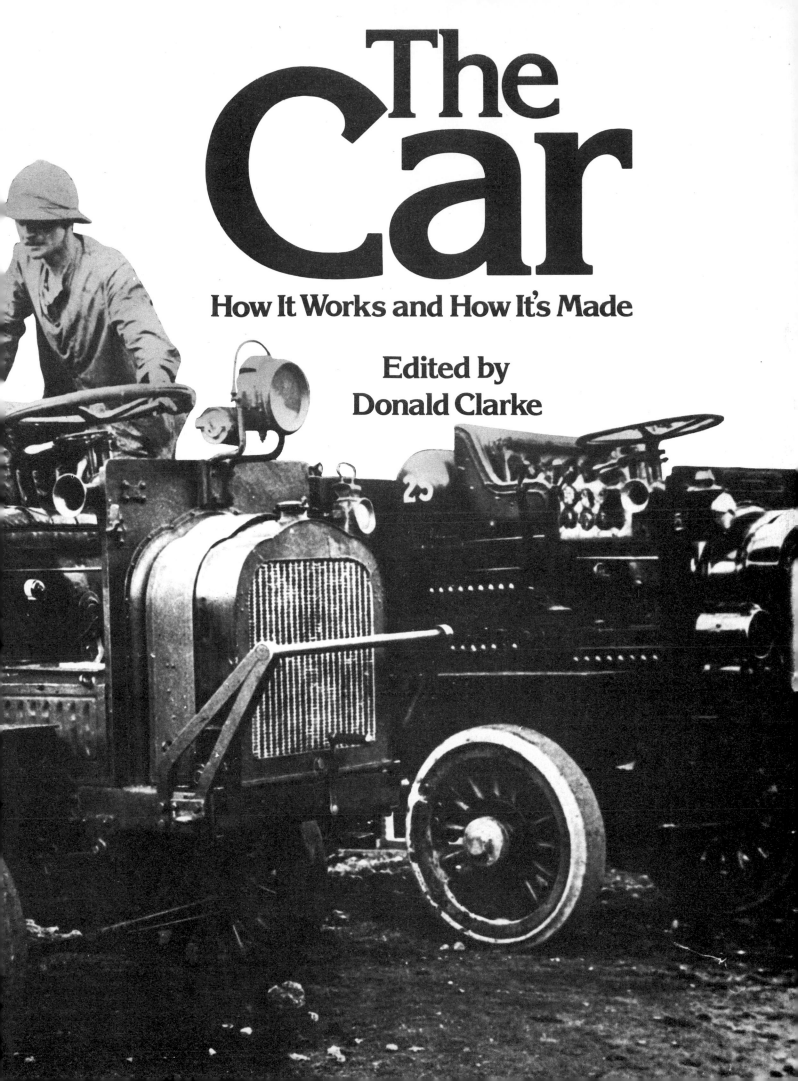

The Car

How It Works and How It's Made

Edited by
Donald Clarke

Contents

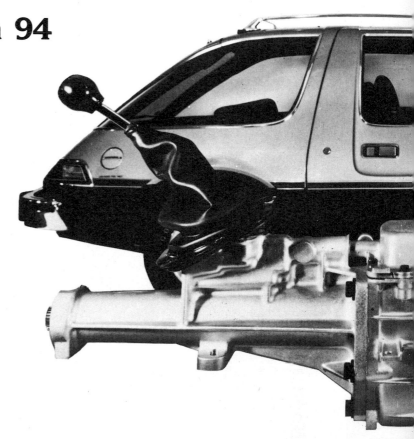

On the previous two pages: Jeffery, a predecessor company of American Motors Corporation, began making the Quad four-wheel-drive truck in Kenosha, Wisconsin, in 1911. By 1918 nearly 21,500 had been built for America and her wartime Allies, making Jeffery the largest truck manufacturer in the world.

On these pages: One of AMC's newest products is the Pacer, which has a new optional four-speed gearbox. The new gearbox weighs only 55 pounds because of its extensive use of die-cast aluminium parts.

Edited by Donald Clarke
Designed by Graham Dudley

Published by Marshall Cavendish Books Limited
58 Old Compton Street
London W1V 5PA

First printing: 1978
© Marshall Cavendish Limited 1974, 1975, 1978

Printed in Great Britain
by Collier Searle, Acton, London, N.W.10
ISBN 0 85685 453 0

Note: British spellings are used
throughout this book; for example,
'tyre', 'carburetter'. Where the
American equivalent is a different
word, it appears in square brackets
after the British; for example,
silencer [muffler], petrol [gasoline].

Introduction

Rapid technological advance during the nineteenth century made the automobile a reality. Henry Ford's mastery of assembly line construction put America on wheels, ending the isolation of rural communities and setting an example of industrial efficiency for the rest of the world to emulate. The car is not an unmixed blessing: cities have been spoiled, their neighbourhoods obliterated as highways smash through; environmental pollution, shortage of natural resources and the survival of public transport are problems caused largely by the car. Yet the car itself is still the object of endless fascination.

History of the Car

*Above: nearly all modern cars are of 'unitary'
construction: a body shell built up from sheet
steel panels, shaped to resist stress, carries all the
components and there is no separate chassis or framework.
Here body shells are being mass produced by resistance
spot welding on an assembly line.*

*Top right: the first car to have a 'unitary' body was
the Lancia Lambda of 1923. The panels would have been
covered with varnished fabric.*

The first practical cars driven by internal combustion engines appeared in the 1880s, but steam driven carriages had been produced with varying degrees of success for over a hundred years previously. The car was not invented by any one man, but was the outcome of the work of many individuals, working either independently or in collaboration with others.

Before 1900 The first workable four-stroke internal combustion engine was invented in 1876 by Nikolaus Otto in Germany, after many years of experimental work into gas engines. Following Otto's work, Karl Benz and Gottlieb Daimler, working independently, produced the world's first cars with internal combustion engines. The Benz, of 1885, was a three-wheeled vehicle with a tubular steel chassis and an open wooden two-seater body. The single front wheel was steered by a tiller, and the two large rear wheels were driven by chains. The single-cylinder petrol engine operated on the four-stroke principle, with electric ignition and water cooling, and was mounted horizontally over the rear axle. At 250 to 300 rpm it produced about $\frac{1}{2}$hp and drove the car at about 8 to 10 mph (13 to 16 kph).

Daimler's car, the first four wheeled design, was a converted carriage fitted with a vertical single-cylinder engine developing $1\frac{1}{2}$ hp and running at up to 900 rpm. It was produced in 1886.

By 1900 in most industrial countries various car designs had appeared, and several important innovations were made during this period. Among them were the introduction of the float-type carburettor by Maybach in 1892; the steering wheel (Vacheron) in 1894; the Michelin brothers' pneumatic tyre, and Lanchester's propellor shaft transmission (1895); multi-cylinder engines by Mors (V4) and Daimler (four in line); in 1899 the honeycomb radiator, gate gearchange, and floor-mounted accelerator (Daimler); and the universal joint for shaft drive to sprung rear axles (Renault).

The first motor race was held in France in 1895, over a distance of about 750 miles (1200 km) from Paris to Bordeaux and back. The overall winner was a 4 hp twin cylinder Panhard and Levassor, driven by Emile Levassor. The race took 48 hours and Levassor averaged 15 mph (24 kph), despite falling asleep once on the return journey to Paris.

In Britain, the law restricting cars to 4 mph (6.5 kph) in the country and 2 mph (3.2 kph) in towns, and insisting that every vehicle should be preceded by a man on foot waving a red flag, was repealed in 1896. This was celebrated by the first Emancipation Run from London to Brighton, about 60 miles (96 km), which is still held annually as a reliability trial for Veteran cars. (Veteran cars are those built before 1918; Vintage cars were built between 1918 and 1930).

Such sporting events served to stimulate design improvements and increase public interest in motoring.

1900 to 1920 By the beginning of the 20th century the car had ceased to be a novel 'horseless carriage' and had become established as an efficient means of transport. The work of two Frenchmen, Georges Bouton and Count Albert de Dion, had led to the development of lightweight, high speed engines. Their 1903 'Populaire' produced 8 hp at 1500 rpm, with a cubic capacity of 846 cm³ (52 in³) and a weight of only 40 lb (18 kg). To handle the requirements of this high speed air cooled engine, Bouton had to design an improved ignition system which bore many similarities to the modern contact breaker ignition.

The improvements in engine design, which led to high road speeds, forced the pace of development in braking and transmission systems. The first brakes were based on those used on horse-drawn vehicles and on bicycles. A solid block of wood, leather or metal was forced against the wheel rims by a hand-operated lever, or a contracting band of friction material acted on the propeller shaft in conjunction with externally-contracting brakes fitted to drums on the rear wheels. Asbestos brake linings were patented by Herbert Frood in England in 1908, and were much more effective than the cotton based linings then in use. The disc brake was invented in 1902 by Frederick Lanchester, then the following year the Mercedes company (formerly Daimler) produced a braking system with internally-expanding shoes inside a brake drum. Four-wheel braking was first employed by the Italian company of Isotta-Franchini in 1911.

The early 1900s saw the growth of the American automobile industry, and the stream of innovations that originated in the USA during this period included automatic transmission (1904), coil and distributor ignition (1908), the electric starter, the dynamo, a car telephone (1911), and hydraulic braking (1920). In 1908 the first Model T Ford came off the production line, and by 1911 Ford of America were producing 1000 per day. During its 19 year production run over 15,000,000 were made.

World War I was the first mechanized war and there was a great demand for mass-produced, standardized engines and components. This led not only to improved production techniques but also to more reliable and efficient vehicles.

1920 to 1940 Between the World Wars a number of very high quality cars were built, and some of these represented such an exceptionally high standard of craftsmanship and durability that owing to changing economic circumstances it is unlikely that cars of comparable quality will ever be built again. Such classics as the Bugatti 'Royale', Hispano-Suiza, Rolls Royce 'Phantom III', Bentley 8 litre, and Delage are unlikely to be excelled.

Mass production methods were now well established, and this led to the availability of a wide range of cheap, reliable and comfortable cars which found a ready market in the relatively affluent 1920s. The main components of the cars were well designed and efficient, and a variety of accessories were introduced, such as reversing lights, radios, automatic chokes, windshield wipers, and chrome-plated trim. During the Depression many smaller firms went out of business or were absorbed by larger ones, but new groups were merging that had better production facilities and more money to spend on sales promotion and market research.

In America the trend was towards power and luxury, while the European manufacturers concentrated on small low priced cars like the Austin 7 in England, and the Italian Fiat 500. In Germany the KDF, which was to become better known as the Volkswagen, was designed by Ferdinand Porsche with the backing of Adolf Hitler. KDF stands for 'Kraft durch Freude'—'Strength through Joy.' The basic shape remains today, and over 12 million have been made.

1940 to 1960 During World War II the production of private cars was severely restricted as raw materials were diverted to military uses and the factories used to make military vehicles, munitions and aircraft components. When car production recommenced the first models were almost the same as the pre-war designs, and it took a few years for the plants to re-tool sufficiently to produce any really new designs.

Many of the new models had powerful high compression engines, independent front suspension, and in styling were longer, lower and more elaborate. Lightweight chassis-less bodies were adopted, and the use of curved glass for windshields and rear windows greatly improved the drivers' visibility. There was extensive, sometimes excessive, use of chromium plating, and styling became one of the major preoccupations of the industry, with new models being introduced annually that were often mechanically identical to those they were meant to replace.

In the USA the tubeless automobile tyre was introduced in 1948 by the Goodrich company. Power steering, air

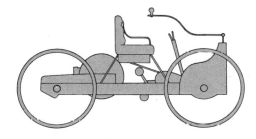

Before 1900, the mechanical parts of cars were arranged wherever they would fit on a bare platform.

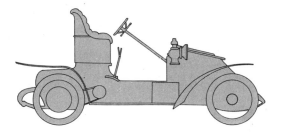

From 1900 to 1910 the layout settled down to front engine, central seating and rear wheel drive.

conditioning, twin headlamps, and wrap-around windshields all originated in the States during the early 1950s. Glass fibre reinforced resins, light and corrosion free, were used on the bodywork of the 1953 Chevrolet Corvette, and for the roof panel of the 1955 Citroen DS19.

Advances in fuel technology allowed the use of higher compression ratios. Overhead valve and overhead camshaft designs, with improved fuel systems (including fuel injection) and better ignition system performance contributed to engine power outputs for a given cubic capacity being greatly increased. The resultant increase in power to weight ratio that was possible improved the acceleration, speed, road holding and braking of cars of that time.

Disc brakes, less prone to failure from overheating than drum brakes, at last became widely accepted, over half a century after Lanchester's original design was patented. Further improvements in roadholding and braking resulted from the introduction of radial-ply tyres in 1953. Due to their higher cost, these tyres were at first used only on expensive high performance cars, but they are now widely used on all kinds of car.

The introduction of new plastic materials for the interior trim was a great asset for the stylists, and a wide range of colour schemes to match the body colours became available. The once universal oil pressure gauges and ammeters were often replaced by simple warning lights, which are cheaper and less complicated but also less informative.

After 1960 Car design in the 1960s was greatly influenced by the new interest in safety and pollution control. Mechanical improvements brought higher speeds, better roadholding, braking and acceleration, but many countries began to introduce laws restricting the maximum speed of vehicles. Cars had to be built to comply with the strict new safety and anti-pollution laws of the United States, which were gradually adopted by many other countries.

In addition to the improved performance, cars became more comfortable and easier to drive. Heating and ventilating equipment became standard on even the small cheap cars where it was previously only available, if at all, as an

Top left: a Bersey electric taxi of 1897. Its rear mounted, battery powered electric motor gave a top speed of 9 mph (14 km/h) and a range of 30 miles (48 km).

Top right: the car built by the Austrian Siegfried Markus in 1875. The single cylinder, ¾ hp engine took it up to 4 mph (6 km/h).

Left: a 1910 Austin 10. It had a single cylinder, side valve engine and three speed gearbox, and was a forerunner of the famous Austin 7 of 1922.

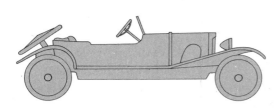

By 1920, cars had full bodywork with doors and windscreens and were longer, lower and more stable.

During the 1930s closed cars became more common, and the lines of the body became more fluid and sweeping.

11

The veterans

The petrol-driven car, first commercially produced by Benz and Daimler 1885–6, slowly began to dominate other forms of road transport. Experimental cars gave way to the production-line model such as the Model T, although racing cars such as the 80 m.p.h. Wolseley 'Beetle' continued the work of innovation. The Model T turned the car from an expensive plaything for the rich into a necessity for the not-so-wealthy; but the luxurious Silver Ghost continued in production for 19 years, one year longer than the Model T. The Grégoire ignored changes in styling, its design still clinging to the more leisurely days of the horse.

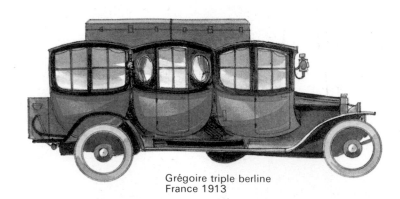

Grégoire triple berline
France 1913

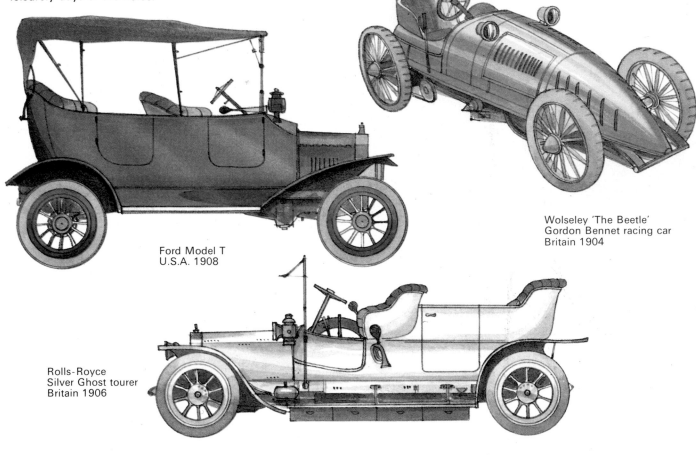

Ford Model T
U.S.A. 1908

Wolseley 'The Beetle'
Gordon Bennet racing car
Britain 1904

Rolls-Royce
Silver Ghost tourer
Britain 1906

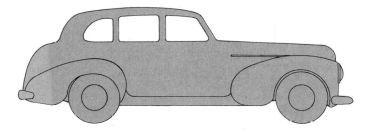

In the late 1930s and 1940s, cars became heavier, longer and simpler and more rounded in outline.

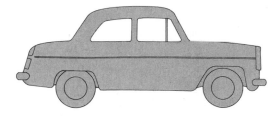

Cars of the 1950s were simplified into a 'three box' shape, without separate wings.

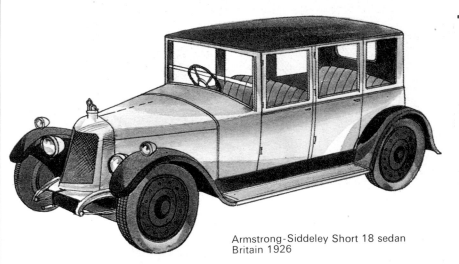

The vintage era

'No car built after 1930 is worth calling a car' could be called the 'creed' of the vintage enthusiast. And indeed, by that date, the great changes had taken place. The first Rhemag was produced in 1924, its front wings looking almost like early aerofoils. The Hanomag, a compact two-seater, contrasts with the 1926 Armstrong-Siddeley, typical in shape of the more luxurious cars of the period. As the family car became more reliable and comfortable, the racing car went faster; the 130 m.p.h. Bugatti won over a thousand races in two years. The 1929 4½ litre Bentley Le Mans was perhaps the zenith of styling and power in vintage motoring.

Armstrong-Siddeley Short 18 sedan
Britain 1926

Bugatti 35B racing car
France 1927

Rhemag Sports roadster
Germany 1924

Bentley Le Mans sports
Britain 1929

Hanomag Kommisbrot coupé
Germany 1928

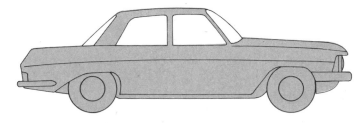

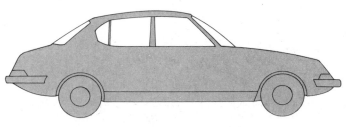

The 1960s saw cars becoming lower, longer and heavier often with aggressive, squared-off lines.

The 1970s trend is to rounder contours, noticeably higher at the rear for a streamlined 'wedge' shape.

13

Fast buses

After the Roaring 20s came the Great Depression of the 1930s. These phrases could also be used to describe the fortunes of the motor-car industries in Europe and the United States. But it was in the 30s that two of America's finest cars were built. Very few SJ Duesenbergs were produced but most are still on the road today. Their maximum speed was 130 mph; 104 mph in second gear. The 1936 Cord, although short-lived, was perhaps the most beautiful car of the period. And in Britain, the impressive streamlined body of George Eyston's Safety Special covered an almost unmodified London bus diesel engine that achieved a record 105 mph — truly the fastest bus in the world.

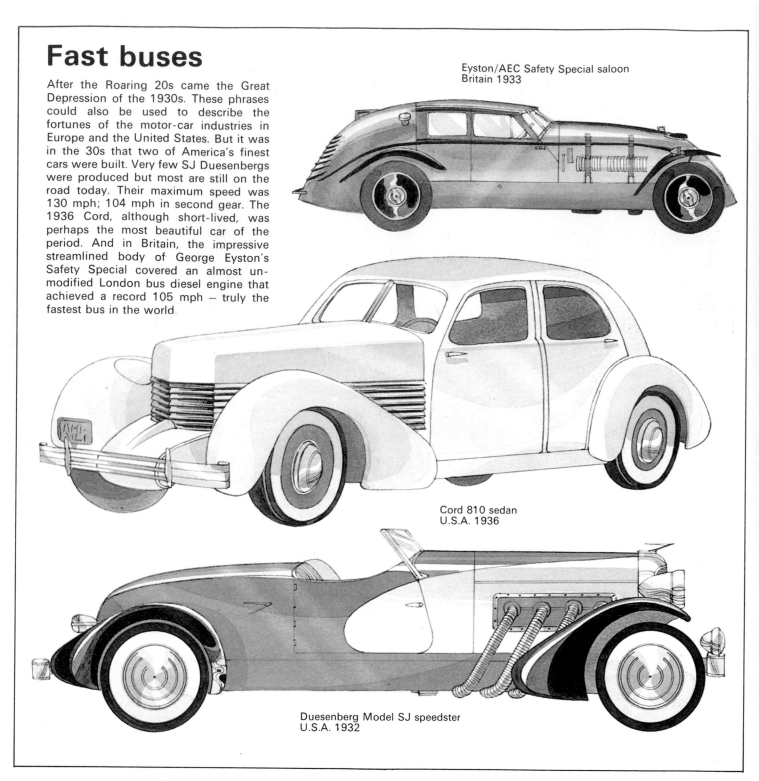

Eyston/AEC Safety Special saloon
Britain 1933

Cord 810 sedan
U.S.A. 1936

Duesenberg Model SJ speedster
U.S.A. 1932

extra. Automatic transmission, power brakes and power steering also gained widespread acceptance.

The electrical system, which had an increasingly heavy load to handle, was improved by the introduction of the alternator to replace the dynamo, and the use of circuit breakers instead of fuses.

One of the most important recent developments in engine design has been the invention of the wankel engine, which has a single three-lobed driving rotor instead of the conventional pistons and crankshaft. The first one was made in 1957 by Felix Wankel of Germany, and in 1964 the NSU company brought out the Wankel-engined 'Spyder', followed a few years later by the R080. The prototype Mercedes C111 and several Japanese Mazda cars also have

had Wankel engines, which are light, compact, powerful and smooth running. One of the early drawbacks of this engine was the relatively short life of the rotor seals, but a great deal of research has gone into overcoming this problem. Diesel versions are being designed for use on buses, trucks and boats.

Steam cars Perhaps the first automobile ever built was a three-wheeled steam-powered vehicle constructed by N J Cugnot in France in 1769. It travelled for 20 minutes at a speed of about 2 mph (3.2 kph) carrying four passengers. In the next 100 years numerous steam carriages and traction engines were built, particularly in England, but it was not until the end of the 19th century that the first steam-powered vehicles recognizable as forerunners of the modern

Left: the 1936 Fiat 500 Topolino (*'Mickey Mouse'*) *brought cheap motoring to thousands.*

Above: the exotic, plastic-bodied 1953 Chevrolet Corvette.

car were produced. The most successful steam car was that built by Stanley in the USA; more than 60,000 were made between 1897 and 1927, and some remained in ordinary service until 1945. A Stanley steam car broke the world speed record in 1906 with a speed of 127 mph (204 kph). The Stanley car had a two-cylinder non-condensing engine with direct drive to the rear axle and a special type of fire tube boiler under the bonnet [hood]. Its range was limited because it needed a full tank of pure water every 20 miles (33 km) at full speed. A condensing model was also made between 1915 and 1927.

Condensing steam cars had a much greater range but were troubled by cylinder oil contaminating the feedwater which upset the boiler and controls. The most successful of these was the car built in the USA by White between 1900 and 1911. This had a compound engine under the bonnet behind an air cooled condenser. A spiral tube boiler was under the driving seat. The usual fuel in steam cars was paraffin [kerosene], and elaborate controls were needed to ensure that the supply of steam matched the driving conditions without burning out the boiler or starting a fire from excess fuel. Steam cars went out of favour when electric starting for petrol engines was introduced.

In spite of their drawbacks, steam cars do have two important advantages over cars powered by internal combustion engines. First, the torque developed by a steam engine is independent of speed, so a complex gearbox is not re-

quired, and second, combustion of the fuel at atmospheric pressure outside the cylinders eliminates the need for additives and substantially reduces pollution. This second consideration has led to a revival of interest in the steam car; modern research is concentrated on developing control mechanisms to replace earlier ones (now prohibitively expensive) and boilers suitable for mass production, but serious problems remain.

Electric Vehicles Electric vehicles are often thought of as a new development, but as long ago as 1837 Robert Davidson of Aberdeen built an electric carriage powered by a crude iron-zinc battery and driven by a very simple electric motor, which contained all the basic elements of the modern electric vehicle.

The advent of the lead-acid battery allowed the first commercial battery-operated vehicle to be introduced in 1881 by the Paris Omnibus Company. London had its first electric bus in 1888, and also the world's first mechanically propelled taxicabs which were built by W C Bersey in 1897 for the London Electric Cab Co Ltd, and operated for two years.

Around the turn of the century the first land speed record was set in France by a battery-driven car. In 1898 the flying kilometre was completed at an average speed of 39 mph (63 kph), and in 1899 this was raised to 66 mph (106 kph), by the Belgian, Camille Jenatzy, in his bullet-shaped electric car called *La Jamais Contente*. By 1902 technical improvements enabled Charles Baker, an American, to attain over 85 mph (137 kph), but unfortunately on his third and officially timed run the car suffered a mechanical failure and so no official world record was obtained. The most recent speed record for an electric car was attained by the 'Silver Eagle' developed by Eagle Picher Industries in the USA. In August 1971, at Bonneville, the car completed the flying kilometre at an average speed of 152.59 mph (about 245 kph) and one mile from a standing start at an average of 146.437 mph (about 236 kph).

By the early 1900s a high proportion of the cars on the

15

Above: the first road
going locomotive (it
could scarcely be called
a car) was designed and
built by the Frenchman
Nicholas Cugnot in 1769.
This improved model of
1770, now in a Paris
museum, was so hard to
steer (the heavy boiler
turned with the front
wheel) that on its first
public trial Cugnot drove
it through a wall; he was
imprisoned.

Right: over a century
later, steam cars
achieved a short lived
popularity. The most
successful were the
Stanleys, such as this
1899 model.

roads of London, New York and Paris were battery electric, and electric cars became very fashionable. The rapid development of the internal combustion engine, however, accelerated still faster by World War I, meant that by the 1920s electric cars could no longer compete in terms of speed, acceleration and range. Between the wars many electric car companies came and went. One of the best known English makes was the Partridge Wilson 'Brougham' of 1936, powered by a 60 volt 324 ampere hour battery which gave it a claimed maximum speed of 32 mph (51.5 kph) and range of 60 miles (97 km) per charge. This was typical for most electric cars of that time, and would be considered insufficient for most purposes today.

The factors which lead the private buyer to reject the electric car did not affect the commercial user in the same way. Electric vans and trucks were developed in parallel with the cars, and today in Britain for example there are some 55,000 electric vehicles in use performing a variety of tasks such as local authority duties, milk delivery and postal work, all of which involve a significant amount of stop-start driving. The electric milk truck is ideally suited for this arduous stop-start kind of work, and whereas the diesel powered version lasts only 3 to 5 years the electric one has a useful life of over twenty years. Electrically powered fork lift trucks are in common use the world over.

The electric vehicle is basically a very simple machine; it can be said to have only five basic components and eight moving parts, four of which are wheels. In essence it consists of the battery, a controller, the motor, the transmission, and the vehicle chassis and body, and it was for this reason that so much interest was shown in it in the early days of powered transport. Apart from the battery, controller and motor, the design of electric vehicles usually follows conventional lines.

Most batteries in use today are of the lead-acid type. Originally based on the flat plate design, modern traction cells are now of tubular construction. This type of battery, provided it is regularly charged and the electrolyte level is maintained, has a guaranteed life of four years, which is regularly exceeded in practice. It is, however, rather heavy and the energy density (the amount of energy produced per unit weight) is only about 11 watt-hours per lb (approximately 5 Wh/kg), and this is the feature principally responsible for the poor road performance of most electric vehicles. Where vehicles are used comparatively infrequently, as in mining and tunnelling, nickel-iron batteries are often used as they can stand long periods of non-use without attention.

The motor in most electric road vehicles is a low speed DC series wound type driving the rear wheels through a conventional back axle arrangement. Speed control is carried out in two main ways. The simplest is to change the voltage applied to the motor by tapping the battery in a combination of series-parallel connections. For example, if a 48 volt battery is used it is initially connected for 12 V to limit the high current needed for starting, and once the vehicle is on the move the controller switches the connections to give 24V, then 36 V and ultimately the full 48 V. Most electric vehicles are controlled via a conventional type of accelerator pedal, the only other foot pedal being that for the brake. As the only controls needed in electric vehicles are the accelerator, brakes, and steering they are particularly easy to drive.

A more advanced form of control of the motor speed can be provided by the use of thyristors, which are solid state 'switches' that allow the current to be supplied in bursts. For starting and acceleration the thyristor conducts for short periods limiting the energy supplied. As the speed increases the length of the thyristors' conducting periods are increased so that maximum power can be developed.

Considerable interest has been shown recently in electric road vehicles, because the high levels of noise and pollution so common with petrol and diesel engines are absent. In terms of resources, the electric vehicle also competes on equal terms, being no less efficient and frequently more efficient in overall energy consumption than its internal combustion counterpart.

Extensive research programmes are under way in many parts of the world to produce designs which will provide road performances comparable to conventional vehicles. The major difficulty with the electric vehicle has been to find a battery which will give sufficient energy from a realistic weight. The standard lead-acid traction cell is really too heavy, although the most recent designs will now give 16 to 18 watt-hours per lb (7 to 8 Wh/kg) and working lives of up to 800 charging cycles are predicted. Using this type of battery, Chloride/Selnec in Britain and RWE/Varta/MAN in Germany have produced buses capable of carrying 50 passengers and operating conventional services, both types being capable of about 45 mph (72 kph) with a range of about 40 miles (64 km). To prevent the vehicles having to stand idle for lengthy periods while their batteries are recharged, they are designed so that the run-down batteries can be quickly exchanged for a fully charged set. The MAN bus carries its batteries in a trailer, and in the Chloride bus they are under the floor.

The US Post Office is now
trying out electric vehicles in
Massachusetts. This one is bu[...]
by Electromotion Inc. of Bedford. Its battery pack is
recharged by plugging it in
overnight.

Above: Camille Jenatzy of Belgium with his record-breaking electric car La Jamais Contente, *in which he raised the world land speed record to 106 km/h (66 mph) in 1899 at Achéres, France.*

Below: the ideal conditions for an electric vehicle in contrast to a conventionally engined one are short, urban journeys not exceeding a known length, followed by a regular return for recharging. This German MAN electric bus sidesteps the recharging delay by having exchangeable batteries on a trailer. Here they are being slid into the charger.

Many light electric vans are now being developed. In Germany a conversion of the standard Volkswagen van is so designed that the battery can be rapidly charged, and in Britain the Electricity Council and J Lucas Ltd have produced modified versions of British Leyland and Bedford vans. The former uses a mechanical gearbox and a high speed motor and the latter a variable speed motor controlled by thyristors. Both are capable of up to 50 mph (80 kph). In the USA the Electric Vehicle Council have ordered a large number of vans from Battronic for use by electricity utilities throughout the country. Similar schemes are being undertaken in many other countries; Japan in particular is investing heavily in research.

The van is a particularly useful test vehicle in that the extra space available compared with a car allows new energy sources to be tested easily. In the USA for example General Motors have produced a van powered by a fuel cell with liquid hydrogen and oxygen being carried in cryogenic (low temperature) tanks. In Britain the Electricity Council has used one of its van conversions to demonstrate the first sodium-sulphur battery, which gave an energy density of 30 Wh/lb (13.5 Wh/kg). Later developments are expected to give as much as 70 Wh/lb (31.5 Wh/kg). Many other types of battery are also being tested such as the zinc-chlorine (Udylite, USA) and the zinc-air (Sony, Japan).

The electric vehicle development which creates most public interest is the battery car. To date no really successful product has been sold, and early visions of cheap electric town cars are receding. The majority of cars so far produced have been conversions of existing products, and although the major car manufacturers have produced or sponsored prototype designs they have as yet made no really significant contribution. In France, Electricité de France have produced conversions of the Renault R4 (reducing it to a two seater in the process) and in Italy ENEL have converted a Fiat. In the USA there have been successful conversions of large-bodied cars which have speeds of up to 60 mph (97 kph) and ranges of up to 100 miles (161 km), but no large scale production has been started.

The electric car as a product presents several design problems. It is becoming more difficult to design small cars which will comply with new safety regulations, and the extra mass of batteries in the electric car present additional difficulties. The majority of purpose-built cars have so far been lightly constructed vehicles unlikely to pass stringent tests. The Enfield 8000, which has been ordered by the Electricity Council in England, has overcome these problems. This two seater, which is designed to have a low aerodynamic drag and rolling resistance, is powered by electric batteries and has a top speed of over 40 mph (64 kph), rapid acceleration and a range under normal conditions of 40 to 50 miles (64 to 80 km). This performance allows it to operate well in normal traffic, making it an attractive town car.

A recent development is the introduction of lightweight electric motorcycles, such as that produced by the Austrian firm of Steyr-Daimler-Puch, which may prove to be a useful form of personal transport in busy city centres.

Pioneers of the Motor Industry

Benz, Karl (1844-1929) Karl Benz, a German engineer, was a pioneer of automobile construction. He was the son of a railway engineer, who died when Karl was only two years old. But Karl seemed to have inherited a flair for engineering, and studied mechanical engineering at his home town of Karlsruhe. He left his studies to work for a locksmith,

Private electric vehicles are also coming, despite high cost and weight, and limited range.

Left: the chassis of the Ford Comuta (still in the experimental stage) showing the bulky lead acid accumulators.

Right: this car, the Enfield 8000, is in full production. Expensive to buy but cheap to run, it makes a useful town car.

Below: scooters are also suitable for electric power, since they are not required to go very far or very fast.

and made designs for a 'horseless carriage' in his spare time. Originally, he thought of adding an engine to his bicycle, but soon decided that a three-wheeled vehicle would be a better idea.

Benz designed a simple two-stroke engine on the principle used by the French engineer Etienne Lenoir, whose engine ran on coal gas. He risked his life savings to build a prototype engine, but the result was so successful that a backer put up money for Benz to establish a small manufacturing plant at Mannheim, which opened in 1879.

Meanwhile, the German Nikolaus Otto had produced an engine working on a four-stroke cycle and Benz turned to this as the power source for the automobile he still hoped to build. By 1885, Benz had produced a prototype horseless carriage. This was a three-wheeled vehicle using a four-stroke engine with a horizontal cylinder. The engine ran on benzine, a highly volatile petroleum derivative based on aliphatic hydrocarbons, not to be confused with the aromatic compound benzene.

This was the first practical petrol-driven engine, and it introduced many features. To vaporize the fuel, Benz designed a small carburettor. He invented an electrical ignition instead of the flame ignition that had been used before, and he covered the engine with a jacket through which cooling water could flow. In 1886, Benz patented a simple radiator to cool the water again for recirculation.

The engine ran at 250 to 300 rpm, instead of the 120 rpm of his gas engines, and developed about $\frac{3}{4}$ hp. The drive was transmitted by two chains to the rear axle via a primitive clutch.

On 29 January 1886, Karl Benz received a patent for the Patent Motor Car. Its top speed was less than 10 mph. He exhibited an improved version at the Paris Exhibition in 1887, but it was not until he drove through the streets of

handbrake

petrol tank under seat

brake block

chain

Above: Karl Benz built this three wheeled, petrol driven car in 1888—one of his four improved cars based on his experimental model of 1885. The wheels are wooden, iron tyred at the rear, soild rubber tyred at the front. Wooden brake blocks work directly on the rear tyres. The single cylinder, four stroke engine already has electric ignition by coil and spark plug (unlike many successors). The cooling system works by boiling water away at the rate of about $\frac{1}{2}$ litre every hour.

Left: Benz in his old age, standing in front of one of his firm's cars.

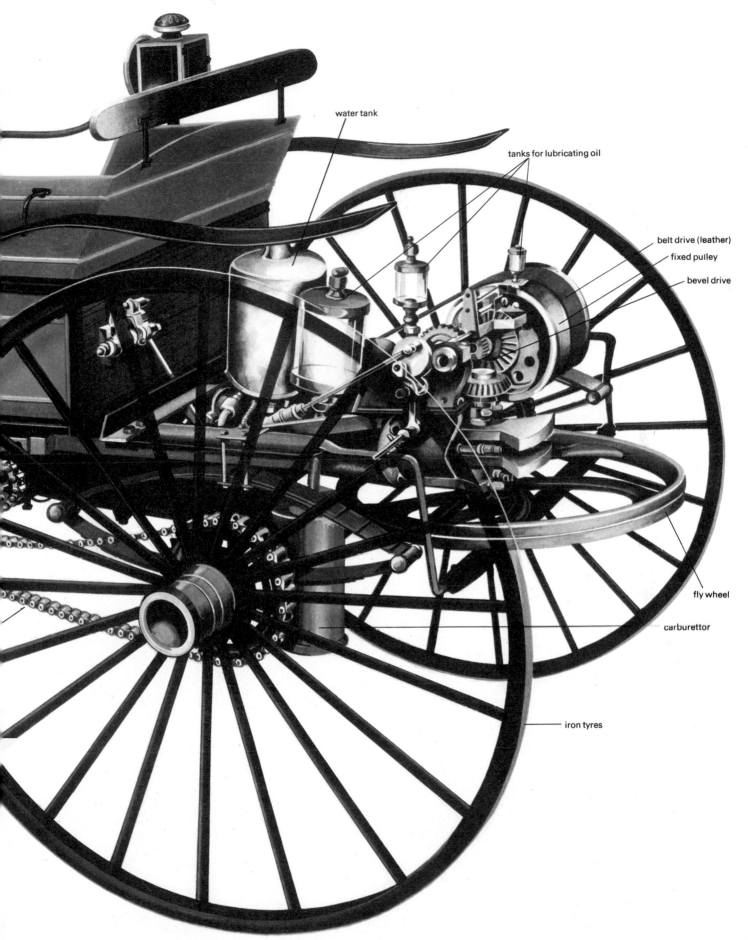

water tank

tanks for lubricating oil

belt drive (leather)

fixed pulley

bevel drive

fly wheel

carburettor

iron tyres

23

Above: a Benz omnibus of 1895, with a five horsepower engine. Despite its apparently small size, it could carry up to eight people.

Below: another version of Benz's car: 1886; 0.9 hp; top speed 9 mph (15 km/h). This already has the wire wheels and rubber tyres which later became universal.

Munich the following year that his orders grew. In another model, his two teenage sons drove their mother for 125 miles —then the longest automobile journey ever made.

His original backers were not impressed with the idea of motor vehicles, so Benz had to find alternative financial support and start a new factory. In 1890 he built his first four-wheeled car, and a Benz car exhibited in Chicago, in 1893, influenced American motor pioneers. Two years later, Benz built the world's first bus.

By 1900, 4000 three-gear 'Comfortable' models, with a 3-horsepower engine, had been sold, and the Benz company was the largest automobile manufacturer in Europe. Benz retired from the management in 1903, and in 1926 the firm merged with the Daimler company to form Daimler-Benz AG, the makers of Mercedes-Benz cars.

Ford, Henry (1863-1947) Henry Ford, the pioneer car-maker whose assembly line methods have largely been responsible for the tremendous outpouring of consumer goods in this century, was born on his father's farm, near Dearborn, Michigan. He never liked farm work; when he was twelve years old, he saw a steam tractor moving down the road under its own power, and realized that the drudgery of life on the farm would be relieved by machinery.

Ford left school at the age of 15 and went to work as an apprentice in a machine shop, working at night repairing watches. He then spent two years investigating the possi-

bility of a steam tractor, powerful enough to do farm work yet small and light enough so that any farmer could afford to buy one. He was forced to abandon steam as impractical for his purposes, and built a four stroke, one cylinder internal combustion engine. It was based on the model of the Otto engine, which he had worked on as an apprentice, when nobody else knew anything about them. He discovered that a one cylinder engine was impractical for a road vehicle because of the weight of the flywheel necessary to balance it.

In 1893 Ford built his first car, which had two opposed cylinders, one delivering power while the other was in its exhaust stroke. It resembled the Benz car, which Ford had travelled to New York to see, but was lighter. It had a planetary (epicyclic) gearbox and belt drive; shifting the belt gave two forward speeds and a neutral position. There was no reverse gear. One of the things Ford discovered while building the car was the necessity for what he called a 'compensating gear' (differential) to allow equal power to be distributed to each drive wheel while the car turned corners. It was the only car in Detroit; Ford drove it about 1000 miles before selling it, later buying it back.

In the meantime, he had been working for the local electric power company, which offered him a promotion if he would give up tinkering with his 'gas buggies.' Instead he quit his job and went into the car business. In 1903 he built two cars which had four cylinder engines developing 40 hp, and hired Barney Oldfield to race them. The publicity brought him enough backing to form his own company.

Above: Henry Ford and his wife seated in the earliest Ford car, which he built in 1893. It had belt drive and no reverse gear. Ford drove it around Detroit for about 1000 miles (1600 km) and then sold it, but later bought it back and put it in a museum.

Left: Model Ts, on which the early success of the company depended, just off the assembly line: 'You can have any colour you want so long as it's black.'

25

Over the next few years, Ford experimented with manufacturing methods and building different models, gathering enough experience to build the kind of car he had in mind: cheap and reliable enough so that anybody could drive one. He proved that the lower the price of the car the more people would buy it. He discovered vanadium steel, which has twice the tensile strength of ordinary steel, and thus could be used to reduce the weight of the car. He was able to buy enough stock in the company to have a controlling interest, and in 1908 he began to build the famous 'Tin Lizzie': the Model T. In June of that year the factory built 100 cars in one day for the first time.

The Model T had only four sub-assemblies: the power plant, the frame, the front axle and the rear axle. It was available with four different bodies, and the cheapest model sold for $825. During the first year, 10,607 cars were built. More than 15,000,000 Model T cars were sold by 1927, when the last one was made; the Ford Motor Company, having begun with $100,000 worth of capital in 1903, had in 1927 $700,000,000 of reserve balance alone.

Henry Ford was a man of great practical ability and strong opinions. He believed that the purpose of manufacturing industries should be to offer the public the best quality product at the lowest possible price, and that profits would take care of themselves. He attributed the fantastic success of the Model T to the fact that it was simple and reliable (the slogan was that anyone could drive a Ford) and to the fact that it never went out of date, because the only changes made in the car were towards higher quality at a lower price, and never made obsolete cars already sold.

Ford perfected the assembly line method of manufacturing, reducing the duty of each employee to one simple operation which required no thought or skill. He managed to reduce the price of the car while the costs of labour and materials were rising. He foiled every attempt to take over his company, saying that bankers should stick to banking, and the money to operate a manufacturing concern should come out of the sales of the product. In 1914, he instituted a profit-sharing plan and offered the highest wages in the industry; the crush of people wanting to work for him was so great that the police had to be called out to handle the crowd.

Above: early Fords were not famous for speed or for advanced design features, but later the company took an interest in experimentation. The GT 40 sports car has a carbon fibre-reinforced plastic body, stiffer than glass fibre and needing less support to keep it from flexing at high speed. On the right is a microphotograph of carbon fibres; their structure resembles graphite.

Left: as the Model T came off the assembly line, the body with seats in it was lowered to it and secured. All the Model T cars were identical mechanically; there were four different body styles available.

He never lost his interest in farming, and began to build tractors during World War I. The first models were used in England, where farm women learned to drive them while the men were away at war.

Ford's social and political opinions were sometimes naive and regrettable. He tried to insist that his employees be non-smokers and regular churchgoers. Late in life he began to indulge in anti-semitic activities. His greatest accomplishment was to put the nation on wheels and get the farmers out of their rural isolation; having created an enormous demand for cars, he lost touch with the public, who wanted fancier, more comfortable cars. By the time his factories retooled in 1927 to build a more modern car, he had lost his leading position in the car industry, and never regained it.

Royce, Frederick Henry (1863-1933) At the turn of the century the motor car was still a novelty with tremendous scope for development, and in 1903 when Frederick Henry Royce bought his first car, a second hand Decauville, he already had a reputation for high quality workmanship and refinement of design detail. It was therefore not surprising that he soon began building his own cars.

Royce, the son of a miller, was born in Alwalton near Peterborough, the youngest of five children. From an early age he showed a keen interest in how mechanical devices worked; at the age of three he fell into the mill race while examining the mill wheel and would have drowned had his father not managed to rescue him. When Royce was four his father's business failed and they came to London where he spent an impoverished childhood, his father dying when he was nine. He then sold newspapers until he was eleven, when he managed to attend school for a year. At 14 an aunt paid £20 for his apprenticeship to the Great Northern Railway, based at Peterborough. Here he acquired mechanical skills but no technical or commercial training and was forced to leave through lack of money at 17. In the meantime, however, he had taught himself electricity and algebra and, with electrical lighting gaining acceptance, managed to obtain a job with the London Electrical Light and Power Company who sent him to Liverpool. Two years later he was once more unemployed so, with a friend, set up a workshop in Manchester. At first they made electric light filaments, later electric bells, and business increased greatly

27

when Royce designed a reliable dynamo. Eventually they also made electric cranes. But excellent though these products were, they were not to make his name a household word.

After experimenting with the car he had bought, in 1904 Royce decided to build three experimental cars to his own design. They were two-cylinder 10 hp models which included overhead inlet valves (unusual for those days), ample water cooling spaces to avoid overheating, additional leaves in the springs for more comfort, and a gearbox with three forward speeds and reverse. Royce designed his own coil and distributor ignition system and his own carburettor, which had a float spray feed and was fitted with an automatic valve. In third gear the cars did 30 mph and each car weighed about 1500 lbs.

The Hon Charles Stewart Rolls, who was looking for a reliable British car to promote through his car firm, was introduced to Royce, saw his cars, and in December, 1904, entered into an agreement with him. Royce was to produce 10 hp two-cylinder cars at a cost of £395 under the joint name of Rolls-Royce. Such was their success that by 1908 they had opened a new factory at Derby; by this time the car they were manufacturing was the six-cylinder 40/50 hp Silver Ghost.

In 1911 Royce's health failed and he was brought to London, where doctors gave him only three months to live. Years of working long hours, often without proper meals, and deprivation in childhood had eventually caught up with him. He recovered but was never to return to his factory at Derby again; the rest of his life all his ideas would be generated either at his villa in the south of France or his home in Sussex. But his brain was as active as ever, and so it was arranged for a team of assistants to work on design projects with Royce at his home. It is said that he could design a component entirely in his head without taking a single note, and then explain it in such detail that when drawn by the draughtsman it was invariably correct.

At the outbreak of World War I any Rolls-Royce cars that were around the factory were taken over for military use and the government asked them to produce aircraft engines from both French and British designs. This acted as a challenge to Royce who decided to design his own. It was a water-cooled 12-cylinder engine with two banks of six

Above: Royce at the gate of his house in Sussex, where he retired in 1911 when his health failed. He continued design work here and in the South of France.

cylinders in V formation; it weighed 900 lb and produced 200 hp. In 1915, after only six months' work, the first Eagle engine was tested. This design was followed by the Hawk, Falcon and Condor engines. Great ingenuity was shown in Royce designs; the engines could often keep going after some major parts had been shot away.

Royce was knighted in 1930 and died in 1933. The work he had begun was continued in his tradition of high workmanship. He was an extemely patient man who had never accepted anything as being perfect, even his own designs. Quiet-spoken and modest, he claimed that he was 'just a mechanic'.

Below: the 40/50 hp Rolls-Royce Silver Ghost was years ahead of its time when introduced in 1906, and is one of the most famous cars in the world.

Diesel, Rudolf (1858-1913) Rudolf Christian Karl Diesel was an engineer who perfected the type of internal combustion engine that is named after him. He was born in Paris, the son of a German leather worker from Augsburg. Diesel's parents were strict, and the family was very poor. A harsh, insecure upbringing gave Diesel the drive to accomplish great things, but also had its effect on his mental stability.

Diesel was a brilliant student. As a boy he spent many hours in the Paris Museum of Arts and Crafts, where he made drawings of machines, including Cugnot's steam wagon of 1769. At the outbreak of the Franco-Prussian war of 1870, the Diesel family moved to London, where Diesel was fascinated by the machines in the Science Museum. Then he was sent to Augsburg to live with an uncle who was professor of mathematics at the Augsburg trade school. While in Augsburg he saw a pump which created heat by the compression of air, and his later success began to take form.

In 1875 he began attending lectures at the Munich Technical University. Among the lecturers was Carl von Linde, whose research in thermodynamics had led to the invention of refrigeration machinery. After graduating from the university with the most brilliant record in its history, Diesel went to work for von Linde in his refrigeration company, soon rising to the post of factory manager.

At university Diesel had found that existing engines were not very efficient, and had studied the theories of Carnot on the efficient transmission of energy in the form of heat. He resolved to build a more efficient engine. In his capacity as von Linde's plant manager, he became interested in the possibility of replacing steam with ammonia vapour, but gave that up in favour of the idea of using the heat from compressed air to ignite a fuel mixture in the cylinder. He patented designs in 1892 and 1893. At first he wanted to use coal dust in his engine, as the cheapest fuel available, but his design required a fluid which could be sprayed into the combustion chamber, so he settled on petroleum oil. His first successful engine was a 25 horsepower single-cylinder four-stroke model built in 1897. It was displayed at a Munich exhibition in 1898, and the inventor soon became a millionaire.

A diesel engine needs no spark plugs because the fuel is ignited by the heat of the atmosphere in the combustion chamber, which is compressed by the upstroke of the piston. It will run on cheaper fuel than other internal combustion engines. In 1902 it was first used to generate electricity, and in 1903 the first diesel-powered ship was afloat.

Diesel's engine was not the first compression-ignition engine, and some of his patents were contested. A factory he built in Augsburg failed. Some of his early engines broke down; because of the tremendous pressures required, the earliest designs were not reliable. Diesel was a suspicious, difficult man who insisted that the engines be built to his original specifications, delaying improvements which could have been made. In spite of all this, his ability as an engineer was widely recognized, and there was some talk of a Nobel prize.

In 1913 he disappeared during a trip from Antwerp to Harwich on the mail steamer *Dresden* to discuss the sale of his engines to the British Admiralty. There was some speculation that he had been kidnapped or murdered by government agents in the tense atmosphere of pre-World War I Europe, but in fact he had made special preparations at home before leaving, and had spoken of suicide by jumping off a ship.

Above: 1898 portrait of Diesel by Alexander Fuks.

Below: Diesel's first successful engine, built in the Maschinenfabrik works at Augsburg in Germany. Note the heavy bracing required to deal with the very high compression which is a feature of diesel engines.

Car Safety

Safety in car design was recognized as being important even in the earliest cars. In recent years, however, it has developed into a fundamental subject in its own right. Active safety measures are designed to reduce the likelihood of a car being involved in an accident in the first place, whereas passive safety measures assume that a collision is inevitable and then aim to reduce the severity of the injuries to the road users involved.

Brakes In recent years brakes have changed greatly in design, disc brakes replacing the more conventional drum types. Instead of linings which press outwards against the inside of a drum, a disc attached to the axle is gripped from each side by friction pads attached to calipers. The great advantage of disc brakes is that they are essentially fade free, and repeated applications do not result in excessively high temperatures arising in the linings and drums, which previously had been the reason why brake fade was a hazard. In the near future non-lock or anti-skid brakes will be introduced. Systems have been developed, initially for aircraft, which slow the wheels just to the point of skidding, and then allow some rotation to continue. This has the effect of producing the maximum retardation, and also eliminates the possibility of a wheel locking, with subsequent loss of control of the car.

Tyres Tyres have also changed tremendously since the 1950s. New rubber components have been introduced into tyre compounds and have improved skid resistance. Recently new types have been developed to cope with the dangers of sudden deflation. One of the most interesting is a tyre mounted on a relatively narrow wheel, so that the tyre can be run in a totally deflated condition without damage to the tyre side walls. In addition the tyre contains a special liquid which, when the tyre is run under the deflated condition, vaporizes and generates a pressure so that the tyre can partly reinflate.

Visibility For some years there has been discussion of the advantages of a polarized headlight system. Such a system comprises headlights which produce polarized light in a particular plane. The windscreens of all cars would be fitted with polarizing glass, which would be so oriented that glare

Above: the differences between laminated glass and toughened glass. A laminated windscreen (top picture) hit by a stone stars but does not disintegrate, because the plastic layer holds the fragments in place. A toughened windscreen crazes all over, becoming almost opaque despite a zone of larger chips in the middle.

Below: a Chevrolet Nova crashes into a barrier at 30 mph. The fiduciary marks painted on the sides permit exact measurement of panel deformation caused by the crash.

from an approaching vehicle would be essentially eliminated, while the forward vision would still be maintained at the present levels. The theoretical advantages of such a system are attractive, but the practical problems of making the transition from the present lighting systems to a fully polarized type are very great, because it would not be practicable to convert all existing vehicles to this type of lighting. Also, the benefits would be marginal because glare itself is not a very frequent cause of accidents.

As far as the instruments of a car are concerned, new devices are under consideration which allow certain information, for example the vehicle's speed, to be displayed by creating an image in the windscreen. The image appears to be some distance ahead of the car, so that the driver need not refocus his eyes to read it. This so-called head-up display device would therefore allow the driver to be able to monitor his speed and other functions of the car without having to scan downwards from his forward view.

Research The main concern of car safety research in the last ten years has been the development of passive safety design features, where the aim is to improve the 'crashworthiness' of vehicles. The fundamental aim of good passive safety design is to ensure that only tolerable loads are applied to a car occupant's body during a crash. This is done first by restraining the occupant within the passenger compartment by means of a seat belt or other device, so that the chances of making contact with the interior parts of the car are reduced. Secondly, where contacts cannot be avoided, then the structures which are likely to be hit by the occupants must be designed to collapse and cushion them.

It is essential for the designers to have some knowledge of the forces that the human body can withstand, but as yet this branch of biomechanics has not been fully researched. Work is done at low impact energy levels using volunteers, but for higher speed crashes it is necessary to use dummies. The relationship between dummy performance and that of a real person in a crash is complex, and it may be that these differences are very considerable. To reduce this problem some work is currently being done using human cadavers.

Even though the difficulties of rational design in this area of injury tolerance and 'crashworthiness' are great, many basic improvements have been introduced into cars in recent years. These include anti-burst door latches, safety glass, energy-absorbing steering wheels and columns, head restraints and various seat belt systems.

Safety glass Safety glass for windscreens was one of the first passive safety devices introduced into cars in the 1930s, but its use remains a controversial question. North America and Scandinavia favour a laminated glass, which consists of two sheets of annealed glass separated by a layer of transparent plastic. The rest of Europe and Japan favour toughened glass because it is cheaper. This type is a single homogeneous sheet of glass which is heat strengthened, and which, on impact, fractures into small cubic fragments without very sharp edges. In recent years laminated glass has been improved by changes in the properties of the plastic interlayer. Recent research has demonstrated that this new laminated glass is some four times safer than toughened glass, but because it is more expensive, controversy continues as to whether or not toughened glass windscreens

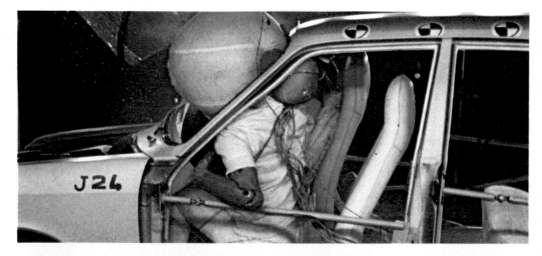

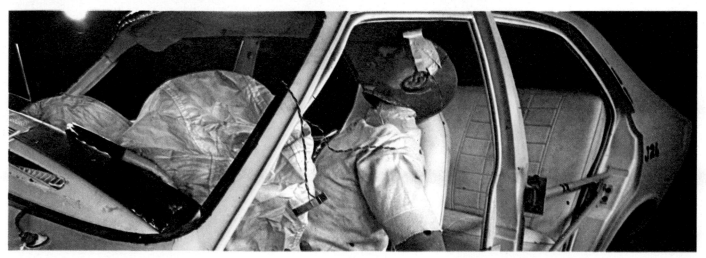

The airbag, which inflates automatically in a fraction of a second on impact, was thought for a time to be the ultimate in passenger protection, but it is not reliable. In this test it inflated just too late: the dummy 'driver' has already crushed his chest against the steering wheel (upper picture), and in real life would have been dead as he fell back (lower picture); the bag has broken his neck.

should be banned by legislative action and replaced by laminated glass.

Further developments in laminated glass have recently taken place. These combine the benefits of both laminated and toughened material in that a laminated construction is used, but the sheet next to the inside of the car is made of toughened glass.

Seat belts The benefits of three-point seat belts have been firmly established; research shows that over 50% of fatal and serious injuries to car occupants would be avoided if all occupants wore their seat belts. A seat belt works by slowing the occupant down by holding him to the seat as the front of the car crushes. The belt also stretches a little, allowing the occupant to move forward in the interior of the passenger compartment, so that he is decelerated in a crash over the distance that the front of the car crushes, plus the distance he moves forward inside the passenger compartment. For such a system to be effective it is obvious that as little slack as possible should be present in the system, and the loads in the seat belt should build up to a tolerable level as soon as possible.

There are two possible improvements over conventional belts which can produce these conditions. The belt can be preloaded by a device which senses that a crash is taking place, and takes up the slack in the belt in a matter of milliseconds. As far as limiting the peak load is concerned, some belts have been designed with tear-webbing sections incorporated in them. These allow the loads in the belt to build up to a predetermined value, whereupon little strips of webbing sewn across a loop in the belt break in series, so that forward movement of the occupant takes place under more or less constant loads.

The air bag controversy Passive restraints are mandated by USA Federal Motor Vehicle Safety Standard No. 208, which was proposed in June 1969 and issued in March, 1971, scheduled to take effect for all cars sold in the USA after January 1st, 1972. This set off a storm of controversy which is still raging. In April, 1971, Chrysler Corporation (followed by other manufacturers) sought a court review of the legality of Standard 208, and interim standards were applied in 1973 and 1974. Standard 208 was on the books for 1975 and deferred again to 1976. Under President Ford the Department of Transportation froze the rule for an 8-year period. The new Carter administration rescinded this suspension. In October, 1977, the mandate by the USA Department of Transportation that passive restraints must be fitted on all cars by 1984, became law. The standard is written so that air bags alone can meet its requirements.

The air bag is an in inflatable balloon, stored in a small folded package and hooked up to a reservoir of pressurized inert gas for split-second deployment, with subsequent deflation through open vents. It is triggered by a crash sensor (which reacts to extreme deceleration force) that opens the valve on the gas tank. With one air bag in front of each seat, the air bag is effective only in frontal impacts. General Motors, which built 11,000 cars equipped with air bags from 1973 to 1976, determined from its studies of accident data that air bags could not approach the effectiveness of three-point belt systems.

General Motors also ascertained that congressional leaders and consumer advocates who had sponsored 'air bag' legislation failed to order cars so equipped when they became available. General Motors had planned to sell 50,000 cars equipped with air bags in the first year (1974), but sold no more than 11,000 over a three-year period. The

air bag was offered as a $300 option for some Buick, Oldsmobile, and Cadillac models, at price levels where an extra $300 was thought to make little or no difference. But the public fears air bags. Customers worry about inadvertent deployment, and about failure to deploy when needed. They have reason to fear. Air bags have failed repeatedly in tests.

Door locks Anti-burst door locks are a relatively cheap development, and have proved to be one of the most successful but unrecognised benefits of crash protective design. Studies have shown that it is much better to remain in a car than to be thrown out, because if a person is thrown out serious injury may result from contact with the road surface, and there is a considerable risk of being run over by one's own or another vehicle. It is therefore very important that the doors should stay shut during a collision, and the design of a latch to do this has now been perfected and introduced into almost all cars in the world. An anti-burst latch provides resistance to tension forces of up to 3000 lb (1360 kg) in all directions, by having a lock striker on the door which completely encircles a ring or plate mounted on the door frame. The system is designed so that it resists the forces generated in a collision both by the occupant striking the door on the inside and by the crash forces themselves due to the distortion of the whole body frame of the car. The result is that ejection, which was established as a leading cause of death to car occupants in 1956, has now been reduced to relatively minor importance.

Steering columns The steering wheel and column have been identified as a major source of injury to the driver, and a range of energy-absorbing and non-intrusion designs have been developed in recent years. There is great variation in these designs, some of which are now thought to be not fully effective.

Energy-absorbing columns have to serve two functions. Firstly they must stop the steering wheel and column being pushed rearwards as the front of the car is crushed in an impact. Before such designs were invented a common

The tests shown here led to a complete redesign of most children's car safety seats. Below: the clip-on type comes away completely in a simulated collision.

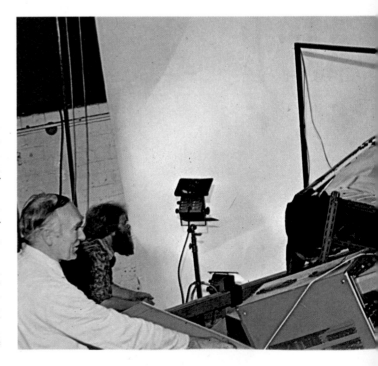

feature of driver injury was for the chest to be speared by the steering column. The second function of the energy-absorbing column is to provide the driver with a tolerable impact as he moves forward and strikes the wheel with his chest. At that point in the crash the column should build up the load on the driver's chest to a tolerable level, and then deform under that load to give a 'ride-down' for the driver. Several design problems are present in providing such a system. In particular the collapse of the column due to the frontal crush of the car should not inhibit its subsequent performance as far as providing ride-down for the driver's chest is concerned. Also the system must be so designed that under crash conditions the wheel stays in such a position that it will strike the driver's chest, and not move upwards into the region of his face, or downwards into the region of his abdomen. At the present time these problems are, in practice, not completely solved, but until knowledge of the tolerance to impact of the human chest is better, rational improvements will remain difficult.

Head restraints Impacts to the rear of cars are relatively frequent and increasing with the greater density of today's traffic. In rear end collisions the car is suddenly accelerated forward, with the result that the head of an occupant is snapped backwards over the seat back. This can cause a serious 'whiplash' injury to the neck. To prevent such injuries cars in some countries have been fitted with head restraints. Many of these, however, are poorly designed because the car occupant must adjust his head restraint to the correct height so that it is in the right position to protect him in a collision. In the United States, for example, where virtually all head restraints are adjustable, field surveys have shown that 80% of the head restraints are in the fully down position all the time. As a result accident studies show that head restraints have had almost no benefits there. An alternative and much better solution, therefore, seems to be that of the fixed head restraint integral with the seat.

Pedestrian injury So far governments and engineers have concerned themselves almost exclusively with the car occupant when crash protection is being considered. In reality, on a world wide basis, there are as many pedestrians who are fatally injured by being struck by a car, as there are fatally injured car occupants. Recently this problem has been recognised and work is under way to produce the optimum dimensions, bumper height and shape for the exterior of cars, and some countries have for many years enforced legislation to restrict the fitting of sharp or dangerous projections on the front and sides of cars.

Below right: only two of all the seats tested passed; this is one of them. It is properly anchored to the car body, not clipped over the main seat back.

Above: the anti-burst door lock completely encircles a pin on the door frame, so that it cannot fly open, but can still be opened if the door is distorted.

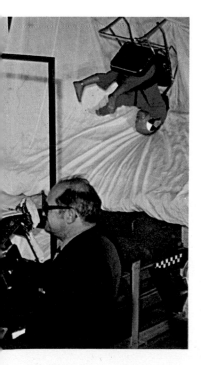

33

An exhaust emission lab at Fiat.

The 1955 Ford (left) featured a 'wrap-around windshield'. In the USA, car manufacturers increasingly concentrated on bodywork design as a means of selling their product. The 'fins' on the rear deck of the 1959 Cadillac (below) were expensive to manufacture and difficult to repair. In the meantime, the distribution of cars and the finance of their purchase had become such a morass of near-fraudulant practices that the business was investigated by Congress; one result was the required posting of the manufacturer's price sticker on each car.

*Below: a Morris Mini-Cooper,
photographed in 1961. It has
a transverse-mounted four-
cylinder engine, front-wheel
drive and front disc brakes.
Bottom of page: the Rolls-
Royce Camargue, which costs
£35,772 in England.*

*Below: the British Leyland
Range Rover, with four-wheel
drive, is a sophisticated
version of the Land Rover,
one of the world's most
versatile vehicles.
Left: a 1961 'E' type Jaguar,
which can do 150 mph.*

Design and Layout: How Cars Work

Introduction

There are many variations in car design—both in exterior styling and in engineering layout—but for most purposes a 'standard' model can be considered with a front mounted engine, rear driven wheels and comparatively simple suspension, brake and steering systems.

Most modern cars consist of a rigid steel monocoque or unit construction which combines bodywork and frame. Most older cars had a separate chassis on which the mechanical parts were mounted.

Engine The heart of any motor car is the engine—the high precision machine which converts the latent energy of petrol into mechanical energy, or movement. Petrol is drawn from the petrol tank by a fuel pump, which can be electrical or mechanical (driven from the engine itself). It is then passed to the carburettor, a device which vaporizes the fuel, providing a highly combustible mixture of petrol and air, the ratio of which changes in proportion with the position of the accelerator pedal. The mixture passes through the inlet manifold and is fed, in turn, to each of the cylinders through the inlet valves. The potentially explosive vapour is compressed in the combustion chamber by the rising piston and fired by a high voltage spark from the spark plug in the top of the chamber. The piston is thus forced down the cylinder, and on its return stroke an exhaust valve is opened to allow the burnt gases to escape through the exhaust manifold, into a silencer to quieten the explosive roar of the engine, and out through the exhaust pipe at the rear of the car.

Each piston drives a connecting rod, the other end of which is connected to the crankshaft; this runs along the length of the engine and converts the up and down movement of the pistons into a circular or rotary movement. At the end of the crankshaft is a heavy flywheel which provides the momentum to keep the engine running smoothly, and because of the great forces involved, the crankshaft is mounted on precision bearings which (like all moving engine parts) are fed with lubricating oil drawn from the sump by a mechanically operated oil pump.

For the engine to run efficiently, it is necessary that the inlet and exhaust valves are opened or closed at exactly the right moment in relation to the position of the piston. The crankshaft therefore drives a camshaft (via a driving chain) which has cams (eccentric lobes) along its length; as the camshaft rotates, the lobes operate pushrods to move rocker arms which in turn open and close spring-loaded valves in synchronization with the movement of the pistons. In some high-performance cars, the camshaft is mounted over the valve assembly—this eliminates both pushrods and rocker gear and increases efficiency by reducing friction.

In the same way that the valves must open and close at the correct moment, the spark at the spark plug must also be accurately timed. This is done by the ignition system. The current for the spark originates from the battery, usually at 12 volts DC; this is passed through the contact points in the distributor, which provides bursts of current at the exact moment required for ignition at each cylinder. In order to provide a good spark, the 12 V current is passed through an induction coil (after the contact break points) and the voltage increased to about 30,000 V. This is then fed to the spark plugs, where the current jumps the gap and provides the igniting spark.

Naturally a machine which contains a series of almost continuous explosions becomes very hot. Most engines are cooled by water which is pumped around the cylinder block by a water pump and through a radiator which can efficiently dispose of unwanted heat. Behind the radiator is a fan which draws air through the cooling vents and increases the efficiency of the cooling system.

Both the fan and the water pump are driven by a belt from the crankshaft; this belt also drives a dynamo [generator] or alternator which, operating through a voltage regulator, continuously charges the battery.

Transmission system A motor car is heavy, and at rest or slow speeds has a great deal of inertia which must be overcome; the function of the gearbox is to transmit power to the driving wheels efficiently. Before the gearbox can be driven there must be a device to connect and disconnect the engine from the gear apparatus in order to change the gears; this is the clutch.

The flywheel at the end of the crankshaft faces a clutch plate or disc covered with a high-friction material; this plate is held against the flywheel by springs and is connected to the gearbox driving shaft. When the clutch pedal is depressed, the clutch plate is removed from the flywheel and the engine disconnected from the road wheels and gearbox. Automatic clutches are used in automatic transmission systems: they may be torque converters operated by fluid pressure or centrifugal clutches worked by centrifugal force.

The gearbox is a complicated system of cogs which provides maximum power to the road wheels. Basically a gearbox contains three parallel shafts—one driven from the engine via the clutch, another connected to the propeller shaft, and a third to link them, each with a cluster of different gears. Operation of the gear lever selects different combinations of cogs which mesh with each other to provide different ratios. In a synchromesh system the driving and driven gears are synchronized in speed before they are engaged, thus eliminating 'grinding' of the gears. In automatic transmissions, the gears, which are generally epicyclic, are selected automatically.

The driven shaft is connected to the propeller shaft, which runs the length of the car, and is in turn connected via universal joints to the differential. The differential gears, besides converting the plane of movement, also allow the two different shafts driving the wheels to rotate at different relative speeds; this is essential in cornering, where the outer driving wheel turns faster than the other. All four wheels of the car are mounted on bearings to reduce friction.

Suspension It is essential that the wheels are connected in such a way as to allow a certain freedom of vertical movement, thus providing a smooth ride for the occupants of the car.

In order to provide this movement, the wheels of the motor car are attached to the body via a suspension system

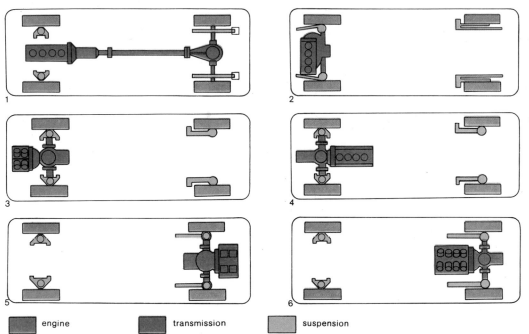

1

2

3

4

5

6

engine   transmission   suspension

Left: component layouts vary widely. 1. 'Normal' front engine, rear drive layout. 2. Front transverse mounted engine, front drive. 3. Front engine in front of front wheels. 4. Front engine behind front wheels. 5. Rear engine behind rear wheels. 6. 'Mid' engine ahead of rear wheels, behind driver.

Below left: wartime cars ran on coal gas.

Below: world's smallest, the Cox .010 cc engine.

Bottom: Triumph Dolomite Sprint head, 4 valves per cylinder (see page 45).

41

which is generally one of two types. A leaf spring system consists of layers of semi-flexible material in a bow shape; each end of the bow is connected to the chassis while the centre is connected to the axle. The coil spring system provides a strong spring directly between axle and chassis. To avoid a 'bouncing' effect, shock absorbers are incorporated into the system to dampen the spring movement.

Brakes and steering On each of the four wheels of the car is a brake drum or disc; when the brake pedal is depressed, the main cylinder hydraulically operates a slave cylinder at each wheel. These, in turn, provide the means to press a pad against the disc (in the case of the disc brakes) or expand a pair of brake shoes (in the case of drum brakes). Both pads and shoes are composed of high-friction material.

The steering mechanism of the standard car is also comparatively simple. The steering wheel rotates a shaft which is connected to the steering box, a system of gears which converts circular to lateral movement. Tie rods are thus pushed or pulled to the left or the right and these are linked to the front wheels, which are separately pivoted. Hydraulic power steering can be used to assist this on large cars.

All that is left are the various electrical appliances needed to drive safely; lighting, horn, turn indicators, windscreen wipers and other refinements. These are all driven through a wiring loom or harness by the battery, a lead-acid accumulator which is constantly charged by the dynamo or alternator.

This is the bare mechanical outline of a standard car, but fifty years of research have provided many refinements and modifications to the standard design. Volkswagen, for example, pioneered and developed the rear-mounted air cooled engine which disposed of the entire customary cooling system and propeller shaft. High performance cars experiment with mid-engine designs for better roadholding. There have been countless refinements in engine, suspension and steering design. The wankel rotary engine could prove to be a major breakthrough in engineering, drastically reducing the number of moving parts in an engine. With the current concern with pollution and a fuel crisis it could be that the internal combustion engine will become extinct and electric vehicles will replace today's cars.

The Internal Combustion Engine

The development of the internal combustion engine was made possible by the earlier development of the steam engine. Both types of engines burn fuel, releasing energy from it in the form of heat which is then used to do useful work.

The steam engine, however, is an external combustion engine; the fuel is burned in a separate part of the engine from the cylinder containing the piston. Anything combustible can be used as a fuel in the steam engine, such as wood, coal or petroleum products, and the liberated energy is used to heat a fluid, usually water. The hot water vapour expands in a confined place (the cylinder) to push the piston. In the internal combustion engine, the burning of the fuel takes place in the combustion chamber (the top of the cylinder). The combustion is very sudden, amounting to an explosion which pushes the piston.

During the eighteenth and nineteenth centuries, as the steam engine was made more efficient, advancements were made in engineering and metallurgy which made possible the first successful internal combustion engines. The opera-

tion of steam engines was not fully understood at first; the French physicist Sadi Carnot published in 1824 his theories which led to the science of heat-exchange thermodynamics. Fifty years before that James Watt had already begun to develop packings and piston rings to prevent the escape of energy past the piston in his steam engines. By 1800, the British engineer Henry Maudslay was making improvements to the lathe which led to machinery capable of producing precision-made parts for engines. In the 1850s more volatile fuels were being refined from petroleum.

In 1860 J J E Lenoir, a French engineer, built a successful engine which was essentially a modified steam engine, using illuminating gas as the fuel. In 1867 the firm of Otto and Langen began producing an engine which transmitted the power of a freely moving piston to a shaft and a heavy flywheel by means of a rack-and-gear device, using a freewheeling clutch in the gear, so that it turned freely in one direction and transmitted power in the other.

Meanwhile, in 1862, Alphonse Beau de Rochas had published in Paris his theory of a four-stroke engine of the type used in the modern car. While de Rochas never built any engines, his theory included compression of the fuel mixture in order to raise its temperature, and he also realized that a four-stroke design would be more efficient at scavenging (intake of fuel mixture and exhaust of burned gases) than the two-stroke.

A two-stroke engine provides for intake of fuel, combustion and exhaust of burned gases with each back-and-forth motion of the piston (that is, with each revolution of the crankshaft). A four-stroke engine requires four strokes, that is, two complete back-and-forth movements of the piston (two revolutions of the crankshaft). The two-stroke engine delivers twice as many power impulses as the four-stroke engine to the crankshaft, but the four-stroke is much more efficient at scavenging, if all other things are equal. The two-stroke design is also wasteful because unburned fuel is exhausted with the burned gases.

In 1876, Otto and Langen began building the Otto 'silent' engine (it was a good deal quieter than their earlier model). It was the first modern internal combustion engine, a four-stroke design which compressed the fuel mixture slightly before combustion. After 1878, it was also manufactured in the United States, where it was an inspiration to Henry Ford in his early research.

The four-stroke cycle operates as follows: on the first downstroke of the piston, the intake valve opens and the fuel mixture is pulled into the combustion chamber. On the following upstroke, all valves are closed and the fuel mixture is compressed. At the beginning of the second downstroke, combustion takes place; the fuel mixture is ignited by the spark plug and the expanding gases drive the piston downwards. On the second upstroke, the exhaust valve opens and the burned gases are expelled. Thus the four parts of the cycle are intake, compression, combustion and exhaust.

The fuel mixture is a mixture of fuel and air in the form of a vapour which is prepared by the carburettor. The fuel is usually petrol [gasoline], but engines can be designed to run on anything from paraffin [kerosene] to high-test aviation fuel. The carburettor must be adjusted properly; if the mixture is too lean (does not contain enough fuel), the engine will not run properly; if it is too rich, the result will be carbon deposits fouling the spark plugs, the valves and the inside of the combustion chamber, wasting fuel and affecting the performance of the engine.

The two-stroke engine must accomplish intake, combustion and exhaust in one back-and-forth movement of the piston. Since scavenging is incomplete and inefficient, the proper mixture is difficult to obtain. Small two-stroke engines such as are still used in some motorcycles, lawn mowers and small cars must have oil added to the petrol, and constitute an air pollution problem; the blue smoke from the exhaust pipe of these engines is one of their familiar characteristics.

One way of improving the scavenging of the two-stroke engine is to build opposing pistons, which reciprocate in opposite directions and share a common combustion chamber. This design was chosen by Henry Ford for his first car, which was built in 1896. A big disadvantage is that each piston must drive a separate crankshaft, and the motion of the two crankshafts must then be combined through a system of gearing.

Another way of improving the scavenging of a two-stroke engine is to use a turbocharger, which is a supercharger driven by the energy of the exhaust gases, and resembles a pump for blowing air into the cylinder. This is combined with a fuel injection system instead of the usual carburettor. The modern diesel engine pulls in only air on the intake, and compresses it to between a twelfth and a twenty-fifth of its original volume, compared to a sixth to a tenth for compression in a petrol engine. This raises the temperature of the air to over 1000°F (538°C). At this point the fuel is injected and ignites spontaneously, without the need for a spark plug. Diesel engines may be of two- or four-stroke design (both types can be turbocharged), though most roadgoing diesels are four-stroke.

The engine block, the head and the crankshaft are all castings that require extensive machining before the engine can be assembled (some larger crankshafts are forgings, for extra strength). The cylinders must be bored and finished precisely in the block. The top of the block and underside of the head are planed or milled to fit smoothly together, and

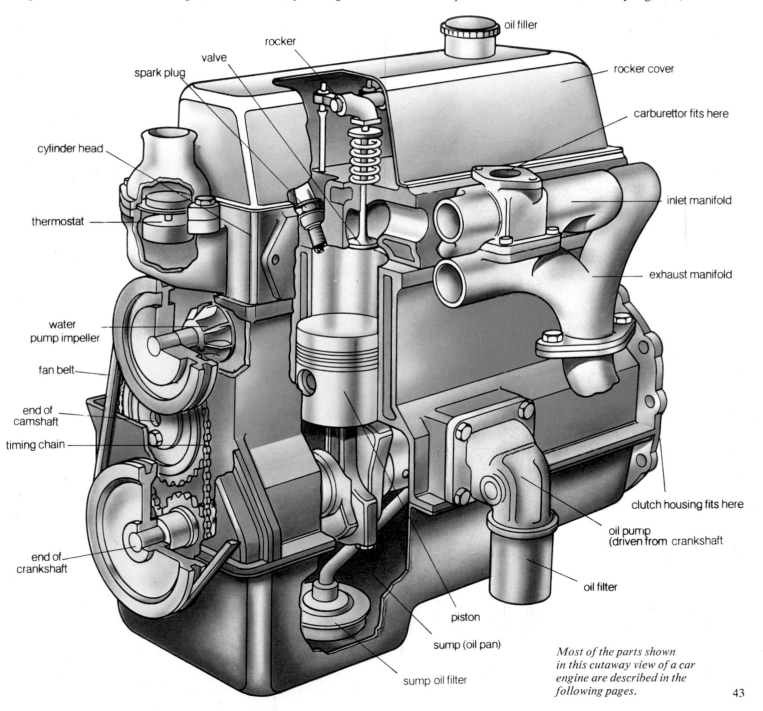

Most of the parts shown in this cutaway view of a car engine are described in the following pages.

43

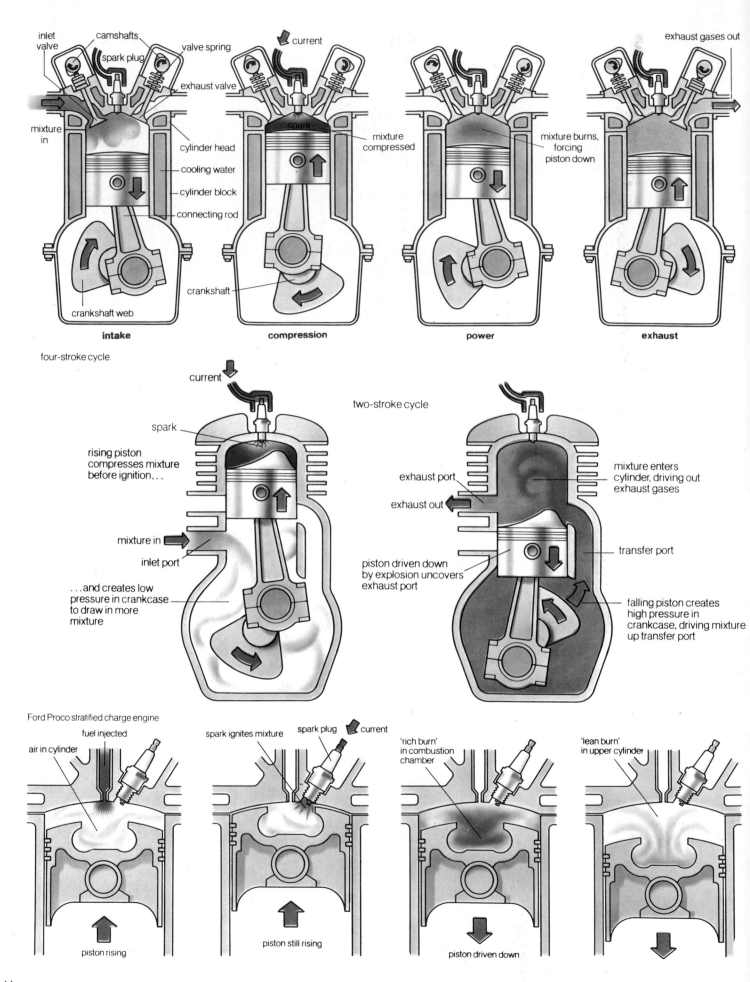

inlet valve
camshafts
spark plug
valve spring
exhaust valve
current
cylinder head
mixture in
cooling water
cylinder block
connecting rod
mixture compressed
spark
mixture burns, forcing piston down
exhaust gases out
crankshaft
crankshaft web

intake　　**compression**　　**power**　　**exhaust**

four-stroke cycle

current

spark

rising piston compresses mixture before ignition...

mixture in
inlet port

...and creates low pressure in crankcase to draw in more mixture

two-stroke cycle

exhaust port
exhaust out

piston driven down by explosion uncovers exhaust port

mixture enters cylinder, driving out exhaust gases

transfer port

falling piston creates high pressure in crankcase, driving mixture up transfer port

Ford Proco stratified charge engine
fuel injected
air in cylinder

spark ignites mixture
spark plug
current

'rich burn' in combustion chamber

'lean burn' in upper cylinder

piston rising　　piston still rising　　piston driven down

Opposite page, top row: how a four stroke engine works. This one is shown with twin overhead camshafts for clarity. Camshafts turn at half engine speed, opening each valve once in the cycle. Intake: the rotating crankshaft pulls the piston down, creating low pressures in the cylinder. The inlet valve opens and mixture enters. Compression: the crankshaft raises the piston, compressing the mixture. At the top of the stroke, the spark plug fires. Power: the mixture, ignited by the spark, expands, forcing the piston down and turning the crankshaft to give power. Exhaust: the piston rises again. The exhaust valve opens, so that the burned gases are forced out of the cylinder.

Middle row: two stroke engines, used on motorcycles, use both the cylinder and the crankcase below the piston in their operation. While the piston rises to compress the mixture above it, it creates low pressure below it, drawing mixture into the crankcase through the inlet port (there are no valves). When the piston is at the top, the mixture in the cylinder is ignited, driving the piston down to open the exhaust port. While the exhaust gases leave, mixture, compressed by the falling piston, is forced up the transfer port into the cylinder. A shaped piston separates mixture and exhaust.

Bottom row: part of the cycle of an experimental stratified charge engine with fuel injection. The mixture is burned in two stages, first inside a shaped piston crown, then more completely outside it, which gives a cleaner exhaust and slightly improved fuel economy.

Above: the action of the cam, pushrod and rocker assembly found on most car engines. The cam is like a wheel with a bulge on one side; as it turns it pushes the pushrod up and so the valve is pushed down. (The four-valve engine shown on page 41 works all its valves from a single overhead camshaft by means of rockers moved directly by the camshaft, with no pushrods between.)

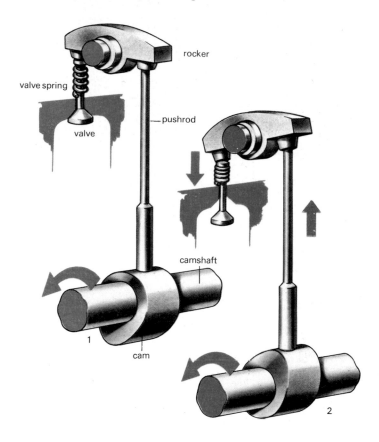

Below: a Ford V4 engine, cut away to reveal the normal arrangement of pushrods, rockers and valves.

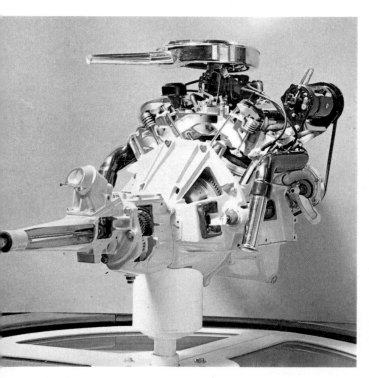

Below: a high performance Ford straight 4 engine with twin overhead camshafts driven by a toothed belt.

the tops of the compression chambers are also machined on the underside of the head—except in 'bowl in piston' designs, where the head is flat and the tops of the pistons are recessed. Both the block and the head must have numerous surfaces machined and holes drilled and tapped where various components will be mounted. Where the head is bolted to the block, a head gasket is included in order to prevent escape of compression in the assembled engine.

The underside of the block is open; at the bottom of each cylinder wall, bearing surfaces are machined to accept the main bearings of the crankshaft. Bearing caps are screwed down to hold the crankshaft in place. The pistons slide up and down in the cylinders and are connected to the crankshaft by means of connecting rods which pivot in the pistons and turn on the throws of the crankshaft. A sump, or oil pan, made of sheet metal or cast light alloy is screwed to the bottom of the block, covering the crankshaft; a gasket is included to prevent leakage of oil, and there is also an oil seal at each end of the crankshaft where it protrudes from the block.

The crankshaft itself is a mechanical adaptation of the hand crank, used for centuries to operate simple machines such as early lathes. For each cylinder in the engine there is a separate throw (offset section forming a crank) which revolves around the axis of the crankshaft, pushed by the operation of the piston when the engine is running. Opposite each throw on the crankshaft is a web (a mass of metal) to balance it. The throws in a multi-cylinder engine are arranged equidistant around the circle described by their revolution, and the firing sequence of the combustion chambers, which depends on the crank position, is timed in such a way as to balance the engine and provide for smooth running. Internal combustion engines have been built with as many as sixteen cylinders or more, in several configurations: opposed, radial (in aircraft engines), V-formation, and in-line (all in a row). The most common type of engine today is the in-line four or six cylinder engine used in cars; V-8 engines are also common, especially in American cars.

On the front of the crankshaft, where it protrudes from the engine, is mounted a pulley wheel from which are

operated, by means of a belt, the dynamo or alternator, and the water pump, if the engine is water-cooled. The crankshaft also drives the oil pump (for lubrication of the engine) by means of a skew gear.

Also mounted on the crankshaft is the timing gear. The timing gear is a pair of gearwheels, or a sprocket linked by a chain to a smaller sprocket, which turns the camshaft, which is generally located in the block, at half crankshaft speed. The camshaft in turn operates the valves, and also drives the distributor to spark the mixture at the correct moment. If the valves are located in the block, the engine is a side-valve, valve-in-head, flat head or L-head design. In this case the valve stems ride directly on the cams. If the engine is an overhead valve design, the valves are operated from the camshaft by means of an assembly of pushrods and rocker arms, and access to the valves for repairs is more easily obtained by removing a sheet metal cover on top of the head, instead of having to remove the head itself. In yet another variation, the overhead cam, the camshaft is also located on top.

In all cases, the valves are operated against spring pressure; there are at least two valves for each cylinder (intake and exhaust); and the adjustment of the timing gear is vital to the performance of the engine. Some high performance engines have four valves to a cylinder; some aircraft engines have sleeve valves, in which a tubular sleeve with holes in it covers and uncovers the ports.

At the back end of the engine, where the crankshaft protrudes, it is linked to the components necessary for the transmission of its power. In a car, these include a clutch, a gearbox or automatic transmission, and a differential, which transmit the power to the drive wheels. (The Dutch DAF car is an exception; it has none of these components in the conventional sense, but is driven by belts running over conical pulleys, moving up and down the cones to give infinitely variable 'gearing' and the functions of a differential.)

The top speed of an internal combustion engine is limited by, among other factors, the speed at which the combustion chambers can be supplied with the fuel mixture. High performance engines can be fitted with a supercharger to increase the pressure available to the engine.

Horsepower was originally a calculation devised by Watt to enable his customers to determine what size steam engine they needed. For an internal combustion engine, horsepower

Right: cutaway view of a variable jet SU carburettor, with (below) a detail of the float chamber. When the throttle is opened the suction increases and the piston rises, pulling the tapered needle out of the jet and increasing both air and fuel flow to the engine. When the throttle is closed the piston and needle fall and the flow stops. The float chamber attached to the carburettor controls the fuel supply from the main tank.

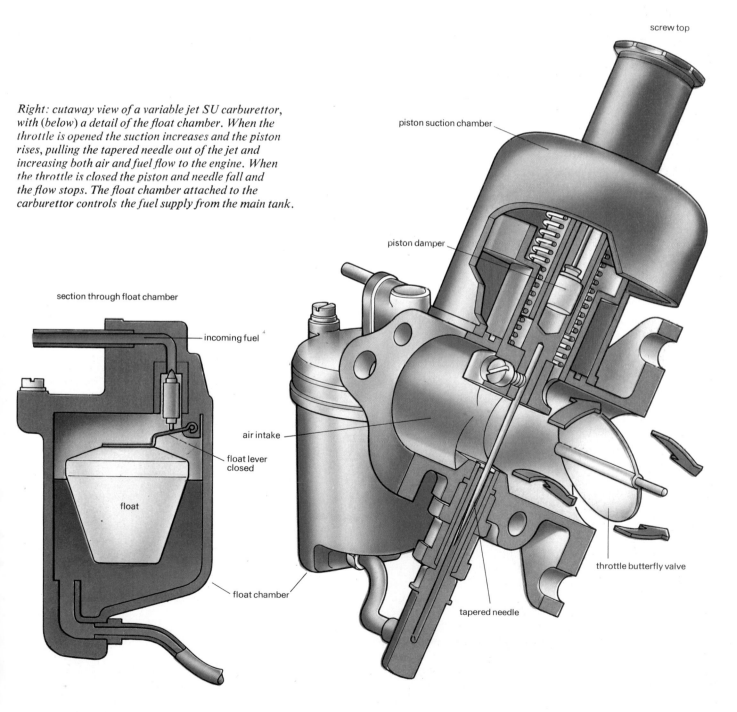

screw top

piston suction chamber

piston damper

section through float chamber

incoming fuel

air intake

float lever closed

float

float chamber

tapered needle

throttle butterfly valve

is determined by using a dynamometer to measure the amount of torque needed to restrain the rotation of the crankshaft. A horsepower rating should always be accompanied by the number of revolutions per minute of the crankshaft at which the measurement was made.

The configuration of the internal combustion engine is determined by the number of cylinders, the length of the piston stroke, the compression ratio (the ratio of the size of combustion chamber to the volume displaced by the piston) and many other factors, all of which are design decisions affecting the theoretical efficiency of the engine, and which are made on the basis of the intended use of the engine. Total weight for internal combustion engines ranges from a few pounds for lawnmower engines to more than fifteen tons for a V-16 design for locomotives.

The carburettor The carburettor is the device used to mix the air and petrol vapour. This mixture is then fed into the engine to be burned, and provides the power which drives the engine in a variety of operating conditions from cold winter starting to fast acceleration.

The first carburettors appeared at the end of the 19th century and were called surface carburettors. They worked very simply by drawing air over the surface of the fuel, and so mixing its vapour with the air to form a combustible mixture which was fed into the engine. The wick carburettor, developed next, was similar but instead of the air being drawn over the fuel, it was drawn over wicks which had one end immersed in the fuel, which soaked the wick and vaporized into the air. To assist evaporation, hot air from the engine was used. Various versions of these designs were made until the development of the two basic types of carburettor used today: the fixed and variable jet carburettor.

The carburettor works by suction from the engine which helps to atomize (break up into tiny droplets) and vaporize the fuel. The amount of fuel drawn into the airstream in the carburettor to obtain the required air-to-fuel ratio is con-

Right: a carburettor of the type shown on the previous page, sectioned to show internal details. The lever at the far right controls the throttle butterfly valve; the Z-shaped one below it is worked by the choke knob and pulls the jet vertically downwards to open it further, for cold start enrichment, and also moves the stop against which the throttle rests when the accelerator is released, so that the idling speed is increased and the cold engine does not stall.

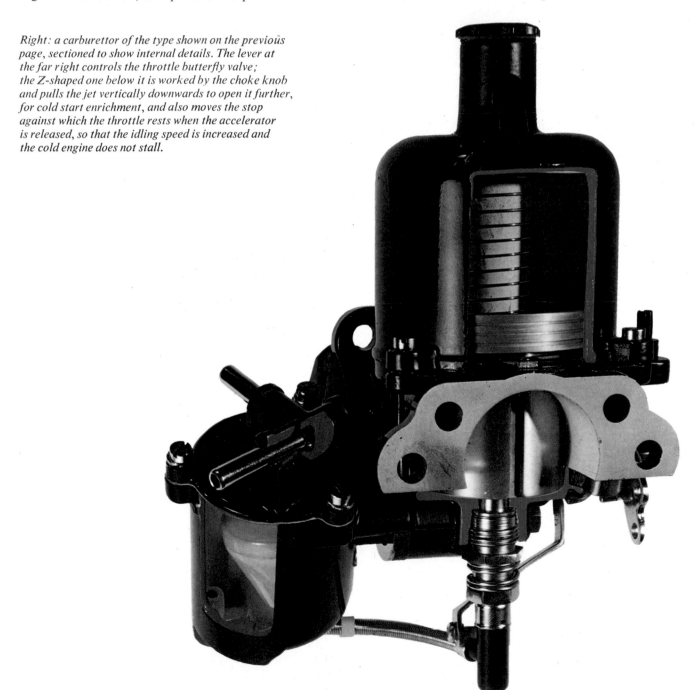

trolled by a narrow passage called the choke, or venturi. As the air flows through this passage its speed increases and consequently the pressure drops, which causes fuel to be sucked into the airstream from a hole or jet at this point.

The fuel atomizes and is mixed with air, usually in the ratio of about 15 parts (by weight) of air to 1 part (by weight) of fuel. In cold starting, however, the mixture may need to be much richer, say 2 parts of air to 1 of fuel.

The amount of fuel-air mixture allowed into the engine is controlled by a butterfly valve or throttle, which is positioned after the venturi. The valve is a simple device which if it is opened (when the accelerator pedal is depressed) allows large amounts of the mixture through, and if it is closed cuts off the supply. The throttle therefore controls the speed at which the engine runs. The petrol-air mixture is sucked into one cylinder of the engine, where a valve closes to seal it in. The piston rises to compress the mixture before it is fired by the spark plug. The force of the burning mixture pushes the piston down, the valve opens, and the cycle starts again.

The fixed jet carburettor has several jets of a fixed size, and an accelerator pump which is used to boost the fuel supply when necessary, as in sudden acceleration. Each jet has a function; the idling jet bypasses all of the other jets and allows a constant small flow of fuel to reach the air flow. It is used to keep the engine turning over at low speeds. The other jets are designed to mix some air with the fuel before it reaches the venturi to prevent the mixture from becoming too 'rich'. They include the main jet which operates once the butterfly valve is opened, supplying fuel for constant high speed running, and the compensating jet. This jet functions when the butterfly valve is opened to supply extra fuel to the engine and enables it to accelerate to a high speed at which the main jet takes over. There may be more jets found in this type of carburettor but basically they just assist the three jets which have been mentioned above.

The variable jet carburettor works on the suction of the engine and also depends on the butterfly valve to control engine speed. Basically it consists of a main jet and a tapered needle which is mounted on a piston. In this type of carburettor the air is always drawn in from the side of the carburettor, as the piston and needle have to be vertical to operate smoothly. They are mounted through the air tube or the venturi. The tapered needle sits in the main jet and as the butterfly valve is opened the suction from the engine is increased; this suction acts on the top of the piston which is sucked upwards. As the piston rises it pulls the tapered needle out of the main jet and so more fuel is allowed to flow through and mix with the air. A damper on top of the piston slows its rise when a richer mixture is demanded for sudden acceleration.

Attached to both types of carburettor is a small reservoir

tank of fuel called the float chamber because it has a float which rises with the fuel level until it reaches a certain level. At this stage it cuts off the fuel supply from the main tank. This means that it also stops too much fuel being passed into the carburettor and so acts as a control valve.

If a better performance is wanted from an engine, as in racing cars, one of the first things to be modified is the carburettor. Engines may have two carburettors instead of one, or a carburettor with two or four chokes side by side. These are said to give a better distribution of the mixture to the engine. Short open pipes may be fitted to the air intakes of the carburettors; these are called ram pipes and are said to improve the air flow to the venturi to give a better mixture. Sometimes larger main jets are fitted to allow more fuel to flow. Other high performance engines have fuel injection systems, where fuel and air are precisely metered and mixed in the engine itself.

Fuel injection Fuel injection has been used since the earliest days of the motor vehicle, but it was largely ignored for spark ignition engines until the needs of the aircraft industry spurred its development in the 1930s. During World War II many military aircraft were equipped with some form of petrol injection equipment, and the success of these systems contributed to the development of fuel injection units for cars. Diesel engines, however, have always used some form of fuel injection, the first engines injecting the fuel by means of a blast of air. There are many claims to the invention of the first practical mechanical fuel injection unit, but the first commercial design was probably that of Robert Bosch in about 1912.

Petrol injection equipment is increasingly being used in place of the more conventional carburettor, the fuel being injected into the engine intake air in the form of a fine spray. This injection takes place either at the inlet manifold or in the cylinder head close to the inlet valves. Control of

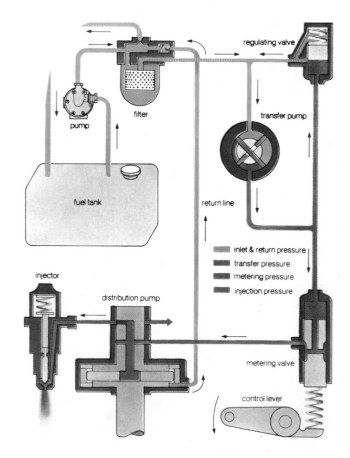

Right: a distributor pump injection system for diesel engines. Fuel is pumped from the tank and passed through a filter to the transfer pump and regulating valve, which maintain a constant pressure feed to the metering valve. The control lever position determines the amount of fuel delivered to the distribution pump.

the amount of fuel delivered to each injector is achieved either by mechanical metering or by an electronic control system, and there is usually one injector for each cylinder of the engine.

A typical mechanical system uses an electric fuel pump to supply petrol from the tank, through a filter, to a metering distributor. Pressure in the fuel line is maintained at around 100 psi (7 bar) by a pressure relief valve regulator. The engine-driven metering distributor measures and distributes the correct amount of fuel to each injector in turn, and works on the shuttle metering principle.

The distributor consists of two main parts, the rotor and the sleeve. The rotor is a hollow tube which has radial ports in its body leading to the centre bore, which contains the shuttle, a small free-moving piston. This shuttle can move along the bore between two end stops, one fixed, the other movable.

The rotor turns within the sleeve, a fixed hollow tube with inlet and outlet ports, and is driven by the engine. As the rotor turns, one of its ports lines up with a fuel inlet port in the sleeve. Petrol enters the central bore under pressure from the fuel pump, and drives the shuttle towards the opposite end stop, filling the bore behind the shuttle with petrol, and at the same time expelling the petrol in front of the shuttle through additional ports in the rotor and sleeve to a fuel line leading to an injector. There is an outlet for each cylinder.

As the rotor continues to turn this fuel inlet port is covered, and another is uncovered which allows fuel in to drive the shuttle back again, expelling another charge to a second fuel line and injector. This process is repeated as the rotor turns, the shuttle oscillating between the two end stops. The quantity of fuel delivered is varied by altering the length of travel of the shuttle, which is determined by the position of the movable stop. A control unit attached to the metering distributor unit alters the position of the movable stop.

On high performance racing engines this control takes the form of a cam actuated by the throttle linkage. Passenger cars employ manifold depression (vacuum) forces for control purposes, as this gives finer control resulting in greater fuel economy and smooth running at low speeds. The engine speed is governed by the control unit acting in conjunction with the throttle, which regulates the amount of air entering the manifold.

An excess fuel control is used for starting, which alters the position of the movable stop to allow additional fuel to be delivered by the shuttle, and also partially opens the throttle to provide extra air.

An electronic petrol injection system consists of two distinct systems, namely the fuel system and the electrical-electronic control system. The fuel system comprises a pipe line known as the fuel rail, which contains petrol at a pressure of about 30 psi (2 bar) fed by the fuel pump, a fuel filter, and a pressure relief valve. Branches of this fuel rail feed the injectors, which are electromagnetic valves operated by the electronic control system. The fuel feed to the injectors is kept at a constant pressure, and the amount of fuel supplied to the engine is metered by controlling the length of time that the injectors are open.

The central feature of the electronic system is the control box. This is connected to several sensors which measure the engine speed, crankshaft position, throttle setting and manifold depression. The circuitry in this unit interprets the signals from these sensors, and generates output signals to open the injectors at the correct moment and for the precise length of time required. Features built into the control system provide for mixture enrichment for cold starting, engine warm up, full load running and acceleration, fuel cut during engine overrun, and corrections for changes in air density (due to changes in altitude, for instance).

Cooling systems Because of very high operating temperatures within an engine, the system must be cooled in order to prevent seizing of moving parts, that is, jamming of the pistons in the cylinders. There are two main types of cooling system: water cooled and air cooled.

Water cooled systems employ a radiator made of copper and brass. Such a radiator is expensive but does not rust. A brass tank at the top of the radiator is connected to a brass tank at the bottom via a mesh of copper tubing. The other major component is the water pump, which is usually mounted on the front of the engine and driven by the fan belt from the crankshaft.

The engine cylinder block and the cylinder head are

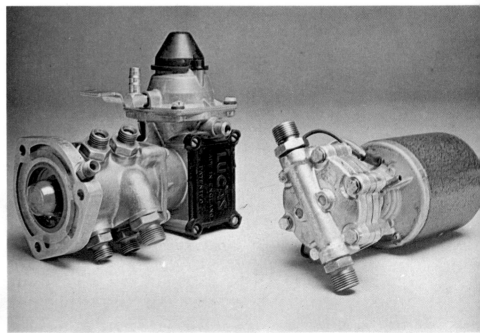

Left: the high performance Porsche 2.7 litre engine. It has overhead valves and camshafts, six cylinders arranged in two horizontally opposed banks, eight main crankshaft bearings for stability, and is air cooled. The belt-driven fan and its ducting are in the foreground of the picture. One of the exhaust valves is shown on p 52: it is sodium-filled to aid cooling of the valve head; the sodium melts and circulates. The lubrication system is also designed for maximum cooling: the oil filter does not restrict flow and there is an oil cooler with a thermostat.

castings which have waterways cast into them. The block and head are connected to the radiator at the top and bottom by rubber hoses. When the engine is running, the water is pumped out of the bottom of the radiator into the block, where it circulates around the cylinders and through the head gasket into the head past the combustion chambers (the hottest part of the engine, where the fuel mixture is ignited). Then it reaches the thermostat, a valve which is operated by heat. The thermostat stays closed if the engine is cold until the water is heated to the correct operating temperature. Then it opens and the water flows through the top hose back into the radiator, where it is cooled as it passes down through the copper tubing.

The fan is mounted on the front of the engine just behind the radiator. When the vehicle is moving, the air rushing through the radiator may be sufficient to cool the water, but the fan is necessary to cool the system when the engine is idling. The fan is normally operated by the fan belt from the crankshaft, but there are some types of fans with blades whose pitch is variable. The blade-pitch variation is controlled by another thermostat, or by the speed of the fan by means of centrifugal force. Other types of fan are driven by electric motors, turned on and off as necessary by a thermostatic switch.

Water expands when frozen, and if allowed to freeze in the engine block will crack it, so in cold weather anti-freeze must be added to the system. Anti-freeze is essentially alcohol, which has a much lower freezing temperature than water. Nowadays most cars are equipped with 'permanent' anti-freeze at the factory and are designed to operate on it all year round.

Water cooled systems are usually pressurized to raise the boiling point of the system, thus improving the efficiency of the engine and the thermal coefficient of the radiator. The radiator cap on such a system will be designed to cope with the pressure, and if the system overheats great care must be taken if the cap is removed while the fluid is still hot.

Although the radiator will not rust, it may become clogged up with particles from dirty water or rust from the inside of the engine. When this happens, the best treatment is to flush the radiator with chemicals in a reverse direction from the usual water flow, that is, from bottom to top, and under pressure.

The most common failure of water cooled systems is

Far left: a new type of fuel injection system: electro-pneumatic, controlled by manifold depression and by an electronic switching unit. Compared with similar engines fitted with carburettors, an engine using this system will have improved performance and fuel consumption and cleaner exhaust.

Centre left: two components of a fuel injection system: a metering distribution pump (left), which feeds fuel to the injectors, and (right) its supply pump.

Left: injector nozzle.

failure of the rubber hoses, causing leakage. A temperature gauge used to be provided on the dashboard of the car, but for reasons of economy many manufacturers have replaced it with a warning light.

Air cooled engines (for example, Volkswagen) have fins on the cylinder bores to give the largest surface area for dispersal of heat. The air is drawn in by a large fan. A thermostat, which is operated by the heat of the engine, directs the air toward or away from the fins. The main advantages with this system are that the engine casting is simpler, and the radiator, water pump, hoses and anti-freeze are all unnecessary.

The larger the engine, however, the less efficient the air cooling system becomes, because much larger fans would be needed. Water is a far more efficient coolant than air. Air cooled engines also tend to be more noisy in operation, because fans are more noisy than pumps and because the water jacket in a water cooled engine block deadens much of the mechanical noise from the engine. Aircraft engines are usually air cooled because the propeller acts as a cooling fan.

The lubrication system Lubrication of automotive engines serves not only to reduce friction and wear of the moving parts but also to disperse heat, reduce corrosion, and help the sealing action of the piston rings.

Modern lubrication systems used in diesel engines and four-stroke petrol engines have developed by stages from the crude 'total loss' systems used in early engines. In these early systems the driver operated a manual pump which delivered oil to the crankcase, from where it was splashed around the engine by the moving parts. The oil in the engine was eventually 'lost' by being burned in the cylinders or by leakages through joints and bearings, and then was replenished by further operation of the pump.

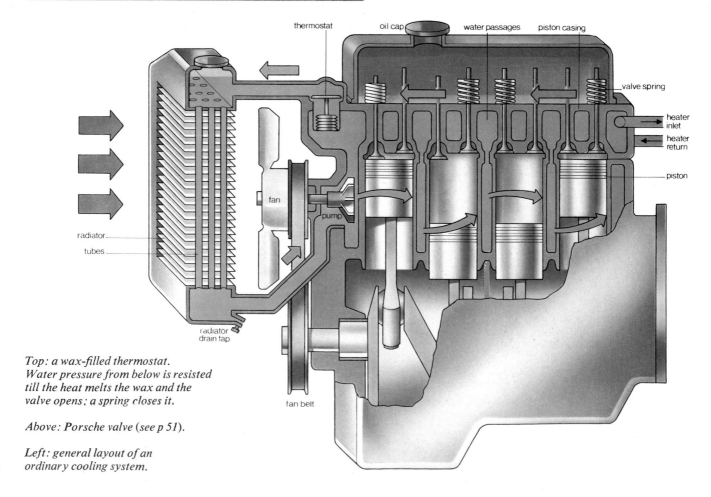

Top: a wax-filled thermostat. Water pressure from below is resisted till the heat melts the wax and the valve opens; a spring closes it.

Above: Porsche valve (see p 51).

Left: general layout of an ordinary cooling system.

This method was eventually replaced by a pump system in which oil was pumped to a trough beneath the crankshaft, where it was picked up by scoops on the big-end bearing caps and carried to the big-end bearings.

In most modern engines, oil is carried in a sump and fed to the moving parts by a pump via a filtration system. The sump is a sheet metal pan screwed to the bottom of the engine block, including a gasket to prevent leakage. In other English-speaking countries it is called, appropriately enough, the oil pan. It forms the lower part of the crankcase and fulfils the combined duties of reservoir and cooler. Cooling is achieved because the sump protrudes into the airstream below the vehicle, and can be improved by adding cooling fins to increase the surface area. The pump is normally fitted to the crankcase and its drive is taken from the camshaft or the crankshaft. The most common forms of oil pump in use are of the gear type, using two intermeshing gears to pump the oil up, or the rotor type.

The rotor type pump has a rotor mounted off-centre within the casing, and sliding vanes around the edge of the rotor carry the oil from inlet to outlet in a similar manner to the operation of a rotary vane compressor.

Oil usually enters the pump through a strainer, submerged in the oil, which is designed to trap any large particles of dirt. The oil then passes through a fine filter of either the bypass or full flow type. In the bypass system, some of the flow is fed to the filter and then returned to the sump while the rest is fed direct to the engine. Full flow filters handle all the pump's output before delivery to the engine, and incorporate a pressure relief valve which returns oil to

Below: how an oil film forms as a bearing turns till the bearing 'floats'; and general layout of a car engine lubrication system (oil shown in brown).

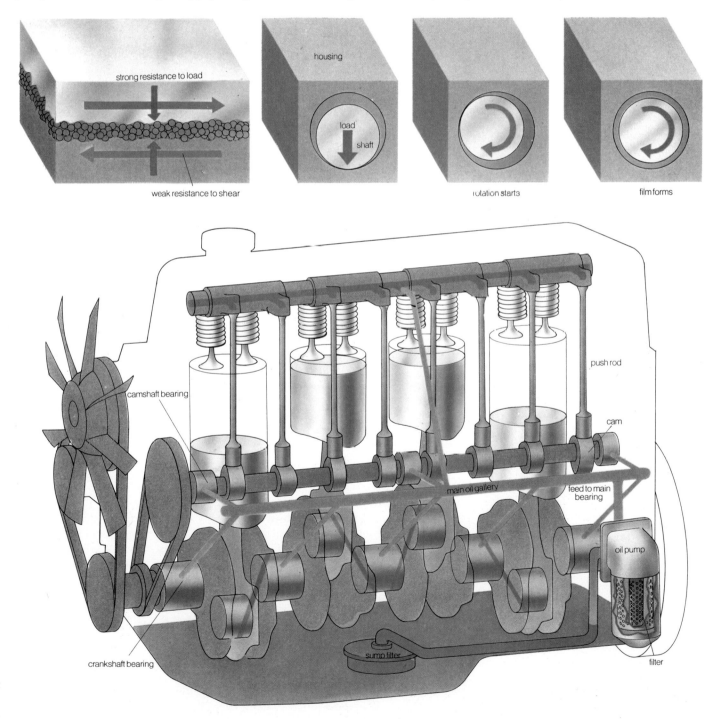

53

the sump if the filter element becomes blocked or when the oil is cold and too thick to flow through the filter.

Filter elements can be made from various materials, but must be capable of restricting the flow of fine particles without restricting oil flow. A common filter element comprises resin-impregnated paper folded into a multi-pointed star, enclosed in a perforated cylinder. Oil enters the filter through the perforations in the cylinder, passes through the filter element, and leaves through a central outlet tube.

Typical full flow filters retain all particles over 15 microns in diameter, 95% of all particles over 10 microns, and 90% of all particles over 5 microns. During use the elements eventually become blocked and therefore less efficient, and so have to be replaced periodically.

From the filter the oil, at a pressure of about 40 to 60 psi (2.76 to 4.14 bar) in modern engines, is fed to a main passage or gallery, which is connected by drillings in the cylinder block to the moving components such as the main bearings, camshaft bearings, valve rockers and timing gears. After passing through the main bearings some of the oil drains back into the sump, and the rest passes through drillings in the crankshaft to the big-end bearings.

Cylinder walls and gudgeon pins are generally lubricated by oil thrown out of the big-end bearings, or else via an oil channel in the connecting rod.

In engines where high oil temperatures are expected an oil cooler may be installed in the pressurized circuit. On some high performance engines a 'dry sump' system is employed. In this system oil is retained in a storage tank, which may also function as a cooling radiator. The oil is pumped to the engine through a filter and then scavenged by a second pump in the sump and returned to the tank.

In most two-stroke petrol engines the crankcase is used to provide initial compression of the fuel-air mixture, and cannot be used as a sump. In these engines lubrication is usually provided by adding a small percentage of oil to the fuel.

Above left: greasing the front suspension of a car. Oil is used to lubricate engine and transmission, but elsewhere grease is the lubricant.

Top: some components are prepacked with grease and sealed, so that they never require lubrication. Here grease is being forced under pressure into rear wheel bearings.

Above: a complete oil filter assembly (right) with its replacement paper filter element.

To monitor the performance of a pressurized system many vehicles have oil pressure gauges. These are connected to the main oil gallery by a thin pipe, and any drop in oil pressure or persistent low pressure will warn the driver that there is either a fault in the lubrication system or else a lack of oil in the system. On many cars the oil gauge has been replaced by a warning light which comes on when the oil pressure is low. It is connected to a pressure-operated switch in the oil gallery, whose contacts close when there is insufficient pressure in the system.

The exhaust system The engine gets its power from a series of explosions in the combustion chambers. The hot gases expand against the pistons and are then allowed to escape through an arrangement of pipes, the exhaust system. As the gases are not only poisonous but at a temperature of about 1700°C (more than 3000°F) and a pressure of about 100 psi (7 bar) when the exhaust valve opens, one of the main functions of such a system is to dispose of them without harm to the occupants of the car or to passers-by. Another function of the exhaust system is to reduce the noise generated to an acceptable level.

An exhaust system starts with an assembly of several pipes collectively called a manifold (meaning 'many branched') bolted to the engine and usually converging to a single steel pipe which passes underneath the car to the silencer, the main noise-reducing component. (The silencer doesn't really

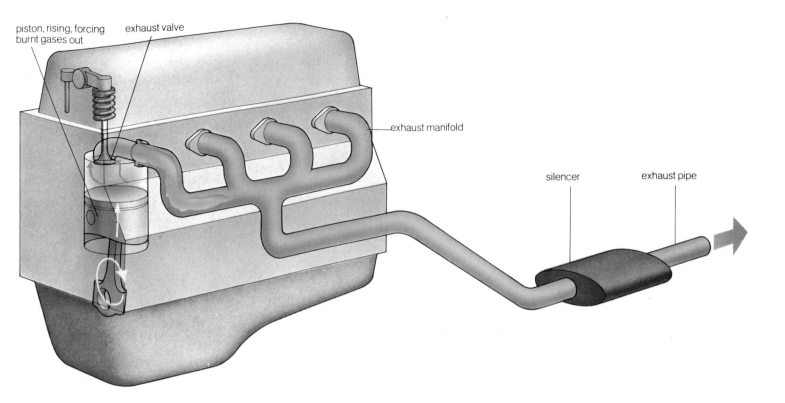

piston, rising, forcing burnt gases out

exhaust valve

exhaust manifold

silencer

exhaust pipe

silence the engine, but considerably muffles the sound, so in North America it is called the muffler.) The silencer is in turn connected to a short length of tailpipe which finishes at the rear of the car several inches above the ground. Sometimes an additional expansion chamber located near the manifold is fitted to absorb more exhaust noise.

Gaskets are fitted where the manifold is bolted to the engine and where the manifold pipe is bolted to the manifold, to ensure a tight connection and prevent the escape of gas and noise. The rest of the system is fastened together and suspended from the underside of the car by a variety of clamps. The entire system, especially the silencer, is exposed to the road surface and subject to a great deal of corrosion and vibration. It is often the first component of a car to fail. In an attempt to make their exhaust system last longer, one American car manufacturer tried coating the components with a ceramic material, but the coating was very brittle and prone to chipping. Longer lasting systems are made of aluminized or aluminium coated steel, or stainless steel, which is very expensive but lasts longest of all and may be cheapest in the long run.

The high temperature of the exhaust gases is reduced to a safe level by cooling in the several feet (2 to 3 m) of pipe which make up a typical system. (In cars with aircooled engines the exhaust gases provide warmth for interior heating), The poisonous nature of the exhaust gases, mostly from carbon monoxide, is not a problem to the occupants of the car (except in a small, closed garage when it is very dangerous) so long as the exhaust system is completely gas-tight and does not leak fumes into the interior of the car. There is a low-pressure area immediately behind a moving car, however, which can cause fumes to be sucked back into it, so the exact location of the tailpipe and the proper sealing of the boot lid or tailgate are also of importance. Exhaust gas toxicity is seldom an immediate danger to pedestrians in the open air, though in most countries, cars now have to conform to exhaust emission regulations, to ensure that

Above: general layout of an exhaust system; and below: two types of stainless steel silencer, one with sound absorbing glass fibre packing.

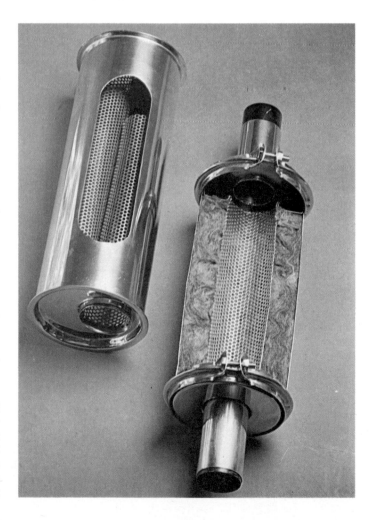

dangerous pollutants are kept to a safe minimum.

For mass-produced engines, the exhaust manifold is usually a single unit made of cast iron, incorporating separate pipes from each cylinder or pair of cylinders which join together into a single outlet of larger diameter. The lengths and geometry of these manifold pipes determine the back-pressure on the engine and so affect its performance and economy. Hence the exhaust manifolds of more highly tuned or expensive engines are sometimes made of very gently curved separate steel pipes of carefully chosen length. When there are two banks of cylinders, as in a V8 engine, two exhaust manifolds are required, and these either lead to a pair or more of entirely separate exhaust systems or are joined to outlet pipes which meet fairly close to the engine at a single final pipe.

The supersonic shockwaves of which exhaust noise is partly composed are reduced in intensity by allowing the gases to expand several times in succession, first in the separate expansion chamber if fitted, and then at perforations in tubes inside cavities within the silencer. The low frequency sound waves also generated are weakened by out-of-phase vibrations of the gases in the expansion chambers, which tend to cancel out the sound waves. In some silencers the perforated tubes are surrounded by an absorptive material such as glass wool which has a high resistance to air movement and cuts down the remaining high-frequency noise.

Cars built since 1970—and especially those sold in the USA—may have exhaust systems which have been modified to meet the pollution laws. In one such emission control system, air from an engine-driven pump is injected into the exhaust manifold to help the completion of the combustion process begun in the cylinder head so that the gases can become more completely consumed. In another system, a proportion of the exhaust gas may be fed back into the engine to dilute the incoming mixture, reduce combustion temperatures and minimize another pollutant. Other cars may use what are called catalytic converters, which purify the exhaust gases and are fitted instead of the silencer or in addition to it.

Supercharging With an internal combustion engine, there is basically only one way to extract more power: burn more fuel. It is a basic law of chemistry that when a given quantity of fuel is burned an exact amount of oxygen is required if the mixture is to be burned without leaving any excess fuel or oxygen. Most petrol engines have to operate at or near this chemically correct mixture, called *stoichiometric*, as do diesel engines at full load. It follows that in order to burn more fuel it is necessary to somehow get more air into the combustion chambers. This is what a supercharger does, by acting as an air pump and as a compressor, compressing the air at the engine intake.

For automotive applications, there are two distinct types of superchargers: the mechanically driven, which includes eccentric drum, lobed or Roots types, and centrifugal; and turbochargers, which use excess energy in the exhaust gases.

An eccentric drum supercharger has an offset drum in which vanes slide radially, being thrown outward by centrifugal force. As the drum rotates the vanes trap the air between the drum, the housing and each other. As rotation continues this space contracts, and the air is thus compressed.

The loading on the tips of the vanes can get quite high at excessive speeds; one way to avoid this problem is to use a Roots type blower. In its simplest form this consists of two rotors, each shaped like a figure 8 in cross-section, running in an oval-shaped housing on parallel shafts and geared together so that their lobes are always in line contact. Clearances between rotors and housing are kept to a fine minimum so that they do not actually touch (and therefore need no lubrication), but the gap is so small that not much leakage of air takes place past the rotor tips. As the rotors rotate, they collect air at the inlet, carry it around the outside and deliver it to the outlet (to the engine intake) at a higher pressure. The Roots type is probably the most common of the mechanically driven devices and is used extensively on the GMC two stroke commercial vehicle engines in the USA.

The basic centrifugal compressor fan is a plate-like rotor with curved axial vanes: as the vanes rotate they collect air at the centre and by centrifugal action fling it towards their outer periphery into a volute or spiral-shaped housing, which by its shape slows down the air and converts its velocity to pressure.

Mechanical superchargers can be driven by belts, by a chain or by gears. The eccentric drum and Roots types can

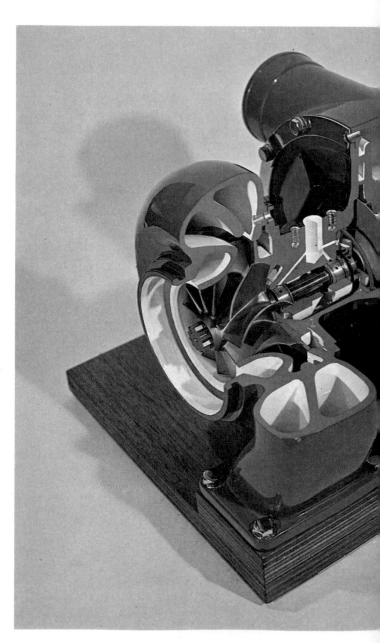

Left: a Roots blower, the type of supercharger used on dragsters.

Below: in the Roots blower, two sets of vanes turn very closely together, not quite touching so as not to need lubrication. They compress the air and drive it into two sets of ports, one for each bank of a V8 engine.

Bottom and centre left: a turbocharger, as used on the diesel engines of trucks. Exhaust gases turn the shaft, driving air through a centrifugal compressor.

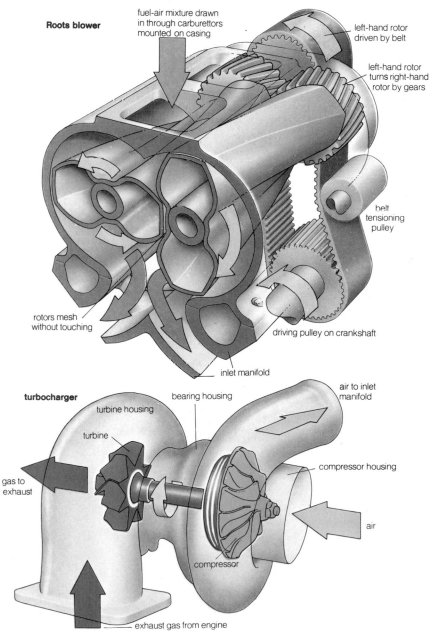

Roots blower

fuel-air mixture drawn in through carburettors mounted on casing

left-hand rotor driven by belt

left-hand rotor turns right-hand rotor by gears

belt tensioning pulley

rotors mesh without touching

driving pulley on crankshaft

inlet manifold

turbocharger

bearing housing

air to inlet manifold

turbine housing

turbine

compressor housing

gas to exhaust

compressor

air

exhaust gas from engine

57

give fairly high boost at low speeds; one of the drawbacks of the centrifugal compressor is that boost is low at low speeds, with the pressure curve rising sharply as speed increases.

If instead of the mechanical drive to a centrifugal compressor fan, another similar fan is attached back-to-back on the same shaft in a suitable housing, and the exhaust gases from the engine are directed into the volute, these gases will turn the blades of the first fan and hence drive the compressor as well. This is the principle of the turbocharger. This is a more efficient and technically elegant way of supercharging, since the energy of the exhaust gases, which would otherwise be wasted, is made to do useful work.

Turbochargers really came into their own on trucks, where a high power-to-weight ratio is more important than first cost; even now their use on cars is rare. If cost is no object, their benefits are enormous: the Porsche 917 Can-Am racing car developed 580 bhp in unblown form, and over 1000 bhp when turbocharged.

Historically, mechanically driven superchargers were first used successfully on Mercedes-Benz racing cars just before World War I. They were expensive and so were limited to expensive cars or racing cars, reaching their peak just before and after World War II on Mercedes, Auto-Union and Alfa-Romeo Grand Prix cars. Nowadays turbochargers are superseding earlier superchargers. It was the development of jet engines which gave impetus to the development of turbochargers, for early jets used centrifugal fans: on the exhaust side these had to cope with very high temperatures and rotational speeds, which required the development of special alloys. When these alloys became more readily available (though still expensive) after World War II, the small, light turbocharger became more practical.

The diesel engine The diesel engine is named after its inventor, Rudolf Diesel, whose first working prototype ran in 1897 after many years of research work. Until the late 1920s most of the development of diesel engines took place in Germany, and a great deal of experience was gained from the production of engines for submarines during World War I. The main companies involved at this time were MAN and Daimler-Benz.

The first successful diesel engines for road transport appeared in 1922, although unsuccessful attempts had been made to produce such engines since as early as 1898. Diesel engines of this type during the 1920s were of two, four or six cylinder designs producing about 40 to 50 horsepower.

The use of diesels for marine applications dates from about 1910, but it was not until 1929, with the introduction of designs by Cummins in the USA and Gardner in Britain, that they became a practical proposition for powering small boats. These engines were subsequently adapted for road use.

Power outputs increased steadily during the 1930s, and by the beginning of World War II diesel engines were in widespread use in road transport, rail locomotives, tractors and construction plant, ships and boats, and as industrial power sources (including electricity generating sets). For cars, motor-cycles and aircraft, however, the diesel could not compete with the petrol engine in terms of performance, although it is still widely used for taxis, and where economy and durability are more important than high performance.

The diesel engine, like the petrol engine, is an internal combustion engine, and although the two have much in common there are important differences in their respective operating principles. In a petrol engine, fuel and air are

Below left: a typical six cylinder turbocharged diesel engine. It gives 143 bhp at 2600 rpm and weighs 1060 lb (482 kg). The unturbocharged version weighs only 925 lb (420 kg) but its power output is much lower: 118 bhp at 2800 rpm. The industrial and marine versions give 160 bhp at 2500 rpm (turbocharged) because better cooling is possible than in a truck.

Right: an engine under test in a sound absorbing chamber designed specially for research into diesel engine noise sources.

mixed in the carburettor, and the mixture is drawn into the combustion chamber at the top of the cylinder during the downward stroke of the piston. The next upward stroke of the piston compresses the mixture to between a sixth and a tenth of its original volume, and as the piston reaches its upper limit of travel the mixture is ignited by an electric spark created by the spark plug. The resulting expansion of the burning mixture forces the piston back down the cylinder (the power stroke).

In a diesel engine, however, as the piston moves down, only pure air is drawn into the cylinder and compressed as it moves up again, but it is compressed to a much higher degree than in a petrol engine (with compression ratios of between 12: 1 and 25: 1) with the result that its temperature is raised considerably, to well over $1000\,°F$ ($538\,°C$). As the piston nears the top of its travel a fine spray of fuel is injected into the cylinder by an injector nozzle near the top. The fuel mixes with the air, which has become so hot due to compression that the fuel/air mixture ignites spontaneously without the need for a spark.

As the volume of air drawn into the cylinder is always the same in a diesel engine, its speed is controlled by the amount of fuel that is injected.

A diesel engine can be adapted to run on almost any fuel from vegetable oils to natural gas and high octane petrol, but the most suitable and widely used diesel fuel is distilled from crude oil and closely related to kerosene. (Kerosene is the name used in technical literature and in English-speaking countries, except Britain, for paraffin.) It is much less volatile than petrol, with a flash point (temperature at which a heated petroleum product gives off enough vapour to flash momentarily when a small flame is placed nearby) of around $168\,°F$ ($75\,°C$) whereas the flash point of petrol is between $70\,°F$ ($21\,°C$) and $100\,°F$ ($38\,°C$).

Diesel fuel injection produces the high pressure fuel supply needed by the diesel engine, and ensures that it is injected in the required quantity and at the correct moment. A complete system consists of fuel filters, injector nozzles,

a high pressure metering injection pump, and usually a low pressure fuel lift pump to feed the fuel in from the tank.

The heart of the system is the injection pump, of which there are two main types, the in-line multi-cylinder pump and the distributor pump; both are engine driven. The in-line pump uses a separate pumping element for each cylinder of the engine, each element consisting of a plunger inside a barrel. With the plunger at the bottom of its stroke, fuel can enter the top of the barrel, either by gravity feed from an overhead tank or by force feed from a low pressure feed pump. The plunger is operated by a cam driven by the engine, and as it rises it closes off the inlet and forces the charge of fuel through a non-return delivery valve to an injector. There is an injector for each cylinder, consisting of a spring-loaded valve which opens as the pressure rises in its fuel feed line from the delivery pump, and sprays a fine jet of fuel into the combustion chamber. As soon as the charge has been sprayed into the cylinder the fuel pressure falls and the injector closes awaiting the next charge.

Control over the amount of fuel delivered (metering), and thus over engine speed, is achieved by shaping the plunger so that rotating it within its barrel alters its effective stroke. A linkage connected to a speed governor or other control is used to rotate the plunger. For multi-cylinder engines the pumping elements are mounted in line in a single unit, and the cams are carried on a common internal camshaft.

The distributor-type pump has only one pump element, and it distributes a charge of fuel from the element to each cylinder in turn. The unit contains a central rotating member, the rotor, which is driven by the engine and carries the single pumping element. The rotor turns within a cylindrical steel body, the hydraulic head, and has a cylinder bored diametrically through it, together with interconnecting radial ports or holes. This cylinder contains two opposed plungers which form the pumping element. The rotor has an inlet port for each cylinder of the engine, and an outlet or distributor port. The hydraulic head also has radial ports, an outlet for each cylinder and one inlet.

As the rotor turns, one of its inlet ports lines up with the inlet port of the hydraulic head, which is fed with fuel at a pressure of about 30 psi (2 bar). Fuel enters the rotor and its pressure forces the plungers apart and outwards. This is the inlet stroke. As the rotor continues to turn, the inlet port is covered up and the single distribution port lines up with one of the outlet ports in the hydraulic head. At this moment the pumping plungers are forced together by the lobes on a cam ring which encircles the rotor. This action forces fuel through the rotor outlet port and the adjacent outlet port in the hydraulic head. From the head the fuel passes at high pressure to one of the injectors.

With further rotation the relative positions of the ports change and a charge of fuel is delivered to the next injector. In this way each cylinder of the engine is fuelled in turn. The amount of fuel allowed to enter the rotor for distribution to the cylinders is under the control of a metering valve, whose setting is adjusted by the accelerator mechanism.

The fuel-air mixture should burn evenly and progressively, as a violent detonation of the mixture causes an uneven running condition known as 'diesel knock'. To achieve correct combustion the fuel and air must be thoroughly mixed. On engines which have the fuel injected directly into the combustion chamber, more effective mixing may be achieved by creating turbulence in the air in the cylinder as it is compressed. This is often done by contouring the crown of the piston so that the air is moved around within the cylinder during compression.

Other designs of engine use swirl chambers or pre-combustion chambers to improve combustion. A swirl chamber is a small spherical chamber above or at the side of the main combustion chamber, and connected to it by a passage. When the air in the cylinder is compressed some of it is forced into the swirl chamber, where a turbulent effect is created due to the shape of the chamber. The fuel is injected into the swirl chamber, and preliminary combustion occurs forcing the mixture into the main combustion chamber where complete combustion takes place. The pre-combustion chamber is connected to the main combustion chamber by a number of fine passages, and the fuel is injected into it. Part of the mixture in the chamber ignites and expands, forcing the remaining unburnt fuel through the connecting passages, from which it emerges into the main chamber as a fine spray and ignites smoothly.

Many diesel engines work on the two-stroke principle, and as they only need to draw in pure air instead of the usual air-fuel-oil mixture needed by the two-stroke petrol engine they are more efficient. The two most common methods of scavenging (the cycle of intake and exhaust) used on two-stroke diesels are *loop* scavenging and *uniflow* scavenging, both of which employ a blower unit to blow the air into the inlet ports.

Left: cutaway diagram of a turbocharged indirect injection diesel engine.

Key: 1 oil filter, 2 dipstick, 3 oil scavenge pipe, 4 oil pump, 5 crankshaft, 6 connecting rod, 7 crankshaft web (counterbalance weight), 8 oil pump drive, 9 camshaft, 10 cam follower (base of pushrod), 11 piston, 12 oil scraper and compression rings, 13 turbocharger exhaust duct, 14 turbocharger spindle, 15 turbocharger turbine, 16 compressor, 17 air inlet duct, 18 water galleries, 19 cylinder bore, 20 inlet valve, 21 injector, 22 rocker shaft, 23 rocker.

In the loop scavenging system, as the piston nears the bottom of its stroke it uncovers the inlet and exhaust ports; the inlet port directs air from the blower into the cylinder in an upward direction, and this forces the exhaust gases downwards and out of the exhaust port on the opposite side of the cylinder. As the piston moves back upwards it covers the ports which effectively seals the cylinder, and the clean air is compressed before the fuel is injected into the top of the cylinder. The uniflow system also has an inlet port in the side of the cylinder, near the bottom, but the exhaust gases are expelled through one or more valves in the top of the combustion chamber. The valves open just before the inlet port is uncovered, and at this point the gases are still under some pressure which starts them flowing out of the cylinder, the remaining gases being expelled by the upward flow of clean air from the blower.

Some two-stroke diesels work on the opposed-piston principle, with two pistons in the same cylinder acting in opposition to each other, moving towards the centre of the cylinder from opposite ends. The pistons may be connected by a crank arrangement to the same crankshaft, or may have separate crankshafts coupled by a gear train. The inlet and exhaust ports are near the opposite ends of the cylinder, and the fuel injector is at the centre. At the point of ignition the two pistons are very close together, crown to crown, and the force of the combustion forces them in opposite directions down the cylinder. One piston uncovers the exhaust ports slightly before the other uncovers the inlet ports, and most of the exhaust gas rushes out under pressure, the remainder being expelled by the incoming air when the inlet port is uncovered.

The power output of internal combustion engines is increased significantly by supercharging, and the diesel is well suited to this as only air has to be blown in as opposed to a petrol-air mixture needed by a petrol engine. The supercharger drives more air into the cylinders than can be drawn in by the downward motion of the pistons alone, so that more fuel-air mixture can be burnt in a given cylinder volume than on an unsupercharged engine, and thus more power obtained without increasing the size of the engine.

Diesel engines which have the fuel injected directly into the combustion chamber do not present any special difficulties when starting from cold, other than the need for very powerful starter motors on the larger versions. Engines fitted with pre-combustion or swirl chambers, however, can be difficult to start and usually employ some form of heater plugs or coils, electrically powered and usually mounted next to the injectors, which pre-heat the air in the combustion chambers and help the fuel to vaporize until the engine has warmed up.

Hand starting is quite easy with smaller engines, and can be used on larger industrial models by means of some form of energy storage. This can be done by spinning a large flywheel and coupling it to the engine when it is spinning fast enough, or by building up pressure in a hydraulic cylinder by means of a hand pump, then releasing the energy to a toothed rack which engages a pinion on the engine crankshaft. In some cases a small, easily started engine may be used as a starter motor for a large engine.

The diesel engine is a highly adaptable power source, and a very large range is manufactured all over the world. They can be air cooled or water cooled, two or four stroke, supercharged or unsupercharged, and can be adapted to run on a wide variety of fuels. On land, they are almost universally used in construction plant and commercial

61

vehicles, and are widely used in taxis and increasingly in cars which have to cover very large annual mileages. Many rail locomotives are diesel or diesel-electric powered, and most agricultural machines such as tractors and harvesters are powered by diesels. (A diesel-electric locomotive uses a diesel engine to generate electricity which turns the wheels.)

Stationary units provide sources of power for industry, including drives for compressors and generators. Marine diesels are used to power launches, yachts, fishing boats, some high speed naval boats, tugboats, speedboats and many other small craft.

In the future, the diesel engine may face increased competition from small lightweight gas turbines, and development work is also being carried out on rotary wankel type diesel engines, which if successful will combine the smooth running and compactness of the turbine with the flexibility of the conventional diesel.

The wankel engine A piston engine has a working chamber whose volume can be altered by the movement of the piston. The reciprocating internal combustion engine has a sliding piston in a cylindrical chamber; in the rotary engine the volume is varied by two or more elements revolving with respect to each other. Thus the fundamental difference is that the centre of gravity of the moving power output member of the reciprocating engine oscillates to and fro in a straight line, while that of the rotary engine moves in one continuous circular motion. Since there is no to-and-fro movement of the working parts, the rotary piston engine is, or can be, in perfect balance, and so for vehicular applications has the advantage of inherently smoother operation.

Rotary water pumps were used as early as the 16th century, and vane or Roots-type superchargers have been used on reciprocating engines for years. Dr Felix Wankel began to classify as many types of rotary engines as possible before World War II, and from these studies emerged the most successful rotary internal combustion engine yet developed, named the wankel after its inventor.

The wankel has a rotor shaped like a slightly rounded triangle which rotates inside a chamber shaped like a fat figure 8. The geometrical shapes of the rotor and housing are derived from a group of curves generically called

Left: the rotor chamber of the Wankel engine. The inward facing gear teeth in the rotor drive the crankshaft.

Above right: the Wankel engine uses the same four stroke cycle as a conventional piston engine, but the geometry is different. The space between the eccentrically revolving rotor and its housing varies in volume, expanding and contracting twice during each rotation, thus giving the effect of a piston moving up and down twice in a cylinder. The four diagrams show the cycle for one side of the triangular rotor (coloured yellow), but the other two sides are also going through the cycle during this time.

Below right: the Wankel engine has attracted motorcycle designers on account of its compactness, smoothness and good power-to-weight ratio. This is the engine and gearbox unit of a Suzuki RE-5 motorcycle: 497 cc (swept volume) developing 62 hp at 6500 rpm, giving the 507 lb (203 kg) machine a top speed of 115 mph (185 km/h).

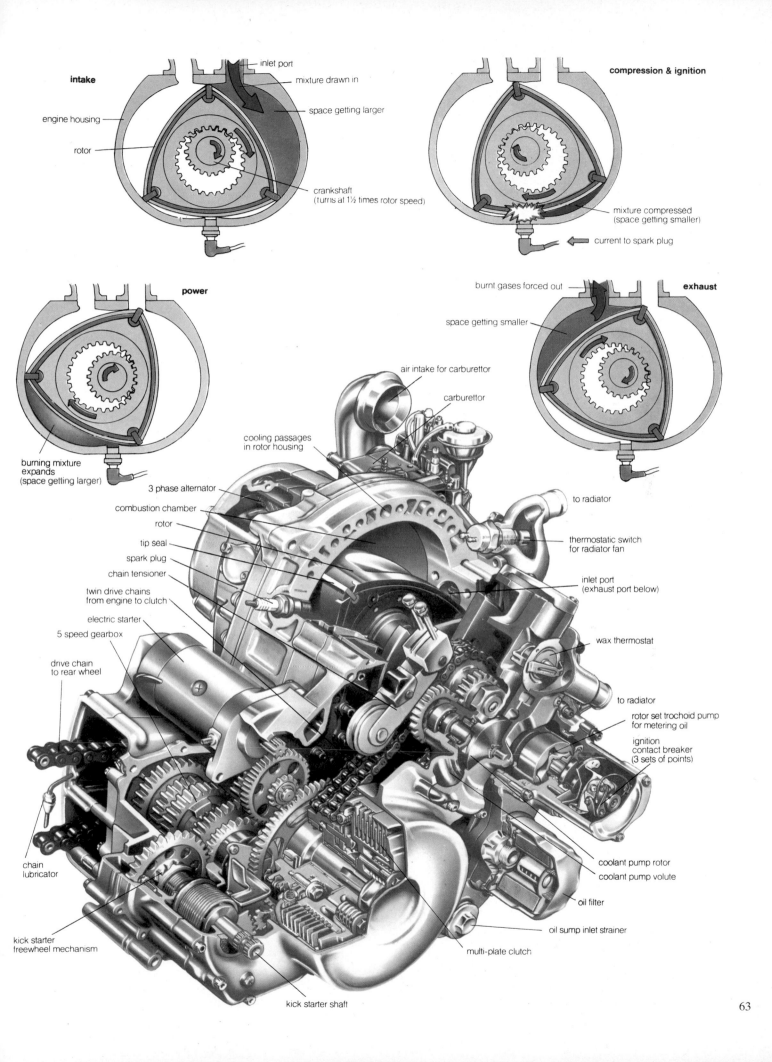

intake

inlet port

mixture drawn in

engine housing

rotor

space getting larger

crankshaft
(turns at 1½ times rotor speed)

compression & ignition

mixture compressed
(space getting smaller)

current to spark plug

power

burning mixture
expands
(space getting larger)

burnt gases forced out

space getting smaller

exhaust

air intake for carburettor

carburettor

cooling passages
in rotor housing

to radiator

3 phase alternator

combustion chamber

rotor

tip seal

spark plug

chain tensioner

twin drive chains
from engine to clutch

electric starter

5 speed gearbox

drive chain
to rear wheel

thermostatic switch
for radiator fan

inlet port
(exhaust port below)

wax thermostat

to radiator

rotor set trochoid pump
for metering oil

ignition
contact breaker
(3 sets of points)

coolant pump rotor

coolant pump volute

oil filter

oil sump inlet strainer

chain
lubricator

kick starter
freewheel mechanism

multi-plate clutch

kick starter shaft

Above: the housing of the Mazda Wankel engine has a coating of a composite nickel-silicone material applied with a spray torch. The heat from the torch causes it to bond to the housing material; it is then ground to its final shape and smoothness.

trochoids, which are found by revolving one circle around another and plotting the path of a point either on the circumference or on an extension of the radius of the revolving circle. The housing of the wankel, for example, is shaped like an epitrochoid.

The rotor has a hole in it with inward-facing gear teeth. It rotates about a smaller gear rotating about a fixed centre; these represent respectively the larger rolling circle and the smaller fixed circle. The shape of the housing can be visualized by imagining an arm of length R attached to the rotor, and following the path faced out by the end of the arm as the rotor revolves around the fixed gear. The centre of the rotor itself describes a circle around the fixed gear, and the radius of this circle is called the eccentricity of the rotor, e. The ratio of R to e determines the basic geometry of the engine. When this ratio is large, the swept volume is comparatively small in relation to the overall size, and the fixed gear must be small, which limits the size of the crankshaft that has to pass through it.

As the rotor rotates, the gap between the flanks of the rotor and the walls of the housing fluctuates cyclically, expanding and contracting to give the four strokes—induction, compression, expansion and exhaust—of the

normal Otto or constant volume cycle, just as in a reciprocating engine. Note that there are three firing strokes per revolution of the rotor (there are three sides to the rotor, so a four-lobed rotor would have four, and so on) but only one per revolution of the crankshaft, since the rotor rotates at one-third the angular velocity of the crankshaft.

Since each flank of the rotor acts effectively as a piston in a reciprocating engine, it is only necessary to consider one flank to follow the sequence of operations. Consider first that the leading seal of one face has just passed the intake port in the housing. As the rotor moves on, the gap between the side of the rotor and the housing increases, and mixture is drawn in. When the trailing seal passes the port the mixture is trapped in the space, and as the rotor continues this gap becomes progressively smaller, compressing the mixture. When the gap is at or near its minimum, corresponding to top dead centre, the spark plug fires and the mixture ignites and expands. Since the centre of rotation of the rotor is eccentric to the centre of the casing, the side of the rotor in question is pushed around, and in turn turns the small gear on the crankshaft. Finally the leading seal passes the exhaust port and the gases escape.

Theoretically the wankel engine has a number of important advantages. One has already been mentioned: its inherent smoothness. Shaft speed in the wankel engine must be high for optimum performance, but this is possible because of the absence of reciprocating parts. The only out-of-balance loads come from the orbital motion of the rotor, and these are easily counterbalanced, for example by having two rotors, each with its own combustion chamber, set at opposite points of their orbit on a common crankshaft. Another advantage is that it has fewer moving parts. Unlike the ordinary reciprocating engine with pistons, connecting rods, crankshaft, camshaft and valve gear, the wankel has effectively only two moving parts: the rotor and the crankshaft. In addition it is basically an extremely compact unit for its output. It generated considerable interest among engineers almost from the outset.

In 1954, in cooperation with NSU, Felix Wankel presented his ideas on a rotary engine. Initial studies took place on a compressor rather than an engine, but by 1957 a prototype engine was running, in a version wherein both the rotor and housing rotated at different speeds. This meant a fairly complex structure, and in 1958 the basic construction was changed to the planetary or epicyclic rotation type with a fixed housing. Shortly thereafter it appeared in production, buried away in the tail of a small sports car, the NSU Spider.

The first serious problem to appear was seal wear. (Wankel himself had begun as a specialist in sealing devices.) The three tips or lobes of the triangular rotor must be fitted with seals to serve the function of piston rings in a conventional engine: to maintain compression by preventing the escape of gases. Seals are not a problem in rotary pumps and other devices, but the high pressure and operating temperature in an internal combustion engine caused seal wear, manifested by 'chatter' marks on the housing. An intensive investigation by NSU and other licensees resulted in special materials which solved the problem, but at some cost. NSU use Ferrotic (a ceramic/metal material) for the apex seals and a coating of elnisil (a composite nickel-silicone material) on the housing, which is first sprayed on and then ground. Other materials used include special cast irons or tool steel for the seals and hard chrome or tungsten carbide coatings for the housing.

Another problem was the result of two inter-related factors. Like a conventional two-stroke engine, the wankel runs on a mixture of petrol and oil so that the apex seals can be properly lubricated, which leads to a smoky exhaust. In addition the combustion chamber is long and narrow,

having a high quench action, which cools the mixture and 'puts the flame out' at an early stage in the cycle, as it were: the result is a very high HC (hydrocarbon) content in the exhaust, and the wankel would have had trouble meeting the American emission laws. In fact this problem was easily solved, for the exhaust was rich enough to maintain combustion in the exhaust pipe; all that was required was the addition of a thermal reactor and an air injector to get one of the cleanest engines in production, as used by the Japanese firm of Mazda for its REAPS (Rotary Engine Anti-Pollution system) equipment.

The Wankel has thus been developed to a stage where the mechanical problems are no longer major problems; but the high fuel consumption is. The wankel is a relatively new engine compared to the reciprocating engine, and the latter has had years of development behind it, particularly in relation to the shape of the combustion chamber, the design of which (after taking into account compression ratios, ignition timing and intake and exhaust systems) probably has more effect on engine efficiency than any other single factor. The wankel combustion chamber will require research breakthroughs before the specific fuel consumptions (a measure of the efficiency of the engine in converting fuel energy into useful mechanical work) approach those of the reciprocating engine: the simple bathtub-shaped cut-outs in the rotor sides may well have to be modified in some way to improve matters. Other ideas which may prove useful include stratified charging by injecting the fuel directly into the combustion chamber as close to the spark plug as possible, reducing the R/e ratio to give a more compact chamber (although this may create mechanical problems), and further investigation into ignition timing and the number and position of the spark plugs.

In spite of the fact that some of the early promises of the wankel remain unfulfilled it is certainly a viable power source. Given that the fuel consumption problems may be overcome, the advantages of its mechanical simplicity, low bulk and weight and inherent smoothness could still lead to a higher penetration into world markets.

The Drive Train

The clutch A clutch is a device which allows two components, usually drive shafts, to be engaged or disengaged

Below: a twin plate clutch used on Formula 1 racing cars to transmit the extremely high torque of the engine; ordinary cars have a single plate.

by its operation. There are various types of clutch available for industrial applications, but the most common application is on motor vehicles.

The job of the clutch on the motor vehicle is to disconnect the engine from the road wheels while changing gear and then to allow the engine to pick up speed smoothly, which is especially important on starting. There are several designs used: the single dry plate type for vehicles with a manual gearbox, and the vane type fluid coupling or torque converter, or centrifugal clutch, for automatic transmissions.

In a single plate clutch system, a flywheel made of cast iron is bolted to the rear end of the crankshaft. The face of the flywheel which touches the clutch plate is very smooth, so as not to promote wear. The clutch plate is a two-piece disc about eight inches (20 cm) in diameter. In the centre of the plate is a hole with splines (similar to gear teeth) in it which correspond to the splines on the input shaft of the gearbox. The inner splined portion of the plate is connected to the outer friction part via 'buffer' springs which absorb the initial take-up shock. Both sides of the plate are covered with friction material on the outer one and a half inches (4 cm) of the diameter. This is a high friction, low wearing, heat resistant material, and is attached to the plate by rivets and bonding. The clutch cover consists of a pressed steel casing which houses a pressure plate backed up by several coil springs or a diaphragm spring, which provide the force to press the plate hard up against the flywheel.

Right: an industrial sprag clutch, which is very like a bicycle freewheel mechanism, turning only one way.

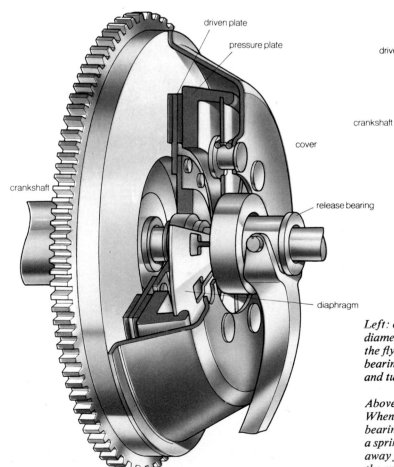

driven plate
pressure plate
cover
crankshaft
release bearing
diaphragm

engaged
driven plate
crankshaft
pressure plate

disengaged
friction pad
spring

Left: cutaway view of a clutch assembly. The largest diameter of the assembly, with the gear teeth on it, is the flywheel. The small shaft which carries the release bearing is the transmission shaft. The cover is fixed to and turns with the flywheel.

Above: engaged and disengaged positions of the assembly. When the driver depresses the clutch pedal, the release bearing is thrust against the diaphragm, which acts as a spring on pivots, allowing the friction pads to come away from the flywheel and thus breaking contact between the engine and the transmission.

When the clutch pedal is pressed down, a release bearing under hydraulic pressure presses down on the centre of the clutch cover and forces the pressure plate away from the clutch plate. This action allows the clutch plate to remain stationary between the revolving flywheel and clutch cover. Gears may now be selected and the slow release of the clutch pedal gradually clamps the clutch plate to the flywheel, allowing a direct drive from the crankshaft to the gearbox.

On automatic gearboxes, a fluid type clutch is used. As with the dry clutch assembly, a large casing bolts onto the flywheel and contains all the parts. The casing is a casting which has impeller vanes attached to the inside of it. Another large wheel, which is attached to the gearbox input shaft, has the output vanes around the edge of it. It is fitted inside the outer casing, to allow both parts to turn independently. The inside of the device is filled with oil, and sealed. As the flywheel rotates faster around the inner—output—vanes, the oil sets up a turbulence which makes the inner wheel rotate. This action now provides drive from the flywheel to the gearbox through the oil. The design allows the car to remain stationary when the engine is idling, but when the engine revs up, the oil is disturbed, thus giving a smooth take-off. Apart from the convenience of the automatic feature, this sytem eliminates a lot of moving parts. The only maintenance which is required is the periodic replacement of the oil.

The gearbox A gearbox is a set of gears with a shifting lever which provides a selection of gear ratios between two components of a machine, such as an automobile. The gearbox, or transmission, is located in the drive train between the engine and the drive wheels, and is a necessary part of the car because an internal combustion engine does not have much torque at low speeds. In order to move the car from a standing start, the gear ratio between the engine and the driving wheels must be such that the crankshaft of the engine is turning over at a relatively high speed. A simple three-speed gearbox allows the crankshaft to turn at roughly four, eight or twelve times for each revolution of the wheels, depending on the gear selected.

A three-speed gearbox consists of a clutch shaft with a clutch gear on it which is turning when the clutch is engaged; a layshaft [countershaft] has several gears, one of which is always meshed with the clutch gear and is turned by it; and a transmission shaft, which transmits the power to the propeller shaft and which has two gears on it, one larger than the other, splined so that they can slide on the shaft. Each of the two gears on the transmission shaft is fitted with a shifting yoke, a bracket for pushing it back and forth on the shaft. The shifting yokes are selected and shifted by the driver by means of the shifting lever, which pivots between the driver's compartment and the top of the gearbox case.

When the driver selects first gear, or low gear, the larger of the two gears on the transmission shaft is pushed along the shaft until it meshes with the smallest gear on the layshaft. Then the clutch is engaged, allowing power to be trans-

Below: the cutaway view of a British Ford gearbox designed for use with their V4 engine. The shifting lever protrudes from the housing on the upper right.

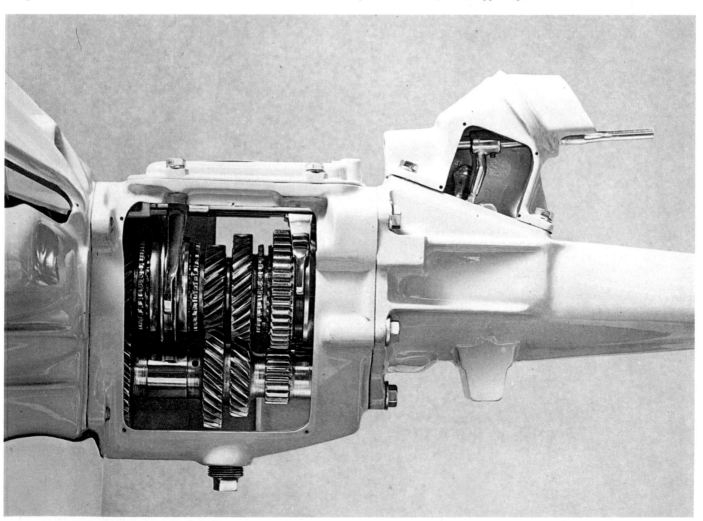

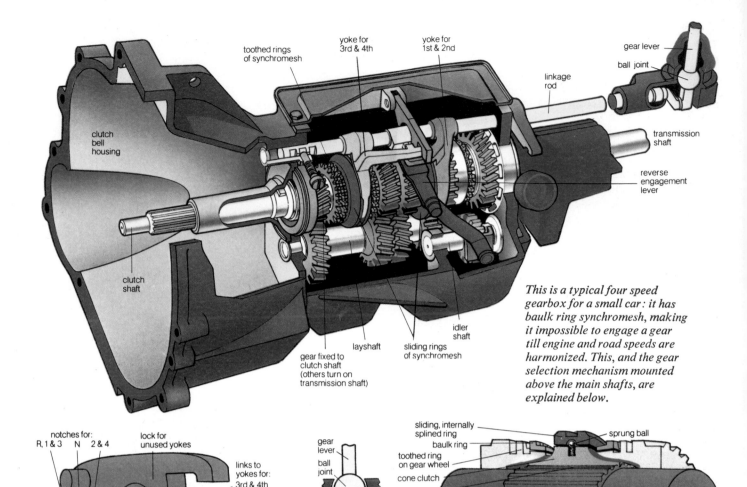

toothed rings of synchromesh

yoke for 3rd & 4th

yoke for 1st & 2nd

gear lever

ball joint

linkage rod

transmission shaft

clutch bell housing

clutch shaft

reverse engagement lever

gear fixed to clutch shaft (others turn on transmission shaft)

layshaft

sliding rings of synchromesh

idler shaft

This is a typical four speed gearbox for a small car: it has baulk ring synchromesh, making it impossible to engage a gear till engine and road speeds are harmonized. This, and the gear selection mechanism mounted above the main shafts, are explained below.

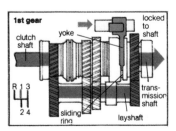

notches for: R, 1 & 3   N   2 & 4

lock for unused yokes

links to yokes for: 3rd & 4th   1st & 2nd

gear lever

ball joint

reverse engagement lever

linkage rod

sprung peg   cam   actuating tooth

gear selection mechanism

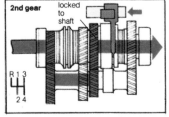

sliding, internally splined ring

baulk ring

sprung ball

toothed ring on gear wheel

cone clutch

splines

transmission shaft

splines

main gear teeth

synchromesh

The gear lever moves in two planes: fore and aft, which moves the linkage rod fore and aft in the other direction, and sideways, which twists the rod. Twisting makes the actuating tooth on the rod engage with one of three links, two to the sliding yokes for forward gears, one to the reverse idler gear. Unused links are held still by a locking bar moved up and down by a cam on the linkage rod.

All forward gears are permanently engaged, but freewheel until locked to the transmission shaft. They are locked gradually, for smoothness, by sliding a splined ring which first engages a clutch to synchronize gear and shaft, then moves on to bridge the two sets of teeth, providing a rigid drive. The baulk ring gives an intermediate semi-locked stage to prevent premature locking. (Reverse gear is unsynchronized.)

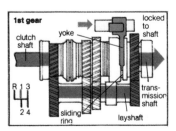

1st gear

clutch shaft

yoke

locked to shaft

transmission shaft

sliding ring

layshaft

2nd gear

locked to shaft

3rd gear

yoke

locked to shaft

4th gear

clutch shaft locked to transmission shaft

layshaft unused

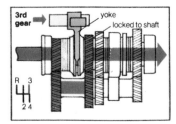 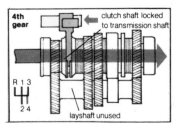 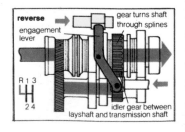

reverse

engagement lever

gear turns shaft through splines

idler gear between layshaft and transmission shaft

1st gear: rear yoke slides back, locks rearmost gear to transmission shaft. Gear on clutch shaft drives layshaft; this drives transmission shaft (line of power shown in red). 2nd: rear yoke slides forward, locks another gear to shaft. Layshaft ('countershaft' in USA) works as before.

3rd: front yoke slides back. 4th: front yoke slides forward, locks clutch and transmission shafts to give direct drive. Reverse: idler gear, inserted between layshaft and teeth on rim of rear synchro ring, turns transmission shaft backwards.

mitted from the engine through the gearbox to the wheels. The gear ratio between the transmission shaft and the layshaft is 3:1, and the effective ratio between the crankshaft and the wheels is about 12:1 (because of further reduction gearing in the differential, the set of gears which transmits power between the propeller shaft and the drive wheels).

When the car is moving fast enough, about ten mph (16 kph), the driver shifts to second gear, engaging the small transmission gear with the large layshaft gear. The gear ratio is now 2:1 and the ratio between the crankshaft and the wheels about 8:1. For cruising speed the driver shifts to third gear (high gear), forcing the smaller transmission gear axially (lengthwise) against the clutch gear. These have teeth on the sides of them which engage, and the gear ratio is now 1:1; that is, the transmission shaft and the clutch shaft (hence the crankshaft) are turning at the same speed. The ratio between the crankshaft and the wheels is now about 4:1. Thus the speed of the engine is always within the range of efficiency for the engine while the car moves from a standing start to speed.

The reverse gear is at the back end of the layshaft, and turns a small idler gear which meshes with the large transmission gear when the driver selects reverse. (When spur gears mesh, they turn in opposite directions; the interposition of an idler gear between them means that they turn in the same direction, so that the car reverses its direction.)

In a gear system, speed reduction means an increase in torque. (Torque is a twisting force, such as the effort needed to loosen a tight cap on a jar). Thus the gearbox, when first gear is selected, transmits less speed from the small layshaft gear to the large transmission gear (because when two gears turn together the larger gear turns slower), but transmits more torque from the crankshaft, to 'twist' the propeller shaft and overcome the inertia of the car to get it moving.

American cars with large engines have usually had three-speed gearboxes, but smaller European cars usually have four or five forward gears, because the usable range of speed of the engine is smaller. The gearbox on a large lorry may have sixteen forward gears or more, because of the torque required to get the great weight of a fully loaded lorry moving.

In the early days of motor cars, gearboxes were simple devices such as described above, and it took some muscle power and skill to shift the gears smoothly. The edges of the gear teeth were chamfered (rounded) so that they would mesh as smoothly as possible. Down-shifting was particularly complicated, requiring double-clutching (disengaging the clutch, revving the engine to a higher speed, and re-engaging the clutch after shifting gears).

As more and more people took up driving, it became necessary to make shifting easier, and gearbox design became more complicated. Syncromesh gears were designed, in which the gears are made to run at the correct speed before they mesh so that they can do so without grinding. One way of doing this is to provide conical sections on the sides of the gears which fit into one another; friction starts the gear turning before the teeth actually mesh. A balking provision is made in some designs to prevent the gears from meshing until they are running at speed. Some syncromesh gearboxes may have all the gears meshing all the time; power is not transmitted until a sliding 'dog' axially engages the appropriate gear. At first most gearboxes provided syncromesh only on the upper gears, but most models nowadays provide it on all gears.

Nowadays nearly all American cars, and many others as well, have automatic transmissions, but some drivers like the feeling of control over the vehicle that they get from operating a manual gearbox. People who drive in competitions prefer manual gearboxes because skilful gear-changing can mean split-second advantages when negotiating hills and curves.

Automatic transmission In an automatic transmission the most appropriate gear is selected without any action from the driver. There is no clutch pedal for the driver to control, and selection and engagement of gears are performed automatically. All the driver does is operate a control lever for a number of guiding positions: P for park, R for reverse, N for neutral, D for forward drive, and L to hold the lower gear. There are stopping devices to prevent the accidental selection of reverse and park while the vehicle is in motion, and another safety feature ensures that the engine only starts in neutral or park. Fully automatic gear changes, both up and down, occur with the lever in the D position.

Automatic transmission should not be confused with semi-automatic where the driver changes gears manually but is assisted by an automatic clutch. With the self-changing or preselector gearbox, the driver predetermines the choice of gear and controls the clutch, but the gear-change is performed automatically.

Automatic transmission must provide smooth acceleration from rest without jerking. The engine must therefore be allowed to slip with respect to the wheels, so that it can turn over while the vehicle is stationary, then by increasing the engine speed progressively transmit more and more power to the wheels. In addition, it should provide a sufficient range of gear ratios to accommodate all possible vehicle loads and speeds.

Normally a range of three or four gear ratios is provided, but one system has been developed which provides a continuously variable gear ratio over a certain range. This is the Daf Variomatic transmission manufactured in Holland for a low-powered range of cars. A continuously variable gear ratio can be achieved by a system of friction belts running over pulleys of varying diameter, provided that the amount of power to be transmitted is not great. Such schemes have been tried at various times since the beginning of the century, but the Variomatic is the only one now in use. In this, a centrifugal friction clutch forms the coupling mechanism and takes up the drive when the engine is accelerated. The final drive is provided by belts of wedge section passing over pulleys that expand or contract to alter their effective diameters.

The pulleys are controlled by centrifugal governors, built into the driving pulleys and sensitive to engine speed, and by vacuum servomechanisms which respond to the degree of vacuum in the engine inlet manifold. These two devices are balanced against each other so as to achieve gearing which is a reasonable compromise between performance and economy. When maximum acceleration is desired, the accelerator pedal is fully depressed. This floods the inlet manifold with a mixture of fuel and air, reducing the vacuum (increasing the pressure) and cancelling the vacuum servomechanism. The transmission therefore responds to engine speed alone and assumes a gear ratio which maintains the engine at the speed which produces maximum torque.

Such a mechanism is limited in its capacity, and is at present suitable only for cars of fairly low power. In such applications its high mechanical efficiency is important. Mechanical efficiency is the ratio of the work output of a machine to the work input and for the Variomatic is in excess of 90% over most of the working range, reaching a maximum of 94%.

Vehicles with larger engines use an automatic gearbox offering a series of gear ratios which are selected and engaged automatically by clutches energized hydraulically or (less commonly) electrically. The controls for these are still governed by the inlet manifold vacuum and engine speed, with additional overriding controls linked to the accelerator pedal and the gearbox output shaft, which gives a measure of the vehicle's speed.

The gears themselves are almost invariably planetary or epicyclic sets in constant mesh. The term 'planetary' is sometimes used for epicyclic gears because the system is made up of an inner 'sun' gearwheel which is in mesh with two small 'planet' gears. These planet gears rotate about the sun wheel, and are themselves surrounded by a toothed outer ring. The various gear ratios are produced by locking one or other of the gear elements, for example the planet carrier, by means of a clutch. In an automatic gearbox there are several of these systems interconnected to provide the necessary gear combinations. Epicyclic gearboxes of this kind are invariably associated with some form of fluid drive or hydrokinetic coupling—a form of clutch in which a fluid (oil) transmits torque from the input member (called impeller or pump) driven by the engine, to the output member or turbine which drives the gearbox.

The simplest kind, first used in 1929 by Daimler in conjunction with a preselector gearbox and featured in Rolls-Royce and Mercedes-Benz cars until quite recently, is the fluid coupling. Once known as the fluid flywheel, it consists essentially of two radially-vaned saucers face to face, separated slightly to avoid direct contact. Oil is flung centrifugally from the pump to the turbine, which makes it rotate. This torque is transmitted without any rigid mechanical connection between the driving and the driven members, which can therefore slip relative to each other. (Slip refers to any difference in the rotational speeds.) The important feature of the fluid coupling is that the output and input *torques* are always equal. Any difference between input and output *speeds* is a measure of the slip taking place and of the efficiency of the device. At best, a fluid coupling reaches about 97% efficiency; but until it has reached coupling point (that is, until the slip has been reduced to the minimal 3%) it is very inefficient. Careful matching of the coupling to the engine is essential: if it is to carry the full engine torque at high efficiency and low slip, it must have a torque capacity much greater than that which the engine can deliver. Otherwise, slip would be severe and excessive heat would be generated, eventually boiling the fluid.

A more complex form of hydrokinetic coupling is the fluid converter, so called because it multiplies the input torque. To achieve this, a third element is added between the pump and the turbine, and the blade forms are curved instead of straight. The third element, the reactor or stator, is fixed so that fluid flow from the pump is diverted to strike the turbine blading at a more effective angle, thus amplifying the torque applied to the turbine. Actually the torque on the turbine equals the sum of the torques on pump and reactor, which means that the torque applied to the gearbox can be several times higher than that produced by the engine.

This sort of converter is used in construction machinery, but is unsuitable for cars: it is most efficient at about 40% slip, and is grossly inefficient at the extreme ends of the slip range, where all the engine power is dissipated in heat. The

answer to this problem is to mount the reactor on a free-wheel or over-running clutch; then, when coupling point is reached, the reactor is free to move in the same direction as the turbine but is always locked against rotation in the opposite direction. This system is used in most cars with automatic transmission.

At coupling point, therefore, the reactor automatically removes itself from the circuit, in which it can no longer play an effective part. The mechanism then acts purely as a fluid coupling, with no torque multiplication or conversion. Hence it is called a converter coupling in the strict terminology, though the motor industry casually refers to it as a torque converter. In effect, the device combines the best characteristics of fluid converter and fluid coupling, but at some cost of efficiency to each. The transition from converter to coupling after reaching coupling point is slow, since the curved blading necessary for converter operation is not entirely suitable for coupling operation. Furthermore, the coupling point is normally reached when input and output torques are equal, but at that point the output speed will still be about 10% less than the input speed.

The full load efficiency of a converter coupling is usually below 90% in the converter range, rising to about 95% in

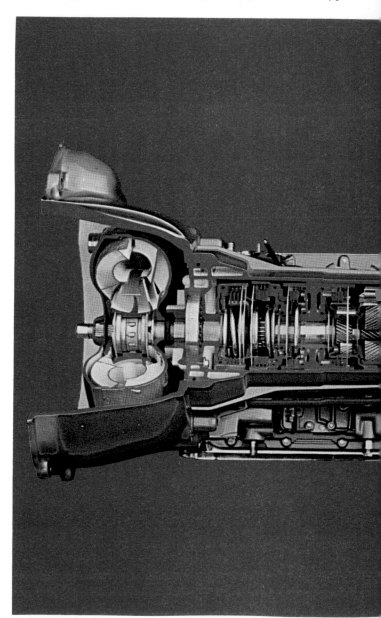

the coupling range. This efficiency is directly related to the product of the torque multiplication ratio and the slip ratio. It follows that when driven gently at low speeds, such a device is of poor efficiency; engine efficiency, however, is low when the load is light and the input speed is high (a situation which favours coupling efficiency), so great care has to be taken in setting the central mechanism to select the most appropriate gear ratio for the circumstances. Careful matching of the converter to the engine is also essential.

The combination of a converter coupling (which slips enough to allow the engine to idle while the car is stationary, and grips enough to transmit most of the engine's power at high speeds) with an epicyclic automatic gearbox is almost universal in the many cars and other vehicles now equipped with automatic transmission. Most developments have been concerned with simplifying (and cheapening) the manufacture of the transmission, together with a number of refinements in the control system. Of the latter, the most important are those which give the driver some means of inhibiting the gearchanges that would otherwise take place automatically, so that he can hold the transmission in a low gear to improve the car's acceleration. Much attention is also being given to making gearchanges smoother.

There have been a number of variations on this basic arrangement. The General Motors Hydramatic transmission has appeared in several versions: some had two fluid couplings, one always being full and operational while the other was drained or filled with fluid according to the gear ratio engaged. Another version had a single coupling with a free-running stator built-in and anchored to the gearbox output shaft rather than to the casing: this gave some torque multiplication, about 30%, but minimized drag losses. Varying the angle of the stator blades has also been tried with some success in the GM Super Turbine 300, and in an earlier Buick transmission featuring a five-element, twin-turbine converter. These refinements, and others such as a lock-up clutch to eliminate slip when in the coupling position, have not been found to justify their cost. Others, such as the substitution of bevel-gear differentials for the conventional epicyclic gear trains in the British gearbox made by Automotive Products, have been more successful.

Universal joints Universal joints, which allow rotary drives to be turned through varying angles, have been in use for hundreds of years: the design of the first is usually attributed to Girolamo Cardano, a 16th century Italian mathematician (hence the term 'Cardan shaft'), but the first practical unit

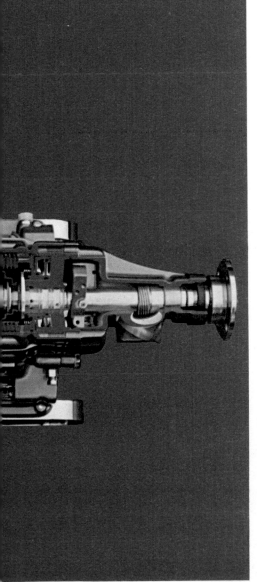

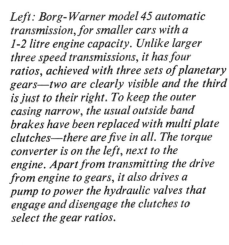

Left: Borg-Warner model 45 automatic transmission, for smaller cars with a 1-2 litre engine capacity. Unlike larger three speed transmissions, it has four ratios, achieved with three sets of planetary gears—two are clearly visible and the third is just to their right. To keep the outer casing narrow, the usual outside band brakes have been replaced with multi plate clutches—there are five in all. The torque converter is on the left, next to the engine. Apart from transmitting the drive from engine to gears, it also drives a pump to power the hydraulic valves that engage and disengage the clutches to select the gear ratios.

Below: Variomatic transmission, installed at the rear of a front-engined car. The front of the unit, at the top of the picture, comprises the drive shaft, two expanding pulleys, and, outside these, vacuum devices to alter the drive ratio by expanding or contracting the pulleys; this is done by moving their sloping sides together or apart. Rubber V-section belts drive the rear wheels via pulleys designed to take up the slack in the belts. The two independent belts avoid the need for a differential, and also reduce the amount of torque transmitted by each belt. High torque would cause slipping, which is why this admirably simple system can only be used on small cars.

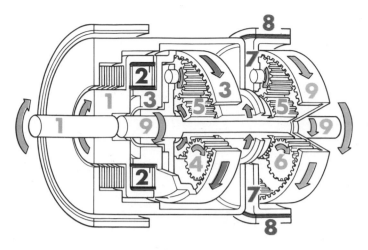

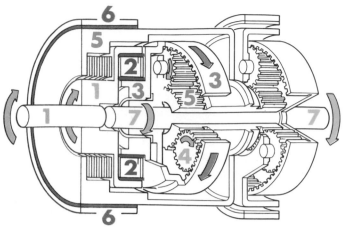

First gear: input shaft 1 turns, forward clutch 2 is locked, driving first annulus 3 and first planet wheels 4, which turn sun wheel 5 backwards. Sun wheel drives second planet wheels 6 forwards; second planet carrier 7 is stopped by band brake 8, so second annulus 9 is turned very slowly, driving car's wheels.

Second gear: input shaft 1 turns, forward clutch 2 is locked, driving first annulus 3 and first planet wheels 4. Common sun wheel 5 is locked by band brake 6, so first planet carrier 7 turns slowly forwards, driving wheels through output shaft linked to it, as well as second annulus, which freewheels.

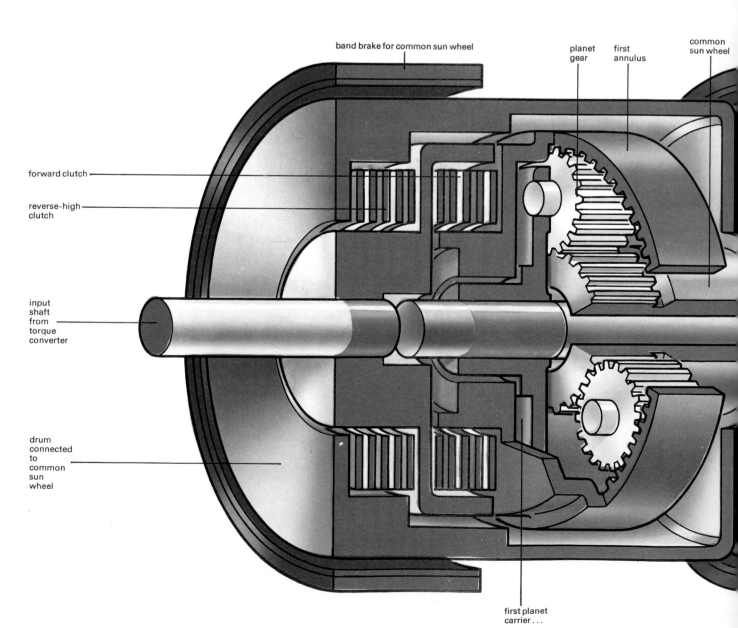

band brake for common sun wheel

planet gear

first annulus

common sun wheel

forward clutch

reverse-high clutch

input shaft from torque converter

drum connected to common sun wheel

first planet carrier . . .

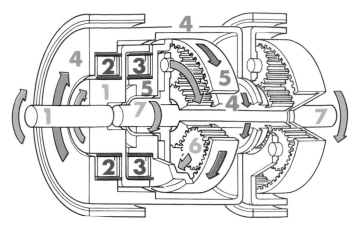

Top gear: input shaft 1 turns, both clutches 2 and 3 are locked, so it drives both common sun wheel 4 and first annulus 5. Planet wheels 6 are between these two and are carried round without themselves revolving, taking with them first planet carrier 7 and output shaft linked to it and driving car's wheels.

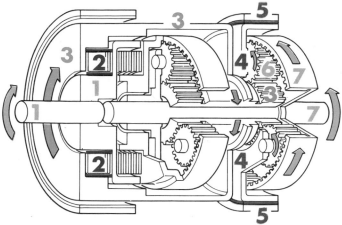

Reverse: input shaft 1 turns, reverse-high clutch 2 is locked, so common sun wheel 3 is driven directly. Second planet carrier 4 is locked by band brake 5, so sun wheel turns planet wheels 6 against second annulus 7, turning it, and car's wheels linked to it, slowly backwards. First planet carrier freewheels.

brake for
nd planet carrier

second
planet
carrier

onnected to second annulus...

and
output
shaft

Left: schematic diagram of three speed automatic transmission with two sets of planetary gears, two multi-plate clutches and two band brakes—the torque converter is not shown. Some parts are permanently linked and turn together: the sun wheels of both gear sets are in one piece and also joined to a drum reaching to the front of the unit. The first planet carrier, second annulus and rear output shaft are also linked. Parts turning together in this way are shown in the same colour. The multi-plate clutches lock together the parts directly to their right and left. The band brakes grip and stop the drum extension of the common sun wheel and the second planet carrier. The operation of planetary gears, clutches and torque converter is shown on pp 74-5; the way all these interact to select three forward speeds and reverse is shown in the diagrams above.

was invented about a hundred years later by Robert Hooke. It consisted simply of two stirrups, one on each end of the two shafts, connected by an X-shaped crosspiece.

Variations of the basic Hooke joint are fairly common: there is the ring type, which replaces the crosspiece with a ring, the ball-type, in which the forked ends of the shafts slide in machined grooves in a ball (if the forked ends carry over more than half the diameter of the ball the latter is trapped and the whole is held together as an assembly), and the de Dion pot-type, which has a T piece on one shaft and a hollow grooved cylindrical pot on the other. Blocks mounted on bearings on the end of the T piece have a curved outer surface and fit into the grooves or slots in the pot: rotation perpendicular to the plane of the T piece is allowed by the bearings, and in the plane of the T piece by the curved edges sliding in the groove.

Where the relative angles between shafts are small, or where unwanted torque reversals and vibrations occur, the joining member between the two shafts can either be made of or covered with rubber to give a degree of damping: the most common in ordinary use are the ring type of 'doughnut' (as used in the rear driveshafts of the Lotus Elan), which also give a degree of relative movement of the shafts towards or away from each other, and the cross type, a Hooke joint with a rubber-covered crosspiece, used on the inner driveshafts of Minis and other BLMC front wheel-drive-cars.

Unfortunately, especially for front-wheel-drive cars, these flexible couplings and the ordinary universal joints suffer from one unwanted characteristic; if one shaft is rotated at a constant speed, and the other shaft is not exactly in line, the second will rotate at a speed that varies cyclically during each revolution. Thus although both sides of the joint complete any given revolution in the same time, the speed of one varies sinusoidally with respect to the other.

This is not much of a problem in linking the gearbox and differential of a front engined, rear wheel drive car, where the angles are fairly small. But in a front wheel drive car, where the outer universal joint has to cope with steering angles of 40° or more, the jerks that this could create would be unacceptable, so it is necessary to use a constant velocity joint.

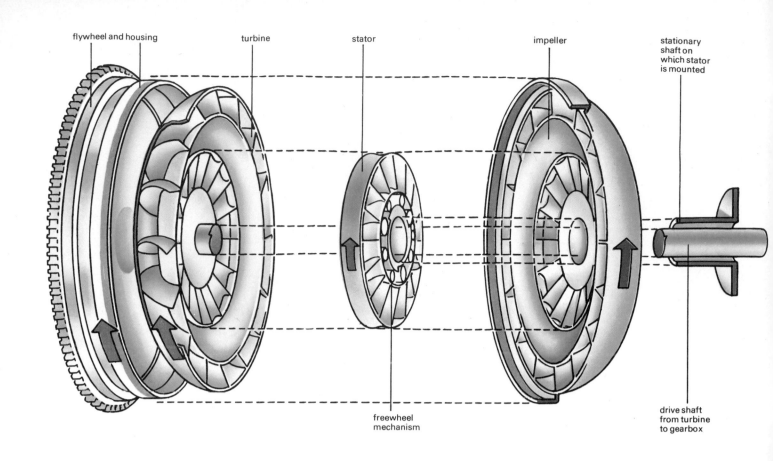

flywheel and housing turbine stator impeller stationary shaft on which stator is mounted

freewheel mechanism

drive shaft from turbine to gearbox

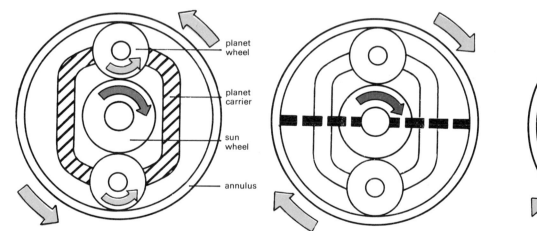

planet wheel

planet carrier

sun wheel

annulus

Directly above: a planetary gear has four main parts: a central sun wheel, an outer annulus, several planet wheels and their carrier. If the carrier is held and the sun wheel turned (left), the annulus turns slowly the other way. If the sun wheel is locked to the annulus (centre), the unit revolves in one piece. If the sun wheel is locked and the carrier turned (right), the annulus revolves faster the same way.

Near right: multi-plate clutch. Red and blue parts spin freely till pressed together, which locks them.

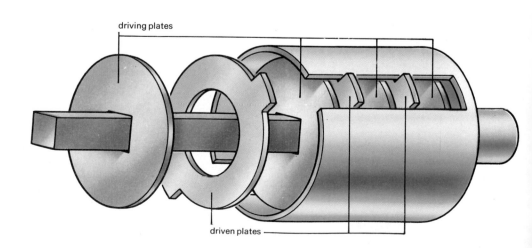

driving plates

driven plates

Left and right: the torque converter is like two fans facing each other: spinning one makes the other turn. It contains oil, thrown outwards by the impeller and returning through the turbine, taking it round with the impeller. At low speeds the turbine slips, but the stator, a slotted disc, angles the oil flow so the torque is transmitted more strongly. The resulting backward push on the stator is resisted by a one-way freewheel; at higher speeds it moves forwards.

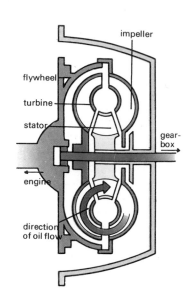

The condition for constant velocity is that the points through which the torque is transmitted from one side to the other lie on a plane which bisects the angle between the two shafts, although there is one simpler way of getting rid of the unwanted speed differentials—arrange two Hooke joints such that the oscillations cancel each other out. But a double Hooke joint is rather long, so in most instances a constant velocity joint is used. The best known of these is the Birfield-Rzeppa unit, in which the drive is transmitted through a set of ball bearings rolling in grooves between a ball and socket: the plane containing the balls always bisects the angle between input and output shaft, so that constant velocity is maintained.

Left: this type of universal joint, used with socket wrench sets, assists the speedy turning of nuts and bolts in hard to reach spots.

Below: the 'Metalastik' universal joint allows relative movement of the shafts towards or away from each other. The cross type is held together by U-bolt clamps, with the cross in the centre. The Birfield-Rzeppa joint is a constant velocity type because the ball race always bisects the angle of the shafts to each other.

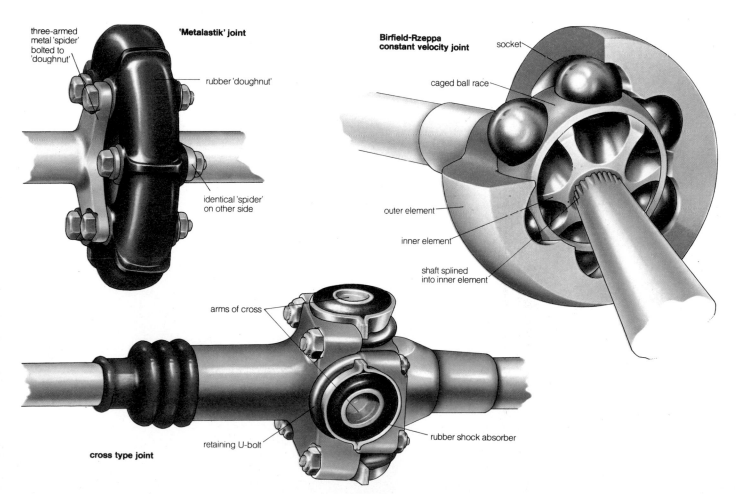

The differential The differential is a gear assembly which transmits power from the propeller shaft to the rear axles, and permits the drive wheels to turn at different speeds when the vehicle is going around a curve. When a vehicle goes around a curve, the wheel on the inside of the curve travels less distance than the other, and so must turn more slowly, for safety in handling and to keep tyre wear to a minimum. A-four-wheel drive vehicle, such as a Jeep or a Land Rover, has two differentials. For maximum traction, a four wheel drive vehicle has been designed with three differentials, separating the front wheels, the rear wheels and the front from the rear, allowing each wheel to turn at its own speed under power. (The only car which does not have a differential is the Daf car, built in Holland, with its Variomatic transmission, which allows belts to slip on pulleys.)

The differential is encased in a casting, which is located on most cars (having rear wheel drive) in the middle of the rear axles between the wheels. (It is sometimes called the 'cabbage head' because of its bulbous appearance.) The drive shaft enters the casting in the front and one axle enters at each side. A pinion gear, which is splined into the end of the drive shaft, turns a bevelled crown gear which is fastened onto the end of one of the axles. An assembly of four small bevelled gears (two pinions and two star gears) is bolted to the crown gear and turns with it. The other axle is driven by the small pinion gear opposite the crown gear. The assembly drives both axles at the same speed when the vehicle is being driven in a straight line, but allows the axle opposite the crown gear to turn slower or faster, as required.

Some units are designed to give a limited-slip or slip-lock differential, to equalize power between the wheels on a slippery or a soft road surface, providing safe handling and minimizing the likelihood of getting stuck in snow or soft earth.

The gear ratio between the crown gear and the pinion gear is one of the factors that determines the performance characteristics of the car, such as acceleration and top speed.

Early cars had pinion and crown gears with straight teeth on them, which resulted in noisy operation of the differential and allowed play in the gear teeth, causing undue wear. Today the pinion and crown gears are helical gears, which means that the toothed surfaces are bevelled and the teeth themselves are curved. This design eliminates play between the teeth, because as the gears spin together one tooth is in full contact before the preceeding tooth leaves. A properly constructed differential should last the life of the car without any maintenance at all.

Brakes In the internal expanding type of drum brake, two brake shoes on a fixed mounting are pushed against the inside of a rotating drum to create the required braking force. Hydraulic or compressed air systems are used for applying the brakes. Brakes of this type are widely used on trucks, buses and motor cycles; on modern cars they are usually found at the rear only.

The metal brake drum dissipates heat quite well, particularly if there are fins on its outer surface to increase the area for heat dissipation, but the internal forces created by the shoes can cause distortion which leads to cracking and failure if temperatures become excessive. Self-energizing types give powerful braking but their effectiveness falls off rapidly at high operating temperatures through what is called 'fade', where the higher temperature reduces the lining friction level. Drum brakes are also particularly liable to lose their effectiveness for a short period after immersion in water—after driving through a flood or a ford it is neces-

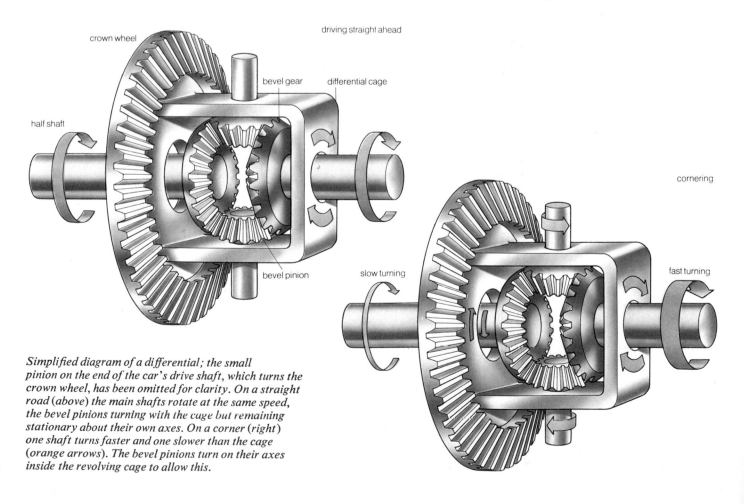

crown wheel   driving straight ahead

bevel gear   differential cage

half shaft

bevel pinion

cornering

slow turning   fast turning

Simplified diagram of a differential; the small pinion on the end of the car's drive shaft, which turns the crown wheel, has been omitted for clarity. On a straight road (above) the main shafts rotate at the same speed, the bevel pinions turning with the cage but remaining stationary about their own axes. On a corner (right) one shaft turns faster and one slower than the cage (orange arrows). The bevel pinions turn on their axes inside the revolving cage to allow this.

Above: a fork lift truck axle. The differential is in the middle. The housings are separate castings to allow for several different axles and wheel offsets to match different motors and gearboxes. The pinion coupling, protruding from the front of the differential casing, can be connected to a gearbox or torque converter directly or via a drive shaft. The wheel hub casings contain additional reduction gearing.

Below: cutaway of a heavy duty truck axle. The large gear at the right is the crown gear of the differential; the chromed disc in front would be connected to one of the half shafts. At the top, far left and right, are two halves of universal joints: one to take power from the drive shaft, the other to transmit it to the other axle of a multi-axled truck. The green casing contains an electrically operated two speed gearbox.

EATON Truck Components

One of the complete line of heavy-duty truck axles.

sary to proceed cautiously and use the brakes frequently but lightly until they dry out.

On a drum brake of the type shown, one shoe is self-energizing and the other is not. If the drum rotation is clockwise, it tends to pull the shoe on the right harder against the inner surface, so that the braking effect is increased; this shoe is called the leading shoe. The other shoe is pushed off by the drum and its braking effect is reduced; this is called the trailing shoe. The leading shoe will wear faster because it does more work than the trailing shoe.

To gain particular advantages of power or wear resistance, drum brakes have also been designed with two leading shoes, with two trailing shoes and with three or even four shoes. The duo-servo type uses two leading shoes linked together in such a way that a very high output indeed is obtained.

The power of car brakes must always be matched to the load carried by each axle and there is also the effect of weight transfer from rear axle to front axle during normal braking. Cars usually, therefore, have more powerful brakes at the front, and, because more energy has to be dissipated, these are often disc brakes.

The disc brake consists essentially of a revolving disc which can be gripped between two brake pads. The caliper type brake commonly found on bicycles is a familiar example but disc brakes for cars are mostly hydraulically operated and the pads cover between one sixth and one ninth of the swept area of the disc. Because the disc is less subject to distortion than a brake drum it can run at much higher temperatures without ill effect; the disc brake can therefore be used for much heavier duty than a drum brake provided an appropriate grade of lining is used.

Disc brakes are now used very widely on the front wheels of cars where, within a given size of wheel, they dissipate about twice as much energy as the rear brakes. High performance cars sometimes have disc brakes on both axles. A rather different design of disc brake, having linings equal in size to the full swept area of the discs, is sometimes found on tractors.

Conventional disc brakes are not self-energizing; to achieve the required braking force very large hydraulic pistons must be used together with a large master cylinder to provide sufficient fluid flow. This might lead to excessive pedal efforts, so many disc braked cars have a brake servo-mechanism to assist the driver. The servo utilizes the difference in pressure between the atmosphere and the carburettor for its source of energy.

All cars need a parking brake which is mechanically operated. Although this commonly acts at the rear, in some cases it acts at the front wheels. When the parking brake is on a drum-braked axle, it usually operates the same shoes that are controlled by the foot brake system; when disc brakes are involved, the parking brake often has its own pads in an attachment to the main brakes.

The materials of which the rubbing surface of brakes are made must give a good level of friction or excessive force would be necessary. At the same time, the life of these parts must be acceptable for the class of application. Experience has shown that the best results are obtained when the moving part is of metal and the stationary parts are lined with a composition friction material which wears much faster than the metal but can readily be replaced.

For general use, such as on vehicle brakes, cast iron has been found to be the metal surface most suitable from all points of view at reasonable cost for both drum and disc

brakes. Drums can be made of a cast iron lining with a light alloy body for improved heat conductivity, but these are expensive; discs can be cast with internal air passages. Brake linings for general use are made of a carefully chosen mixture of asbestos fibre, metallic particles and non-metallic ingredients bonded together with a temperature-resistant synthetic resin.

Power brakes   The force that must be applied to the brake shoes to stop the car is considerably greater than that exerted by the driver's foot, and this is catered for by building mechanical advantage into the system. Suppose that the brake pedal is pivoted so that a certain force applied by the foot exerts three times that force on the piston in the

Below: a publicity stunt demonstrating the value of four wheel brakes fitted to the Rickenbacker car in the 1920s, when not many cars had these. A Los Angeles car dealer drove the car down the steep flight of steps. Midway down, he applied the brakes and the car stopped.

master cylinder (the foot, of course, has to move three times as far as the piston, by the laws that apply to any lever). If the master piston is $\frac{3}{4}$ inch in diameter, each of the front brake pistons is $1\frac{1}{2}$ inch in diameter, and each of the rear ones 1 inch, then the force from the driver's foot will be amplified 48 times at the front and 21 times at the rear, a total of 69. The foot has to move 69 times as far as any of the pistons, but since the brake shoes are already almost touching the drums, this gives an acceptable pedal travel of a few inches.

Despite the mechanical advantage, however, drum brakes on trucks and buses need power assistance because they are larger, and disc brakes require more power anyway, all other things being equal. Power brakes are becoming standard equipment on many cars nowadays, especially in America. Power assisted brakes were originally designed for aircraft, and were gradually introduced on road vehicles from the 1940s on. Nowadays systems on vehicles of all types are designed so that with power assistance, no more pressure on the brake pedal is required to stop a bus than a small car.

Most power brakes on private cars are vacuum servo assisted. A normal petrol engine has a partial vacuum, about 10 psi (0.7 bar) below air pressure, in the inlet manifold while it is running. This can be tapped and used as a source of power; it is particularly useful for brakes because the vacuum is at its highest when the driver suddenly removes his foot from the accelerator, as he would when braking. (On diesel engines, this vacuum is not available, so a separate vacuum pump driven from the engine is used.)

The servo contains a large rubber diaphragm in a chamber connected to the inlet manifold on both sides. One side is directly connected, and the other through an air control valve opened and shut by hydraulic pressure from the master cylinder. The diaphragm is pressed towards this side by a large spring.

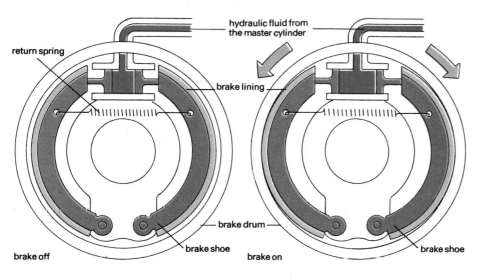

Left: an ordinary car drum brake. The two pivoted brake shoes are pushed outwards against the inside of the revolving drum by hydraulic pressure inside the cylinder. When pressure is released, springs pull the shoes back.

Below: the hydraulic pressure comes from a master cylinder worked by the brake pedal and connected to the four slave cylinders in the brakes.

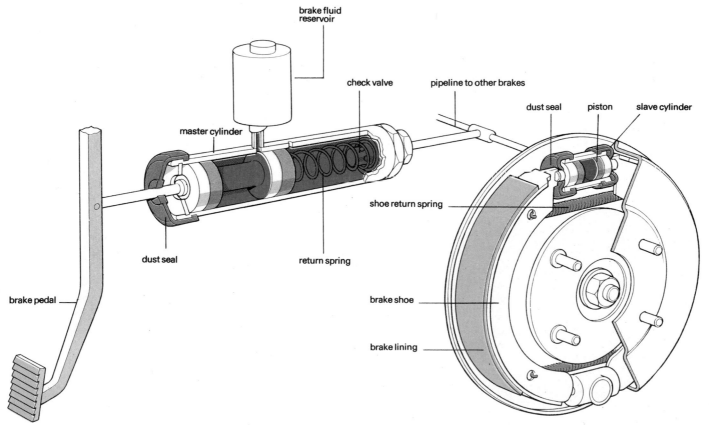

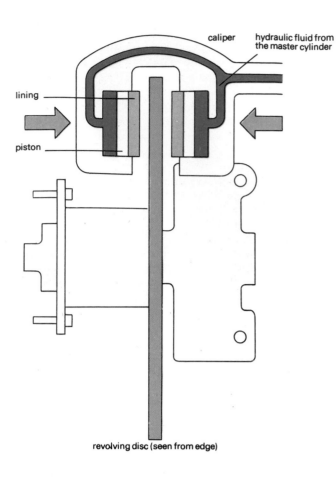

caliper

hydraulic fluid from the master cylinder

lining

piston

revolving disc (seen from edge)

Above: this disc brake on test remains intact at bright red heat, in excess of 600°C. Brakes get hot because they convert kinetic energy—the energy of motion—into heat by their frictional drag.

Above right: in a disc brake, hydraulic pressure in two slave cylinders presses two pads together on to opposite sides of the disc.

Right: the disc is open to the atmosphere except where it passes through the caliper casing so that the heat generated by braking can be dissipated.

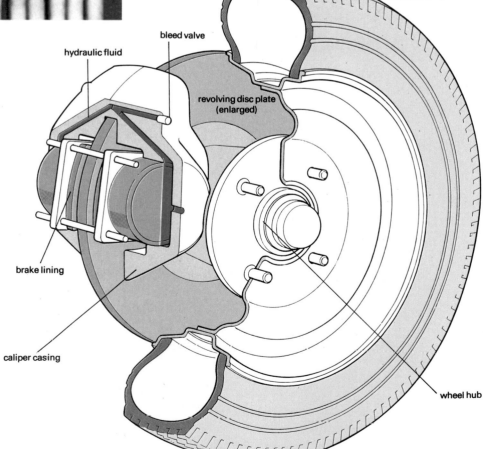

hydraulic fluid

bleed valve

tyre

revolving disc plate (enlarged)

brake lining

caliper casing

wheel hub

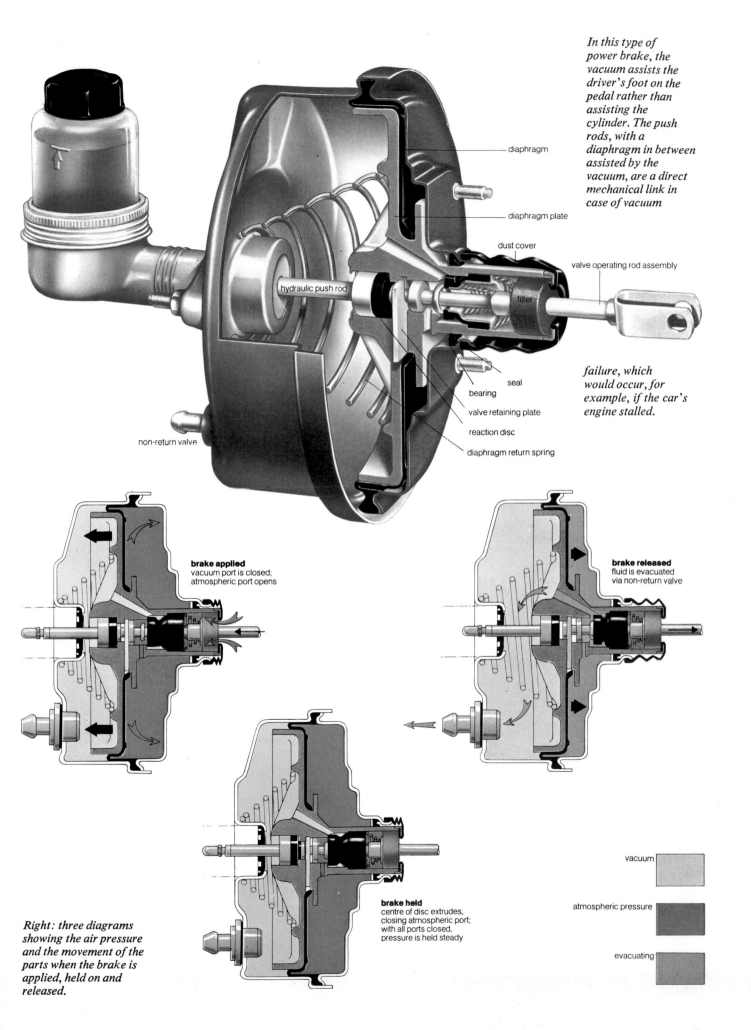

In this type of power brake, the vacuum assists the driver's foot on the pedal rather than assisting the cylinder. The push rods, with a diaphragm in between assisted by the vacuum, are a direct mechanical link in case of vacuum

diaphragm

diaphragm plate

dust cover

valve operating rod assembly

hydraulic push rod

filter

seal

bearing

valve retaining plate

reaction disc

non-return valve

diaphragm return spring

failure, which would occur, for example, if the car's engine stalled.

brake applied
vacuum port is closed; atmospheric port opens

brake released
fluid is evacuated via non-return valve

brake held
centre of disc extrudes, closing atmospheric port; with all ports closed, pressure is held steady

Right: three diagrams showing the air pressure and the movement of the parts when the brake is applied, held on and released.

vacuum

atmospheric pressure

evacuating

81

*Above: vacuum servo unit of the type shown on p 81
installed in a British Leyland Mini. The slave cylinder
is at the top, above the large round diaphragm chamber;
to its right is the air control valve.*

Hydraulic fluid from the master cylinder enters a slave cylinder with a slave piston in it. There is a hole in the slave piston, and if the servo were not working (for example, if the engine stalled) pressure from the master cylinder would pass through this hole direct to the brakes.

A passage leads off the slave cylinder 'upstream' of the slave piston to a small auxiliary cylinder containing a piston linked to the air control valve. Pressure from the master cylinder moves this piston, thus opening the valve, which admits air from the outside to one side of the diaphragm. Since this air is at a higher pressure than the inlet manifold vacuum, it forces the diaphragm across its chamber, against the spring. A rod connected to the diaphragm moves against the slave piston, closing the hole in it and forcing it down the slave cylinder so that it applies the brakes. (If the hole were not closed, the high pressure between the slave piston and the brake would be transferred back to the master cylinder, forcing the brake pedal violently up.)

As soon as the driver feels he has applied enough pressure to the brakes, he stops pressing the pedal down and the air control valve partly shuts, so that just enough air is admitted to hold the brakes as far on as they were. Because the amount of air admitted is proportional to the pressure on the brake pedal, the driver can control the amount of air entering, and thus the pressure on the brakes, exactly. When the brake pedal is released completely, the air control valve shuts completely and the equalized vacuum on either side of the diaphragm allows the return spring to push it back to its original position.

The system is 'fail safe' because a leak in the air system, or failure of the manifold vacuum for any reason, leaves the diaphragm in the 'off' position, so the hole in the slave piston is unblocked and the master cylinder works the brakes directly, without assistance. The extra pressure the driver feels when operating without assistance warns him of the fault.

Large commercial vehicles generally have air pressure brakes. These work in much the same way as hydraulic brakes, but by air, instead of fluid pressure. This is supplied by an engine-driven compressor rather than a hydraulic pump. There is a low pressure warning device, as well as an air pressure gauge, in the cab, and duplicate systems for trailer brakes and as a standby.

Steering gear   The simplest form of steering is that which was used for centuries on horse-drawn vehicles: it consists of a beam axle, pivoted in the middle and having a wheel on each end. It works quite effectively at walking pace, but as many a cowboy movie shows, when cornering at higher speeds it is unstable, because of the difference in track (distance between front and rear wheels) and is liable to overturn easily.

In 1818 a German called Lankensperger took out a British patent on a system of steering in which the steering wheels are separately pivoted at the ends of the shaft. All four wheels follow a true radius about a single point on a line which includes the rear axle. The geometry was named after the patent agent, whose name was Ackermann; in fact few modern cars operate on pure Ackermann principles, but the name and the idea have stuck.

The steering wheel in a modern car is made of a steel skeleton covered with hard plastic or leather. The hub is splined to the steering column (splines are longitudinal grooves similar to gear teeth). The steering column extends from the interior of the car down to the front end underneath, where the steering gear is located. Nowadays both the hub of the steering wheel and the column itself are made to be energy-absorbing, or collapsible, for safety reasons, to reduce chest damage in case of accident. At the lower end of the steering column is the steering box.

The purpose of the steering box is to provide leverage, or mechanical advantage, since the effort required to turn the front wheels is much greater than that which could be exerted by the driver through a direct mechanism. There are four types of box.

The worm and peg (or worm and nut) system consists of a coarse thread (the worm) on the end of the column and a peg mounted on a cross rocker shaft, or a meshing nut

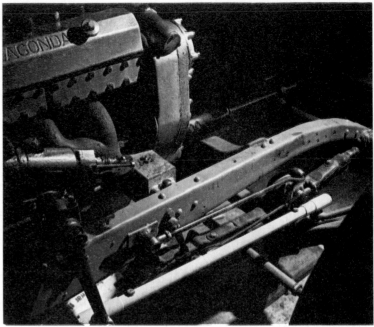

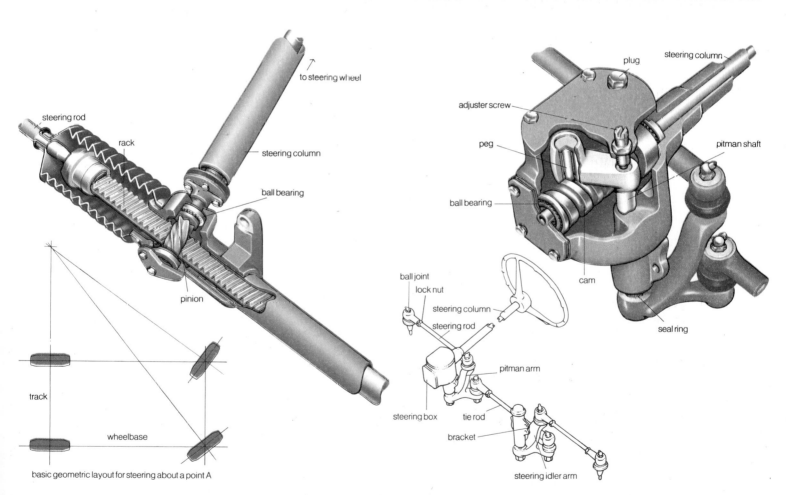

to steering wheel

steering rod

rack

steering column

ball bearing

pinion

track

wheelbase

basic geometric layout for steering about a point A

plug

steering column

adjuster screw

peg

pitman shaft

ball bearing

cam

seal ring

ball joint

lock nut

steering column

steering rod

pitman arm

steering box

tie rod

bracket

steering idler arm

Top: chassis of a Lotus Elan, clearly showing the rack and pinion steering gear, with rubber dust seals.

Above: rack and pinion steering is the simplest of all systems, and therefore the most positive. It is fitted to nearly all small and medium sized modern cars.

Inset: the basic Ackermann steering principle, in which the front wheels adopt different angles to travel on a circular course.

Top: a 1929 Lagonda in process of restoration. At the end of the steering column is the Marles steering box; protruding through the chassis, the drop arm; and, centre of the three rods, the drag link to one front wheel.

Above: such systems use cam and peg steering, as shown here. The cam is really a worm gear. Cars with independent front suspension have a transverse linkage, as in the black and white drawing, to allow for the different movements of the front wheels.

83

surrounding the worm and fastened to the rocker shaft. As the column is rotated the peg or nut rides up and down in the worm, thus turning the shaft. The cam and roller system is a variant of this in which the peg is replaced by a cam (a sort of V-shaped roller) which meshes with the worm. The recirculating ball gear is a more elaborate variant. A bearing casing takes the place of a nut, and instead of threads, ball bearings ride in the coarse groove of the worm. The bearing casing can have one or two 'threads' which are connected end-to-end by a tube (or tubes) to allow the balls to recirculate back to the end of the worm thread when they have in effect rolled off the edge. The rack and pinion system consists simply of a pinion gear on the end of the column meshing with a rack (a flat section of gear teeth).

All but the last type of box require a system of linkages to take the movement created by the drop arm (attached to the steering box rocker shaft) to the steering arms on the wheels. Each manufacturer designs his own systems so as to give the correct linkage geometry, to allow the links to follow vertical wheel movement (for example when the wheels hit bumps in the road) and to fit into the available space. This means a combination of several pieces of linkage: operating arm, idler arm, and track rods [tie-rods]. Here the rack and pinion system scores highly, for its linkage is simple: a track rod from each end of the rack connected to the steering arms on the wheels. Its main disadvantage is that the rack bridges the centre of the car, getting in the way of a front engine.

The attitude or angle of the wheel and axle to the road are

Below: power steering unit on a left hand drive truck, giving a constant ratio from lock to lock and reduced turning circle. The control valves are in the steering box; the actuator is mounted on the chassis.

important in steering. Castor is familiar from castors on furniture, and means that the contact patch of the tyre on the road about which the wheel swivels is slightly behind the axis of the king pin or swivel pin, so that there is a self aligning torque which keeps the wheels pointing straight ahead when travelling in a straight line. King pin inclination has the effect that, as the wheel is turned, it tends to lift the car slightly (like a door on rising hinges) so that in addition to the turning torque required an extra load has to be applied; steering effort rises and is thus partially related to cornering forces, and steering becomes self-centring. Camber is the inclination of the wheel to the vertical; the angle is called camber angle. Modern cars have camber angles of less than one degree, and camber is usually positive (the tops of the wheels are tilted outwards). The purpose of it in modern cars is to prevent the wheels from tilting too much inward because of heavy loads or wear resulting in play in the king pins or wheel bearings. The camber must be carefully adjusted; if the camber of the two steered wheels is not equal, the steering of the car will have a tendency to 'wander' in the direction of the greatest camber and tyre wear will be uneven.

Power steering   The car of today is larger and heavier than earlier cars; the tyres are wider, further apart and inflated to lower pressures. In addition, the trend of development has been to place more than half the weight on the front wheels, especially the weight of the engine, which itself is larger and heavier than in the early days.

To make cars easier to steer, the gear ratio in the steering box at the end of the steering column was changed so that turning the wheel required less torque, but this increased the number of turns of the steering wheel required on modern cars without power steering compared to $2\frac{1}{2}$ or 3 turns for

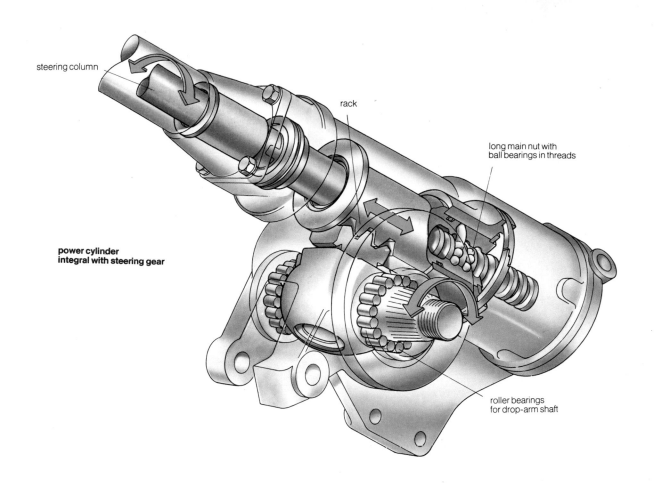

steering column

rack

long main nut with
ball bearings in threads

**power cylinder
integral with steering gear**

roller bearings
for drop-arm shaft

⊠ valves open   ■ valves closed

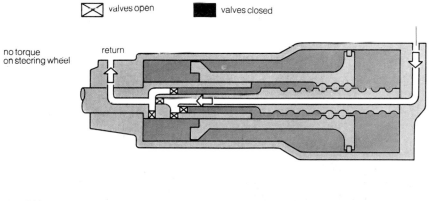

no torque
on steering wheel

return

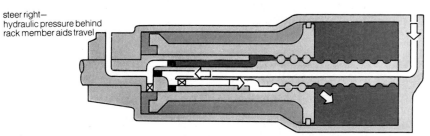

steer right—
hydraulic pressure behind
rack member aids travel

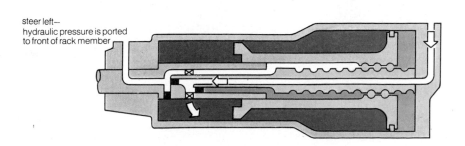

steer left—
hydraulic pressure is ported
to front of rack member

*This power steering design uses
rotary valves within the steering
box. When there is no torque on the
steering wheel—that is, when the
car is travelling in a straight
line—all valves are open and there
is equal fluid pressure at the
front and back of the rack member.
When the steering wheel is turned
one way or the other, appropriate
valves close and the travel of the
rack member on the long main nut is
assisted by the appropriate pressure.
If the pressure fails for any
reason, the mechanical operation
is harder, but still fully
controlled. The steering linkage
itself is connected to the drop
arm shaft and ratios are such that
a short travel of the rack equals
a large degree of turning of the
steered wheels of the car.*

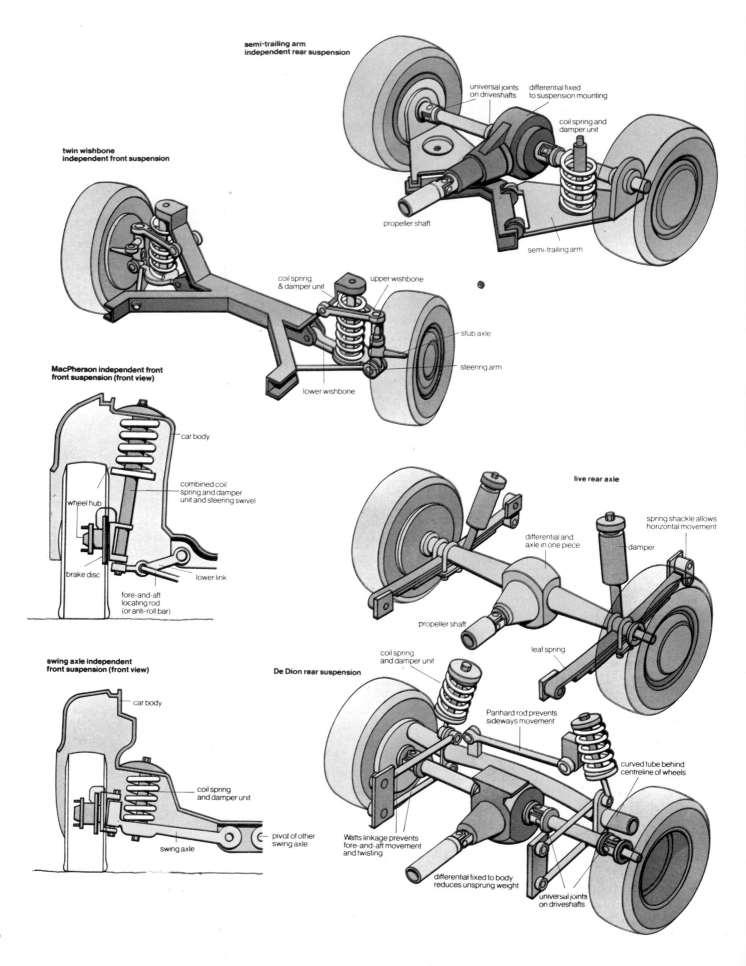

**semi-trailing arm
independent rear suspension**

universal joints
on driveshafts

differential fixed
to suspension mounting

coil spring and
damper unit

propeller shaft

semi-trailing arm

**twin wishbone
independent front suspension**

coil spring
& damper unit

upper wishbone

stub axle

steering arm

lower wishbone

**MacPherson independent front
front suspension (front view)**

car body

combined coil
spring and damper
unit and steering swivel

wheel hub

brake disc

lower link

fore-and-aft
locating rod
(or anti-roll bar)

live rear axle

differential and
axle in one piece

spring shackle allows
horizontal movement

damper

propeller shaft

leaf spring

coil spring
and damper unit

De Dion rear suspension

Panhard rod prevents
sideways movement

curved tube behind
centreline of wheels

**swing axle independent
front suspension (front view)**

car body

coil spring
and damper unit

pivot of other
swing axle

swing axle

Watts linkage prevents
fore-and-aft movement
and twisting

differential fixed to body
reduces unsprung weight

universal joints
on driveshafts

86

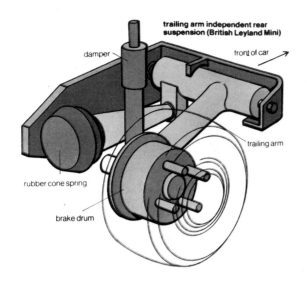

trailing arm independent rear suspension (British Leyland Mini)

damper

front of car

trailing arm

rubber cone spring

brake drum

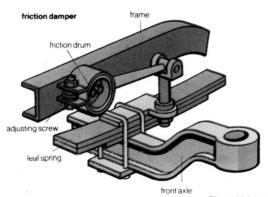

friction damper

frame

friction drum

adjusting screw

leaf spring

front axle

telescopic damper

Citroen high pressure oil-gas suspension unit

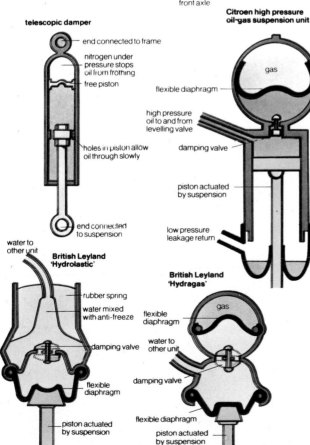

end connected to frame

nitrogen under pressure stops oil from frothing

free piston

gas

flexible diaphragm

high pressure oil to and from levelling valve

damping valve

holes in piston allow oil through slowly

piston actuated by suspension

end connected to suspension

low pressure leakage return

water to other unit

British Leyland 'Hydrolastic'

rubber spring

water mixed with anti-freeze

damping valve

flexible diaphragm

piston actuated by suspension

British Leyland 'Hydragas'

gas

flexible diaphragm

water to other unit

damping valve

flexible diaphragm

piston actuated by suspension

cars built before 1940. Modern cars with power steering only require about three turns.

Power assisted steering was first developed in the 1920s; one of the first devices was developed by an engineer at Pierce Arrow, an American maker of luxury cars. The Cadillac division of General Motors was going to offer power steering as optional equipment on some models in the early 1930s, but the Depression interfered with development. During World War II power steering was fitted to military vehicles; in 1952 Chrysler began offering it, and it is now standard equipment on many of the biggest American cars.

Electric devices were tried, but power steering today is always hydraulic, with oil pressure of perhaps 1000 psi (70 kg/cm²) maintained by a pump driven by the engine of the car. The system is a servomechanism, or servoloop, which makes a correction to compensate for the torque applied to the steering wheel by the driver. It consists of an actuator and a control valve. The actuator is a hydraulic cylinder with a piston, or ram, which is free to travel in either direction from the centre. The function of the control valve is to respond to the torque from the steering wheel by actuating small valves at each end of the cylinder. The system is designed to assist the steering linkage, rather than to replace it, and it does not do all of the work of steering, but leaves some of it for the driver. Thus if the hydraulics fail the car can still be steered, though with greater effort, and at all times the feel of the road is mechanically transmitted from the front wheels to the hands of the driver on the steering wheel, an essential element of safe driving. The power steering makes a positive contribution to safe driving in that if the driver hits a small obstacle in the road or has a flat tyre at speed, the power unit makes it easier to keep the car under control. Many large cars fitted with wide, stiff radial ply tyres would be nearly impossible to steer at parking speeds without power steering.

Hydrostatic systems, designed for off-the-road vehicles, are exceptions to some of this, because they dispense with the steering column and the steering box, and the steering wheel and the steered wheels are connected only by hydraulic tubes or hoses.

The power steering system includes a reservoir to hold the oil. Oil pressure is always provided when the engine is running, but when the system is at rest, that is, when the steering wheel is not being turned, equal pressure is available to each side of the piston in the actuator, so that it does not move.

There are basically two types of power steering systems: those which have the control valve located within the steering box, in which case it is usually a rotary valve, and those in which the valve is integral with the actuator, when it is an axial spool valve.

In a rotary valve system, the valve is integral with the steering column and operated directly by rotation of the steering wheel. In some systems the actuator is part of the steering linkage; in the Adwest rack-and-pinion system, the actuator is mounted on the rack itself. In others, such as the Marles Varamatic, the actuator as well as the valve is in-

Opposite page and above: simplified views of suspension types. The ideals are to keep the wheels upright, unsprung weight low (to stop the wheels from bouncing on bumps), and to be strong and simple.

Near left: damper; gas and fluid 'spring' units.

tegral with the steering box, and operates the Pitman arm, which connects the end of the steering column to the steering linkage between the front wheels. A rotary valve is an input shaft inside a valve sleeve, with longitudinal slots machined on the shaft and on the inside of the sleeve. When the steering wheel is not being turned, the slots are lined up so that oil flows with equal pressure into ports in both directions; when the slots are misaligned by torque on the steering wheel, the oil flows all in one direction. This system can be designed so that the more the shaft is turned the more power assistance is given, with the least assistance near the straight ahead position.

An axial spool valve, which reacts laterally, is usually integral with the actuator in the steering linkage, particularly on commercial vehicles. The axial load fed into the steering linkage by turning the steering wheel actuates the valve. In these systems the actuator is often connected at one end to the cross piece of the steering linkage with the piston end connected to the frame of the car, so that the actuator in effect pushes or pulls against the frame when it is activated.

Suspension Modern car suspension systems have to do considerably more than just cushion the occupants from irregu-

Above: rear suspension of a 1929 Morris Cowley, with leaf springs and friction shock absorbers.

Below: British Leyland Hydragas system, compressed by an L shaped link on the upper suspension strut.

Below: rear suspension of a Lotus Elan, with 'Chapman strut'—the rear equivalent of a MacPherson front strut. Each half axle has a universal joint at each end and the differential is fixed to the frame. The system is only used on sports cars, because it takes up space.

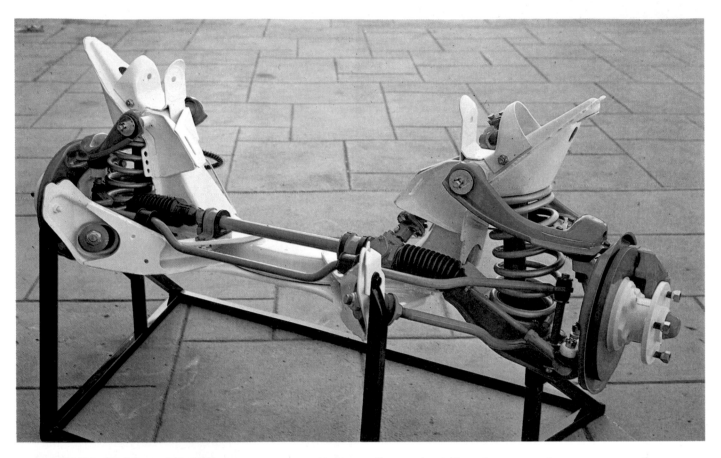

Above: twin wishbone front suspension system, incorporating coil springs, telescopic dampers and rack and pinion steering.

larities in the road surface: they have to ensure that the wheels stay in contact with the road to give adequate grip for accelerating, braking and cornering. The ancient system used on carts of a solid beam axle rigidly attached to the chassis with a wheel at each end would not only be uncomfortable but unstable at anything more than a walking pace.

The first cars drew heavily on carriage practice, and were thus simply sprung on leaf springs, with narrow tyres, and an Ackermann type steering gear. The sophisticated suspension systems of today are the result of development which still continues.

A Scot called Thomson patented a type of pneumatic tyre in 1845, but John Boyd Dunlop is generally given credit for their development. He was the first to realize that a pneumatic tyre not only made a bicycle more comfortable but had lower rolling resistance, and made the bicycle easier to propel. He developed his tyre to absorb some of the road shocks on his son's tricycle, but later it gradually became clear that tyres have another important advantage over solid wheels: when deflected from the straight-ahead, they develop a substantial cornering force, enabling corners to be taken at higher speeds.

For a variety of reasons, tyres until the 1920s were of narrow cross-section and ran at relatively high air pressures. As technology improved tyres were made wider and designed to operate with lower pressures; the wider tyre made greater contact with the road surface at a more uniform pressure, thus giving a better grip, and the lower pressure made a softer spring, giving more comfort.

The tyre alone would not provide much comfort; between the wheel and the body it is necessary to have springs. Some carriages had the body suspended by straps from the chassis

89

extremities, but the semi-elliptical multi-leaf spring was an early development. Leaf springs are still widely used on cars, particularly on the rear axles. One of the advantages is that the inter-leaf friction provides a bit of damping. The leaf spring also performs the function, on a rear axle, of locating the axle, holding it in a set position except for allowing an up-and-down motion.

The other most common type of spring is the coil spring, a helically-wound rod of spring steel, which operates in torsion rather than bending. Closely allied to the coil spring is the torsion bar, which is little more than a straightened coil: one end is clamped to the chassis and the other to the suspension, so that as the latter rotates about its fittings it twists the rod, whose tension then helps to stabilize the suspension.

If a car had only springs without any damping, a road shock would set it bouncing, and theoretically it could bounce for a very long time. This would not only be disturbing to the occupants but would be unsafe, because it might result in the wheels leaving the road, so dampers or shock absorbers are necessary. Early 'shocks' were often of the simple friction type, consisting of a pivoted arm attached to the axle so that its movement turned friction discs like a clutch, whose resistance provided the damping. Nowadays shock absorbers are usually hydraulic and telescopic, consisting of a piston inside a sealed cylinder, one attached to the chassis and the other to the axle. Holes in the piston allow fluid (oil) in the cylinder to leak from one side of the piston to the other, absorbing energy in the process. Some designs use a compressible gas rather than a hydraulic fluid, allowing the shock absorber to perform a spring function as well as absorbing shock.

There are also springs which take advantage of the elasticity of other substances than spring steel. Rubber and air (or some other gas) have their advantages. For example, rubber can be varied in shape and composition to allow it to work in shear as well as compression (shear is a strain or stress in which parallel planes of a substance remain parallel but are allowed to move parallel to each other). Also, owing to its hysteresis properties, rubber can be effectively self-damping. Hysteresis is the retardation of an effect beyond the cause of it: high hysteresis rubber is rubber with less bounce. British Leyland Minis use a simple and elegant form of rubber spring (many had a different system, 'Hydrolastic', described below).

Air springs come in two basic types: high or low pressure. They resemble balloons in principle, which means that in general they act simply as springs and cannot be used to locate any part of the suspension system. Their stiffness comes from three basic parameters: the internal pressure, the load-carrying area, and the volume. A low-pressure spring will have perhaps 70 psi (48 bar) and a high-pressure device up to ten times as much, which means that it can be much more compact.

An example of the high-pressure spring is that fitted to Citroens. It is a metal sphere, divided in half by a flexible diaphragm, on one side of which is a gas, and on the other oil. A piston and connecting rod assembly, attached to the wheel by a system of levers and arms, acts on the oil and thus compresses the gas: as the wheel oscillates the piston moves up and down, alternately compressing the gas and allowing it to expand, providing the springing medium. By including a source of high-pressure oil it is possible to provide a ride of a given height, pumping or bleeding oil from the system as necessary. The British Leyland 'Hydragas'

system is similar, but the fluid used is a mixture of water and anti-freeze, the piston takes the form of a flexible diaphragm, and the hydraulics are connected front-to-rear instead of to a central reservoir. This system is cheaper to build than the Citroen, requiring no extra pump and circuitry, but does not give self-levelling.

Air springs in general give a soft ride, do not require any extra damping, and by means of the fore-and-aft interconnection can be made quite stiff in roll and pitch. The 'Hydrolastic' system is basically a rubber spring as in the early Minis, but with front-to-rear fluid interconnection.

The tyres, springs and so on provide the carrying and comfort function of the suspension system; the axles and other linkage, however, have to do with handling and road-holding, and thus with safety, for they control the movement of the body with respect to the wheels and the road (the suspension 'geometry'). All these functions—comfort, capacity, understeer and oversteer, steering response and so forth—are the result of compromise, and the ultimate handling characteristic of the car depends upon subjective decisions at the development stage.

The ancient solid beam axle is still in wide use, both in front (common on trucks) and in the rear. In the former case, stub axles swivelling on kingpins allow steering to take place. Leaf springs in conjuction with a beam axle at the rear give fore-and-aft and sideways location, and this is still standard on many mass-produced cars. Further location (essential if coil springs are used) can be provided by trailing arms, A-brackets, Panhard rods, Watts linkage and so forth; the more precise the location the more precise the handling of the car. Disadvantages of the beam axle are that a bump on one wheel tends to affect the opposite wheel, and that they tend to be heavy, so increasing the ratio of sprung to unsprung weight, affecting comfort detrimentally, a sort of 'tail wagging the dog' effect. On the other hand, the beam axle keeps the wheels upright, for better cornering.

The swing axle is essentially a beam axle divided in half. VW used it on the Beetle for years, and the British division of Chrysler still use it at the front of the Imp. It has an unfortunate 'jacking-up' effect: when cornering, the body rolls around the heavily laden outside wheel, which then adopts the wrong angle to the road. Thus cornering power is lost and the swing axle can be tricky at high speeds.

The most common independent suspension is the twin wishbone layout, which because of its configuration is compact, allows large vertical wheel movements, gives good camber characteristics and a tight steering lock (small turning radius). Similar characteristics apply to the MacPherson strut type of suspension, but this does away with the top wishbone, using the damper and coil unit as a triangulating locating member.

Some cars (including VW) use trailing arm front suspension, but this means that the front wheels adopt the same angle to the road as the body, which gives undesirable camber change.

Independent rear suspensions follow similar principles to those at the front; the most common is the semi-trailing arm type, which is geometrically a combination of swing axles and trailing arms: such layouts, if well-designed, give acceptable camber change, are compact and are lighter than a beam axle. The de Dion rear suspension system uses a relatively light hollow tube to connect the wheels, and mounts the differential directly on to the chassis, so that the desirable geometric characteristics of the beam axle are kept without the weight.

Tyres The pneumatic tyre was invented by a Scot, R W Thomson, and first patented by him in 1845. A set of tyres made according to Thomson's design were fitted to a horse drawn carriage and covered more than 1000 miles (1600 km) before they needed replacing. It was not until nearly 50 years later, however, that the modern tyre industry was founded by J B Dunlop, an Irishman from Belfast.

A modern vehicle tyre consists of an inner layer of fabric plies which are wrapped around bead wires at their inner edges. The bead wires hold the tyre in position on the wheel rim. The fabric plies are coated with rubber which is moulded to form the sidewalls and the tread of the tyre. Behind the tread is a reinforcing band, or breaker, usually made of steel, rayon or glass fibre. The radial ply tyres fitted to most modern cars differ from cross ply tyres in that they are constructed with very flexible sidewalls and have breakers which are almost inextensible. These properties are achieved by altering the disposition of the fabric plies in the tyre 'carcass'; in particular, the cords in the fabric plies run from one bead wire to the other making an angle of 90° with the 'crown' of the tyre (the circumferential line around the middle of the tread). Radial tyres have better cornering and wear characteristics at high speed than cross ply tyres.

The process of making a modern tyre involves three separate stages: the preparation of the various component

Right: tyre manufacture. Winding rubber coated steel wire tapes on to a former.

Below: removing completed tyres from the mould, which uses heat and pressure to form and vulcanize the rubber.

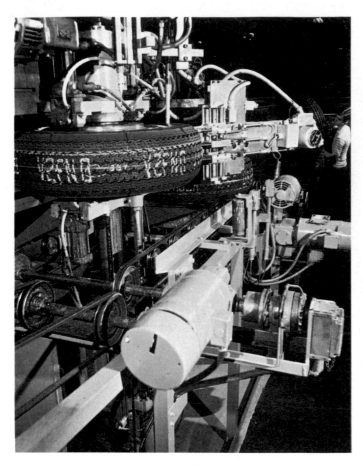

Above: all tyres are tested before sale on a force variation testing machine, which subjects them to stresses in various directions. Slightly substandard tyres may be sold at reduced price for off the road use only; they are clearly marked to prevent unscrupulous dealers from selling them as normal.

parts, their assembly into the shape of a tyre, and finally heating with sulphur in a suitable mould to vulcanize the rubber. During vulcanization the rubber in the tyre structure combines with the sulphur, which sets it in its final pattern and gives the rubber components the required physical properties.

The main materials in tyre construction are steel wire for the inextensible beads, textile fabric or steel for the casing and reinforcing breakers, and of course rubber mixed with various additives to give the required strength and resistance to wear and fatigue. For tyre casings, rayon, nylon and polyester are the most commonly used materials, although thin steel cable is often found in truck tyres. The breaker was originally made of steel, and still is in truck tyres, but nowadays rayon and other materials such as glass fibre are more common in car tyres. The rubber mixes are made from modern synthetic rubbers for car tyres: heavier truck tyres tend to be made of natural rubber because it is cooler running than synthetic rubbers.

The first operation is to prepare the necessary rubber mixes, working the rubber into a plastic state, in an internal mixer, and milling into it sulphur for vulcanization and other ingredients for the different types of rubber mix needed in the various parts of the tyre. In the tread, a relatively high loading of finely powdered carbon black is used to give resistance to tread wear. The casing rubbers are mixed to have strength in the thin layers which bond the

casing cords together, and to have resistance to fatigue under repeated flexings and continuous tension. For use on the bead wires, a hard mix with a high sulphur content is prepared, which will set into a solid mass on moulding.

The bead wires themselves are prepared from high tensile steel wire, assembled as a ribbon of five or six strands, side by side, and enclosed in the hard rubber mix to form a tape. A number of runs of this tape are wound up on a former of the correct size and, on vulcanization, the bead is set in a solid and virtually unstretchable form.

Cotton, which was originally used, has been replaced in tyre casings by modern synthetic textiles, which, as they are made of long continuous filaments, have a much greater strength for a given thickness than ordinary cotton thread spun from a collection of short hair-like fibres.

The material for the plies and for the breakers consists of a practically weftless fabric, with the strength all in the warp, and with the sheet held together only by a system of fine, widely spaced weft threads. This construction is used to eliminate the 'knuckles' which occur in a normal cross-woven fabric, where warp and weft threads cross, and to reduce the sawing and chafing which takes place when such a fabric is flexed under load. The sheet of 'weftless' fabric is made into a sandwich, between two films of rubber, in a calendering operation (pressing between rollers). The rubber-coated fabric is then cut into strips, with the threads running in an appropriate direction, for use in building up the casings of the different types of tyre.

Both radial and cross ply tyres are built up on collapsible steel formers. The layers of fabric plies are secured by turning their edges round the coil of bead wire enclosed in suitable reinforcing and packing strips.

The process of adding the smooth strip of extruded rubber compound which will form the tread differs in the two types of tyre. The cross ply receives its tread while still on the almost flat building drum. Afterwards the complete cylindrical tyre is shaped up to the usual doughnut form as it is introduced into the mould. The radial ply tyre, from its nature, demands different treatment. Here the casing must be taken from the nearly flat cylindrical building drum, and shaped up to the required toroidal form before the unstretchable rigid breaker bands are added. On top of these bands the tread is then fitted.

The final stage in tyre manufacture consists of moulding the built-up raw tyre in a suitably designed steel shell mould. This is either engraved with the tread and wall pattern or has die-castings riveted inside it, to make up the complicated pattern of ribs, blocks, grooves and fine slots, which give the final tyre its road grip and even wear characteristics.

The mould is situated in a press containing a cylindrical rubber diaphragm which is inflated under high pressure inside the tyre as the mould closes. This operation forces the raw plastic tyre into the pattern on the inside of the mould. Heat is then applied, in the form of steam, both from cavities in the press through the outer mould, and by supplying steam to the inside of the diaphragm within the tyre. This heating causes the chemical combination of the rubber with the sulphur which has been included in the various rubber mixes used in the components of the tyre. The result, when the moulding is finished, is a tyre of permanent shape and of suitable physical properties for its intended use.

The outstanding weakness of the pneumatic tyre has always been the risk of puncture. This means that cars have to carry spare wheels, with the necessary tools for wheel changing. The growing speed and density of traffic have made such roadside wheel changes hazardous, and the deflation of tyres, especially on rear wheels, can cause serious loss of control.

Various safety tyres have been developed, one of the most effective of which is Dunlop's 'Denovo' tyre. This tyre can continue to run when punctured without destroying itself. Capsules of liquid fixed inside the tyre rupture in the event of a puncture, and the liberated liquid lubricates the inside of the deflated tyre, thereby reducing the amount of heat generated, and also providing a smallinflation pressure. A locking device ensures that the tyre beads do not move from their seats on the rim, and that the deflated tyre continues to provide the sideways forces which give stability and steering control.

Looking further into the future it is possible to visualize a tyre in which the textile casing will be replaced by a moulded rubber structure, of revolutionary shape, providing all the properties of load-carrying, cushioning, steering, drive and braking, in one simple and readily moulded whole.

Left: testing an aircraft tyre and brakes while wet.

Below: cross ply and radial tyres. The radial's more flexible wall and stiff, braced tread improve its grip and wear resistance. The 'Denovo' tyre (left) is basically an extra-strong radial which keeps in place on the rim when deflated. It contains a gel and a liquid which mix to seal and partly reflate it, so that it can still be driven on, for a limited distance at a limited speed, until it can be repaired.

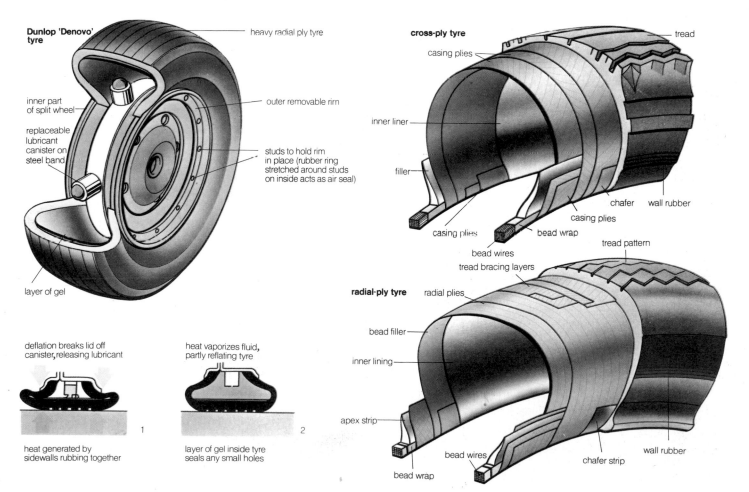

Dunlop 'Denovo' tyre

heavy radial ply tyre

inner part of split wheel

replaceable lubricant canister on steel band

outer removable rim

studs to hold rim in place (rubber ring stretched around studs on inside acts as air seal)

layer of gel

deflation breaks lid off canister, releasing lubricant

heat vaporizes fluid, partly reflating tyre

1

2

heat generated by sidewalls rubbing together

layer of gel inside tyre seals any small holes

cross-ply tyre

tread

casing plies

inner liner

filler

chafer   wall rubber

casing plies

casing plies

bead wrap

bead wires

tread bracing layers

tread pattern

radial-ply tyre   radial plies

bead filler

inner lining

apex strip

bead wires

bead wrap

chafer strip

wall rubber

The Electrical System and the Instruments

Unlike the diesel engine, in which the fuel in the cylinders is ignited by the high temperature of the air compressed by the pistons, the petrol engine uses a high voltage electric spark to ignite the fuel-air mixture. In applications where complete independence from other electrical systems is required, such as some motorcycles, stationary power units and aircraft, the power for the spark is usually provided by a magneto. This is an engine-driven device which not only performs the functions of a coil ignition system, but generates its own electricity. In a car, however, a battery is necessary to provide a satisfactory power supply for its other electrical equipment, and so a battery powered ignition system is used.

Many early engines used 'hot tube' ignition, in which a tube of metal (usually platinum) screwed into the cylinder was heated to red heat by an external flame. The outer end of the tube was sealed, and on the compression stroke of the piston some of the fuel-air mixture was forced into the glowing tube where it ignited, the flame then spreading through the chamber to ignite the remaining fuel.

Reliable electric ignition systems were first developed in the 1890s by several car makers, including Benz and de Dion-Bouton. These early systems worked on essentially the same principles as modern coil ignition systems, and comprised a battery, contact breaker, induction coil and spark plugs. The development of transistors and thyristors during the 1950s led to the introduction of semiconductor ignition systems, which use electronic switching systems to control the ignition coil.

The distributor, containing the contact breaker, capacitor, rotor arm, distributor head and timing mechanisms, is driven at half engine speed through a 2 to 1 reduction gearing from the engine crankshaft. The distributor is set so that the contact breaker is just opening as one of the pistons nears the top of its compression stroke, and at this point the rotor arm carried on top of the distributor shaft is opposite one of the electrodes in the distributor head. A heavily insulated cable connects this electrode to the spark plug in the cylinder about to fire.

The low tension (low voltage) circuit of the ignition system is supplied with current from the battery through the ignition switch. When the contact breaker points are closed, a current of 3 or 4 A flows through the primary winding of the ignition coil, which consists of a few hundred turns of heavy gauge insulated copper wire, and sets up a magnetic field in the laminated iron core of the coil.

As the distributor shaft turns, a cam mounted on it opens the contact breaker points, interrupting the primary winding current. The magnetic field then 'collapses', causing a high voltage (up to 30,000 V) to be induced in the secondary winding, which is made up of 15,000 to 30,000 turns of very fine insulated copper wire wound around the iron core (the primary winding is wound over the secondary winding).

The magnetic field associated with the induced secondary voltage will, in its turn, induce a voltage (the back emf, electromotive force) in the primary winding, and this can be as high as 500 V. This voltage can arc across the opening contacts, dissipating some of the stored energy in the coil and burning the points, and to prevent this arcing a capacitor is connected across the points.

The induced high voltage pulse flows along a lead to the central contact of the distributor, through the rotor arm, and from there to the appropriate spark plug. When the voltage at the spark plug is sufficiently high, the fuel-air mixture in the gap between the plug electrodes ionizes, and the enrgy stored in the ignition coil discharges across the gap in the form of a spark which ignites the mixture in the combustion chamber.

The battery A battery produces electricity by means of a chemical reaction. An accumulator is a type of battery in which the process is reversible; that is, the battery can be re-charged by passing a current through it. A car battery is really a lead-acid accumulator. In its simplest form, it consists of two plates, one of lead and one of lead dioxide, immersed in a weak solution of sulphuric acid known as the electrolyte. There are contacts on top of the plates so that electric current can be drawn from them.

A chemical reaction produces an electric current because the atoms of which chemical elements are made are held together by electrical forces when they react to form compounds. The outer layer of an atom is composed of electrons, tiny particles each carrying a negative electrical charge. These particles are not all permanently attached to their atoms, and are exchanged between them during chemical reactions. When an atom gains an electron, it gains an extra negative charge, and so becomes negatively charged as a whole. When it loses one, on the other hand, it becomes positively charged. Atoms or groups of atoms in this charged state are called ions. Positive and negative ions are attracted to each other, and when circumstances allow, will move together and combine to form compounds. Ions with similar charges repel each other.

The electrons of the atoms of a metal are very easily detached. An electric current consists of a flow of electrons

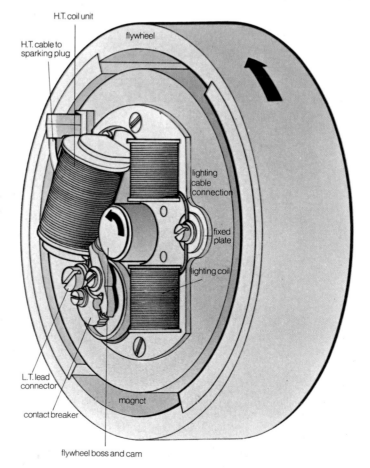

H.T. coil unit

H.T. cable to sparking plug

flywheel

lighting cable connection

fixed plate

lighting coil

L.T. lead connector

contact breaker

magnet

flywheel boss and cam

Above: some of the main components of an ignition system.

Below left: the magneto is a simple combined generator, coil and contact breaker for small engines.

Below: connections of an ignition system. The distributor takes the high tension current from coil to plugs.

through a metal, hopping from atom to atom (this is why metals conduct electricity better than other substances).

Some substances are strongly *reactive*, that is, they have a strong tendency to form compounds. Sulphuric acid is one of these, which accounts for its corrosiveness.

As long as there are no external forces at work, the dissociated ions of the acid do not react either with the pure lead negative plate or with the lead dioxide positive plate. There is a certain amount of chemical activity at the surface of each plate, but a blanketing layer of ions builds up and stops it. But as soon as the two plates of the accumulator are electrically connected (as they would be if a load such as a light bulb or an electric motor were wired up to the cell) this upsets the equilibrium of the cell and a reaction begins at both plates.

Connecting the two plates allows electrons to flow freely from one to the other. Consequently, the lead atoms each give up two electrons and become lead ions with a double positive charge. The positively charged ions attract the negatively charged ions from the acid, and the two combine to form lead sulphate. The process continues as long as electrons flow.

This reaction at the negative plate produces two things: negatively charged electrons flowing along the wire (i.e. an electric current) and positively charged hydrogen ions being discharged into the acid solution. Both move across to the other, positive plate by their separate routes. (The ions and electrons that reach it are probably not the same ones that set out from the far side, but there is a general movement of ions in that direction.)

At the positive plate, two reactions take place. The electrons that reach it through the wire are negative and consequently attract the positive hydrogen ions to the plate. The plate is made of lead dioxide. This, the electrons and

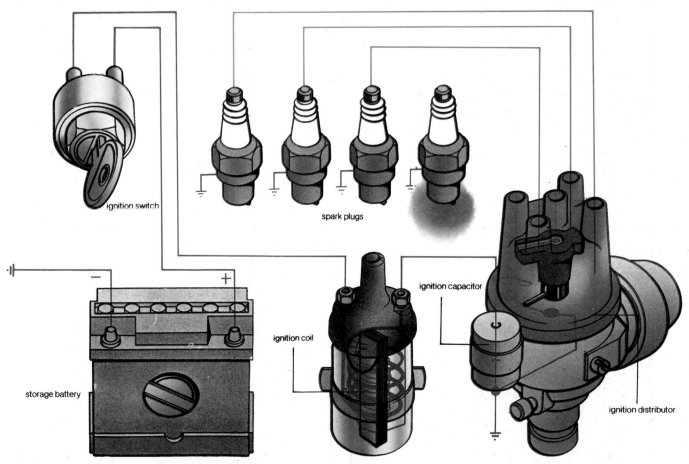

ignition switch

spark plugs

storage battery

ignition coil

ignition capacitor

ignition distributor

the hydrogen ions combine to form lead oxide and water. Unlike lead dioxide, lead oxide is attacked by sulphuric acid even when no current is flowing through the plate. So it immediately reacts with the acid to form lead sulphate and more water. The net result of these three reactions is that both plates change to lead sulphate, and the acid turns to water. When the accumulator has reached this stage no more current flows. It is completely discharged.

The accumulator is recharged by passing electric current from a generator through it in the other direction. This reverses all the electrical forces, and all the chemical reactions reverse themselves as a result. The lead sulphate changes back to lead dioxide in the positive plate and lead in the negative plate. The water changes back to sulphuric acid.

A lead-acid accumulator, as used in a car, does not in practice consist simply of two plates dipped in acid. Lead dioxide is too brittle, and while pure lead is rigid, the lead that is deposited on the negative plate by the charging process builds up as a sort of metal sponge, which is very fragile. Consequently, both plates need some sort of support.

This is normally accomplished by making the plates in the form of grids of an alloy of lead and antimony (which is tougher than pure lead) with the spongy lead or lead dioxide pressed into the grid. There are several grids in each cell of the accumulator arranged so that positive and negative alternate. They are spaced a short distance apart by insulators to make the construction more rigid. The fact that there are several grids does not affect their working.

A single cell, that is one set of plates immersed in a single container of acid, produces electricity at the comparatively low voltage of 2V. The electrical system of most modern cars runs on 12V; this is provided by linking six cells together in series (end-to-end) so as to take advantage of their combined voltage. The six cells are completely separate except for linking bars across the top to carry the current.

A lead-acid accumulator must not be allowed to remain discharged for a long time. This is because the lead sulphate (deposited in small crystals) tends to harden into a solid block. Once it has done this it will not take part in any chemical reaction and the plate becomes partly or wholly dead, depending on how much of it is affected.

The state of charge of an accumulator can easily be told by measuring the density of the acid. The more the battery discharges, the more of the acid turns to water and the lighter it becomes. Its density is measured with a hydrometer. When the battery is recharged, it becomes warm. Some of the water evaporates, so accumulators must be topped up occasionally.

The induction coil The induction coil is an instrument for producing a high voltage from a low one. The principles of the induction coil were discovered by Michael Faraday (1791-1867), and by the early 1900s induction coils were being used to produce electrical discharges in low pressure gases, leading to the discovery, incidentally, of x-rays and cathode rays.

The basic instrument comprises two coils: a primary winding of a few hundred turns of thick insulated wire wrapped around a soft iron core, with a secondary winding of several thousand turns of fine insulated wire wrapped around the primary.

A low voltage DC source provides current for the primary, and is switched rapidly on and off by means of an iron armature similar to that of an electric bell. Current passes through an adjustable screw on which the flat steel spring supporting the armature rests, and into the primary coil. This magnetizes the soft iron core of the coil, which attracts the iron armature towards it. As the armature moves it breaks the electrical contact at the screw, cutting off the current flow and thus demagnetizing the core. The steel spring pulls the armature back to its original position, restoring the current flow, and the cycle of operations begins again and is repeated many times a second.

The magnetic flux produced by the current in the primary winding 'links' with the turns of the secondary, and when the current stops flowing the magnetic field collapses and a high electromotive force (or emf, measured in volts) is

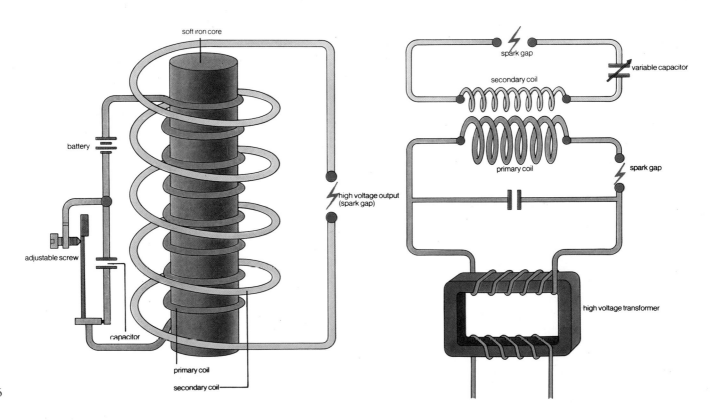

induced in the secondary winding. This induced emf acts in such a direction as to set up a magnetic field which opposes the change in the primary field.

The magnitude of the induced emf is approximately equal to the ratio between the number of turns on the primary and the number of turns on the secondary. For example, if there are a thousand times more turns on the secondary than on the primary then the induced emf in the secondary is approximately a thousand times the emf in the primary.

Self induction in the primary coil slows the rate at which the primary current builds up, and also causes arcing across the armature contacts thus prolonging the duration of the primary current. This reduces the magnitude of the induced secondary emf because this value is dependent on the rate at which the primary flux changes. Placing a capacitor across the contacts is one way of reducing this effect. Instead of arcing across the gap the primary current charges the capacitor, which then discharges through the primary coil, opposing the self-induced emf and giving rise to an increased secondary emf.

The efficiency of a coil is dependent on the sharpness of the break made by the armature, and in larger instruments the armature is replaced by a rotating jet of mercury. Energy losses are created in the core by hysteresis, caused by the interaction between the fields of the core molecules and the induced magnetic fields.

Further losses are caused by eddy currents induced in the core material by the changing flux cutting through it. These losses can be reduced by laminating the iron core and insulating the laminations from each other, by making the core from lengths of soft iron wire insulated from each other, or better still by making the core out of ferrite (a ceramic compound which has ferromagnetic properties).

Ferrite cores are made of materials such as nickel-cobalt ferrite, nickel ferrite or magnesium-manganese ferrite, and they have extremely low losses even with very high frequency currents.

The induction coil finds its most common application in petrol engine ignition systems, where it converts the 6 or 12 volts supply from the battery to as much as 30,000 volts to operate the spark plugs, the make-and-break action in the primary circuit being produced mechanically by a contact breaker set or electronically by a semiconductor switching circuit.

The distributor The operation of the internal combustion engine in most cars depends on each of the spark plugs in the cylinders receiving a pulse of high voltage (or high ten-

Opposite page: in an induction coil, a fast-changing current in the primary induces a high voltage in the secondary.

Below: a distributor, sectioned to show the mechanism.

sion, HT) electricity at precisely the right moment in order to spark off the fuel-air mixture. The HT is produced by the induction coil from the low voltage (low tension, LT) provided by the battery. The distributor is the device which delivers a spark to each combustion chamber at exactly the right moment.

The conventional distributor is a compact unit, housed in a cylindrical aluminium casing about 1 inch (2.5 cm) across at the bottom end, belling out from the middle upwards to about 3 inch (7.6 cm) across. A typical unit is about 7 inch (18 cm) long, and is clamped to the side of the cylinder block, so that it can tap the rotary motion of the camshaft. This is the shaft which operates the pushrods to open and close the valves, rotating once for every firing sequence of the engine. This connection therefore mechanically locks the movement of a central drive spindle in the distributor to the motion of the engine, and changes in the timing can be made by rotating the body of the distributor around this spindle.

As the spindle turns, a rotor arm at its top end points towards a contact for each cylinder in turn, acting as a rotary switch. At the same time, a raised edge on a cam on the spindle separates a pair of contacts in the low tension circuit, so producing the spark. There are as many raised edges around the spindle as there are cylinders.

A voltage of some 30,000 V is needed for a good spark. The induction coil provides this from the low tension (usually 12 V) supply from the battery: every time the LT supply is cut off, a spark is produced. LT current is therefore supplied to the contact breaker assembly continuously; the supply is interrupted as the spindle turns, and is fed to the coil. This produces an HT pulse for every break of the contacts. The pulses then pass along a single lead to the centre of the rotor arm, which distributes them to the cylinder contacts in the right order. The rotor does not need to actually touch each contact—this would result in rapid wear—but the gap is so small that the pulse can easily jump across with very little reduction in voltage. The central contact is provided by a spring loaded carbon rod which can both carry high voltage and form a low friction connection with the moving rotor arm, which has a brass plate mounted on a Bakelite cap to insulate it from the drive spindle.

The contact breaker assembly is mounted on a flat plate which fits into the distributor body over the drive spindle, and can thus be replaced when the 'points' or contacts become worn. One contact is fixed to the plate, while the other is moved by the cam follower, which thus separates the contact points, once for every edge on the cam of the drive spindle.

A means of adjustment for the maximum of the points must be provided, since this affects the duration of the spark and therefore the running of the engine. A capacitor connected across the points acts as a reservoir of electricity to prevent small sparks jumping when the points are open.

The other important adjustment necessary on a distributor is the timing. This can be altered coarsely by twisting the distributor body around the drive spindle, and more precisely by a screw thread which does the same job once the approximate position has been set.

As the engine speeds up, the ignition should be advanced for optimum running—that is, the spark should occur slightly earlier in the cylinder operation. An automatic advance mechanism is usually provided, using the vacuum which occurs in the inlet manifold of the carburettor as the accelerator is pressed down and more air is sucked in. A

small pipe connects this to a diaphragm which moves in and out as the vacuum changes. The movement of this diaphragm pulls the base plate, giving more or less advance to the timing. This device depends upon the accelerator setting rather than the engine speed and has most effect at half throttle, when the engine is not at full speed. To allow for changes in engine speed, the cam is carried on a sleeve which fits over the drive spindle, linked by balance 'bob' weights and springs. As the engine speed increases, centrifugal force throws the weights outwards, causing the points to open sooner.

The various components of a distributor which are not supposed to be at the earth voltage of the chassis have to be well insulated. In the case of the LT, small washers are adequate. The HT, however, can easily jump small gaps so the distributor cover is usually made of a good insulator such as Bakelite. A good seal against water is important, and a rubber or plastic cover over the whole unit is often advisable. It is not uncommon for tracks of carbon to form on the inside of the distributor cover or the rotor arm as a result of moisture. These can reduce the spark voltage and even stop the car if allowed to build up.

The functions of the circuit breaker and distributor cam may be performed electronically, giving more accurate timing, higher spark energy, higher operating speeds and longer life. The circuit breaker has two functions: to interrupt the coil primary current and to time the spark at the correct firing intervals (for instance at 90° intervals for a four cylinder engine).

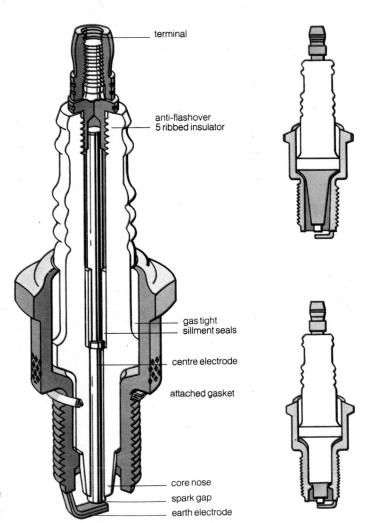

terminal

anti-flashover
5 ribbed insulator

gas tight
sillment seals

centre electrode

attached gasket

core nose
spark gap
earth electrode

Two separate electronic circuits are required to accomplish these two functions. Circuit breaking is achieved by means of a high voltage power transistor and timing by a shaft position sensor. The signal from the position sensor is used, after suitable modification and amplification, to switch the power transistor on and off.

There is a wide variety of shaft position sensors available for use in ignition systems, including opto-electrical units (in which a beam of light focused on a photoelectric cell is interrupted by a shutter) and various forms of magnetic pulse generator. In a typical magnetic unit the distributor cam is replaced by a soft iron reluctor, a device similar in shape to the cam but having much sharper and more pronounced projections, one for each cylinder. The reluctor operates in conjuction with a fixed stator pole carrying a detector coil and the whole assembly is energized by a permanent magnet. As the reluctor revolves its projections pass within 0.02 inch (0.51 mm) of the tip of the stator pole, causing the magnetic field in the detector coil to rise and fall, producing a small signal voltage across its terminals.

The signal voltage amplitude varies in almost direct proportion to the engine speed and its waveform may also change in shape. The most consistent point in the signal waveform for timing purposes is the point at which it crosses the zero point from positive to negative. The input circuit of the electronic unit therefore contains a considerable degree of amplification and a means of detecting the crossover point. When the crossover point is detected, the unit generates a second waveform, usually a square wave,

which after some current amplification can be used to switch the power transistor controlling the primary circuit of the coil.

The power transistor operates in a similar manner to a contact breaker. When it is switched on by the position transducer it allows current to flow from the battery through the ignition coil primary winding, and when a projection on the reluctor passes the stator pole the power transistor is switched off, interrupting the primary current and so causing a voltage to be induced in the secondary winding. The high voltage induced is then switched to the spark plug in exactly the same way as with a circuit breaker distributor. Electronic ignition has been in general use on Formula 1 and Formula 2 racing cars since 1960, and since 1970 has been used on a number of makes of standard production cars.

The spark plug Spark plugs are used in internal combustion engines (except diesel engines) to provide the high voltage sparks which ignite the fuel-air mixture in the combustion chambers. The invention of spark plugs is attributed to Etienne Lenoir (1822-1900), who in 1860 first manufactured an engine which used an electric spark ignition system.

When the engine is running, a pulse of electrical energy at very high voltage is delivered to the terminal of the plug at the correct moment. This causes a spark to jump the gap between the centre electrode and the earth electrode, the latter being earthed to the cylinder block. This spark provides the energy needed to ignite the compressed fuel-air mixture in the cylinder.

Left: the component parts of a modern spark plug. The high voltage pulse of electricity passes down the central electrode and jumps across the spark gap to the other electrode, which is connected to the engine block and thus to the car body. The smaller drawing shows the difference between the core nose lengths of 'hot' and 'cold' plugs.

Near right: This spark plug has been modified to include a thermocouple to enable core nose temperatures to be monitored. The wires that connect the thermocouple are on either side of the centre electrode, and the thermocouple itself is just above the lower end of the core nose.

Far right: effects of various operating conditions on spark plugs. From top to bottom: normal running; carbon fouled by over-rich mixture and too large plug gap; oil fouled by too much oil in combustion chamber; and overheated.

For optimum performance, the temperature of the core nose at the firing end of a spark plug should neither drop below about 400°C (752°F) at 30 mph (48 kph) cruising, nor exceed about 850°C (1562°F) at maximum speed and load. Below 400°C, deposits of carbon and oil are likely to accumulate on the core nose. Carbon, being electrically conductive, can provide a short circuit path for the high voltage pulse and so weaken or eliminate the spark.

Core nose temperatures of above 850°C can cause excessive electrode erosion and, possibly, uncontrolled ignition of the fuel-air mixture in advance of the timed spark. This condition (called pre-ignition) can cause serious engine damage.

As engine designs (and therefore combustion chamber temperatures) vary, it is necessary to produce many types of spark plug to ensure that, as far as possible, plug operating temperatures can be kept within the optimum range in all applications.

The classification of plugs according to their relative ability to transfer heat from the tip of the core nose to the cooling system of an engine is termed the heat range.

A 'hot' (or 'soft') plug has a relatively long core nose, and thus a long heat path from the tip to the metal body. This type of plug tends to retain heat in the core nose, and would be used in a low compression, low speed engine. Conversely, a 'cold' (or 'hard') plug has a shorter core nose, giving a shorter heat path from the tip to the body, and heat is conducted rapidly from the core nose into the cooling medium. This type is used in high compression, high speed engines having higher combustion chamber temperatures.

In order to determine which grade of plug is best for a particular engine design, manufacturers run tests using spark plugs which incoporate thermocouples (temperature sensing elements) at the core nose tips. During the tests, the core nose temperatures of various grades of plug are continuously monitored throughout the entire speed and load range of the engine.

In recent years there has been an enormous increase in the use of plugs on which the core nose projects beyond the end of the threaded body. This design of plug is specified only for overhead valve engines with suitable combustion chamber design. The extra-long core nose runs hotter than a standard type at low engine speeds, giving improved protection against plug fouling. At high engine speeds the exposed core nose tip is cooled by the incoming fuel-air mixture; this avoids the risk of plug overheating. Projected core nose plugs are used in the vast majority of modern overhead valve engines; if such a plug were installed by mistake in a flat-head engine, it would be smashed by the rising piston.

Plug bodies are made of high quality steel, and are zinc plated to avoid corrosion. The threads have to conform to internationally agreed standards and close tolerances. Ranges of plugs with various thread configurations are produced.

The plug insulators are made from a fired aluminium oxide ceramic material which is highly resistant to thermal and mechanical stress and chemical attack. The electrodes

Right: cutaway car alternator. The development of cheap electronics has made it possible to convert the output to DC quite simply. Here, a diode rectifier is incorporated in the unit.

Below: arrangement of a typical alternator. The central rotor is an electromagnet (green winding), powered through slip rings which collect current from brushes, also shown in green. It rotates inside the stationary red, blue and yellow windings, each of which extends two thirds of the way round. This produces one cycle of three phase electricity for each rotation.

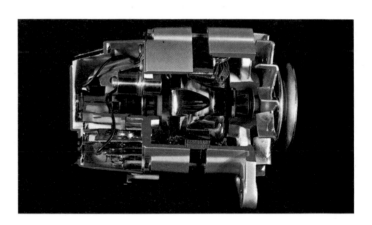

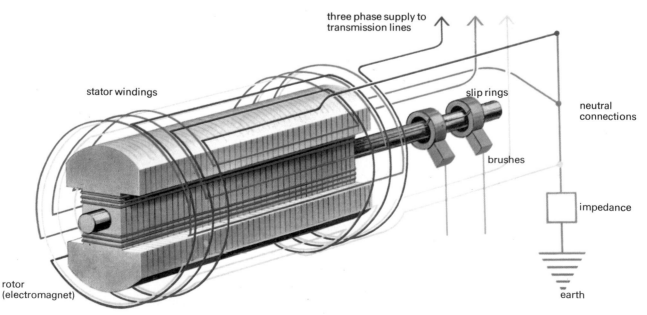

stator windings

three phase supply to transmission lines

slip rings

neutral connections

brushes

rotor (electromagnet)

impedance

earth

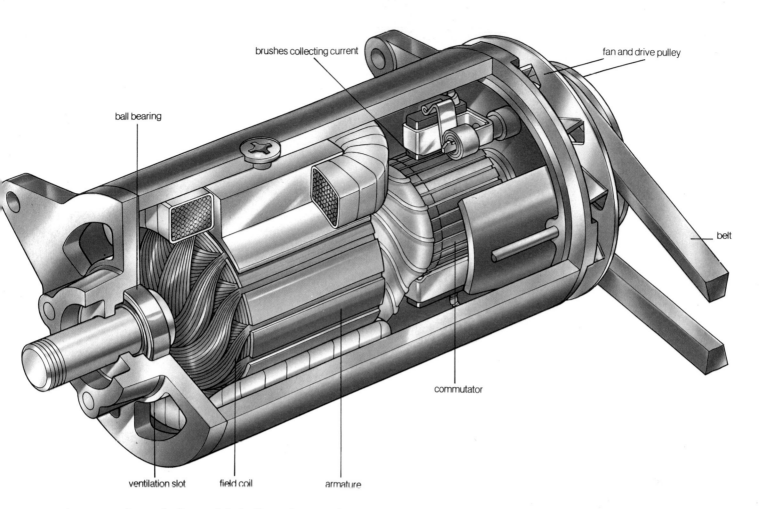

brushes collecting current

ball bearing

fan and drive pulley

belt

commutator

ventilation slot   field coil   armature

are most commonly made from nickel alloys, but precious
metals are sometimes used.

Gas-tight seals are required between the centre electrode
and the insulator, and between the insulator and the plug
body. These seals are formed from aluminium oxide powder
(called sillment) which, when compressed, becomes a rigid
mass which fits the available space exactly. A pre-formed lip
around the top of the body is squeezed downwards on to the
compacted sillment seal.

To keep pace with engine requirements, new construction
techniques and materials are constantly being evaluated.

Alternators and dynamos A device which converts a
mechanical rotation into an electric current is a generator.
Generators and electric motors, like the induction coil, are
electromagnetic devices whose principles were discovered
by Faraday.

In an electric motor, magnetism produced by electric
current induces a shaft to turn. In a generator, the shaft is
the magnet, and induces electric current. Enormous generators are built for electric power plants; they are turned by
turbines whose blades are driven by falling water in the
case of hydroelectric power, or by steam created by heat
from burning fuel or from nuclear fission. The type of small
generator used in a car to re-charge the battery is driven by
the engine, by means of a belt.

In Britain, the type of machine which generates direct
current (DC) electricity is called a dynamo; that which
generates alternating current (AC) is called an alternator.
Both types are used in cars; the use of alternators in cars is a
relatively recent development.

To understand the operation of generators, it will be
useful to briefly examine the principles of electromagnetism.
In an electrical circuit it is voltage that causes the current to

flow. The voltage, or electromotive force (emf), is the cause
and current the effect. By analogy, in a magnetic circuit the
driving 'pressure' is called the magnetomotive force (mmf).
This is the cause and magnetic flux is the result, or effect.
Between the north and south poles of a magnet in the
medium surrounding the magnet can be envisaged a set of
flux lines—the closer these lines are together the greater the
flux density. Flux density is determined by the mmf of the
magnet and the permeability of the surrounding medium.

The emf induced in an electrical conductor, moving in a
magnetic field, is determined by the rate at which the conductor 'cuts' the lines of flux. The induced emf is therefore
related to the speed of the conductor and the flux density.
It is also related to the length of the conductor.

In a simple alternator, a closed rectangular loop of wire
is mounted on a rotating axis (the rotor) and rotated between the north and south poles of a horseshoe magnet (the
stator). When the two sides of the loop parallel to the axis of
the rotor (these are the 'conductors') form a line between the
north and south poles, the rate at which these two conductors cut the lines of flux is at a maximum. The induced
emf in the conductors is therefore also at a maximum
and the current flowing around the loop at its largest value.

When the rotor has turned through 90°, the instantaneous
direction of motion of the conductors is along the lines of
flux. No lines of flux are therefore cut, no emf is induced in
them and the loop current is zero.

When it has rotated by a further 90°, the rate of flux cutting is again a maximum with maximum emf and loop current. The loop is now, however, 'upside down' compared to its position 180° ago and the induced emf and current are a maximum in the opposite direction. A further 90° rotation and the current is again zero.

By breaking the loop at one end near the axis and connecting the ends to two slip rings on the shaft of the rotor, this alternating emf can be tapped using 'brushes' touching the rings to drive an external electrical circuit.

To construct a dynamo, several loops are positioned in sequence around the rotor. This time, instead of taking the loop ends to slip rings, they are connected in the same sequence to individual segments of a commutator (a divided rotating contact). Two brushes are mounted on opposite sides of the commutator such that, as the rotor rotates, the brushes form an electrical contact with the two ends of just one loop at a time.

By positioning the brushes so that they 'tap' that loop which is in the position of maximum flux cutting, then they will tap each loop as it comes into that position during rotation. The induced emf is therefore always in the same direction (that is, a DC voltage) and always with the maximum value possible.

Because alternators use simple slip rings to feed their rotors, instead of the divided commutators used in dynamos, they can be run at a much higher speed relative to the engine, so they give high charging currents even at engine idling speeds. At the same time, because power is generated in the stator and not the rotor, they can be made smaller and lighter for the same power output.

The voltage regulator The output of motor vehicle generators rises with increasing speed. They are driven by the engine at speeds which may vary from less than 1,000 rpm to more than 15,000 rpm. It is therefore necessary to have some form of output control to ensure satisfactory battery charging and operation of the electrical equipment.

Dynamos and alternators require different controls, but the principle of control is the same. In both cases the generator field current is reduced as the voltage rises and increased as the voltage falls. Two basic forms of construction are used for the controls, electromagnetic and electronic. Dynamos use electromagnetic controls; some alternators use electromagnetic controls but the trend is towards electronics.

When the generator is charging the current flow is into the electrical equipment or the battery, but when the generated voltage drops below that of the battery, it is necessary to prevent the battery discharging through the generator windings. The rectifier diodes prevent this happening with an alternator, but it is necessary to provide a switch in the form of an electromechanical cut-out with the dynamo system.

In a dynamo system both cut-out and regulator controls are required. For the cut-out mechanism, the winding of an electromagnetic relay is connected across the generator output and the normally open spring loaded contacts of the relay are connected between the generator output terminal and the battery. When the generator voltage rises sufficiently the relay contacts close and charging current flows from generator to battery. A heavy series coil connected in the generator to the battery lead is wound around the relay shunt coil to assist in holding the contacts closed and prevent 'chattering' when current is flowing from the generator to the battery. When the generated voltage falls, there is a momentary flow of current from battery to generator. This

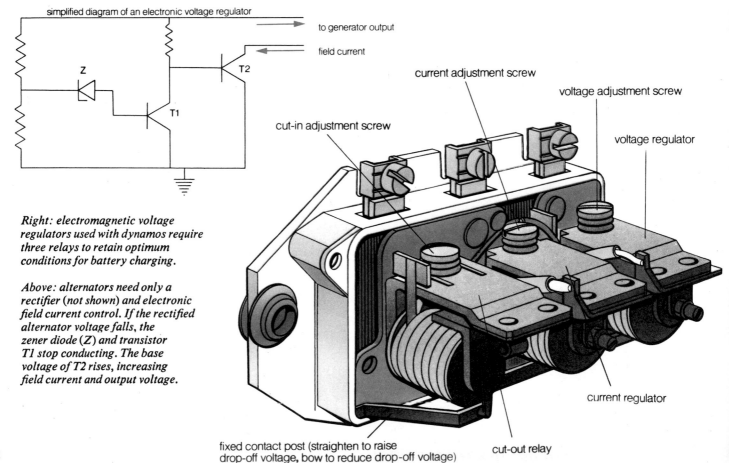

simplified diagram of an electronic voltage regulator

to generator output

field current

Z

T1

T2

current adjustment screw

voltage adjustment screw

voltage regulator

cut-in adjustment screw

Right: electromagnetic voltage regulators used with dynamos require three relays to retain optimum conditions for battery charging.

Above: alternators need only a rectifier (not shown) and electronic field current control. If the rectified alternator voltage falls, the zener diode (Z) and transistor T1 stop conducting. The base voltage of T2 rises, increasing field current and output voltage.

current regulator

fixed contact post (straighten to raise drop-off voltage, bow to reduce drop-off voltage)

cut-out relay

Above: a typical electromechanical regulator used with dynamos. The three relays prevent excessive charging currents from damaging the windings when the battery is low, stabilize the dynamo voltage by controlling the dynamo field current, and cut out to keep the battery from discharging when the dynamo voltage falls.

Below: one of the first electronic voltage regulators made for use with alternators. This can be made very simply because no current regulator is required with alternators, and a cut-out mechanism is unnecessary, as the battery cannot discharge through the rectifier.

causes the series coil to oppose the shunt coil and the contacts open, preventing discharge of the battery.

The voltage regulator is another electromagnetic relay connected across the generator output, but its contacts control the dynamo field supply and are normally closed. As the voltage rises, the electromagnet attracts the armature carrying the moving contact and the field circuit is broken. The generated voltage immediately starts to fall and the armature is released, thereby re-making the contacts and the procedure is repeated. This action occurs very rapidly about 40-60 times per second. The generated voltage is thus controlled at some predetermined level dependent upon the contact spring setting.

If the battery is in a low state of charge, the current generated could be sufficient to damage the windings of the generator and to prevent this, two alternative forms of control are used. One system employs an additional series coil wound around the regulator shunt coil. When a heavy charging current flows through this coil it assists the opening of the contacts and reduces the regulating voltage, which in turn reduces the current flowing. The other system employs another set of contacts in series with the voltage regulator contacts. These contacts are controlled by an electromagnet activated by the load current. If a heavy load current flows, the current-controlled contacts open before the voltage-controlled contacts, and again the generated voltage is reduced below the nominal setting.

The alternator is known as a self-regulating machine; that is, for a given voltage there is a limit to the current which will be generated in the machine. This is determined at the design stage and therefore there is no need for a current limiting device in the control. In addition the output is fed through diodes which only allow current to flow in

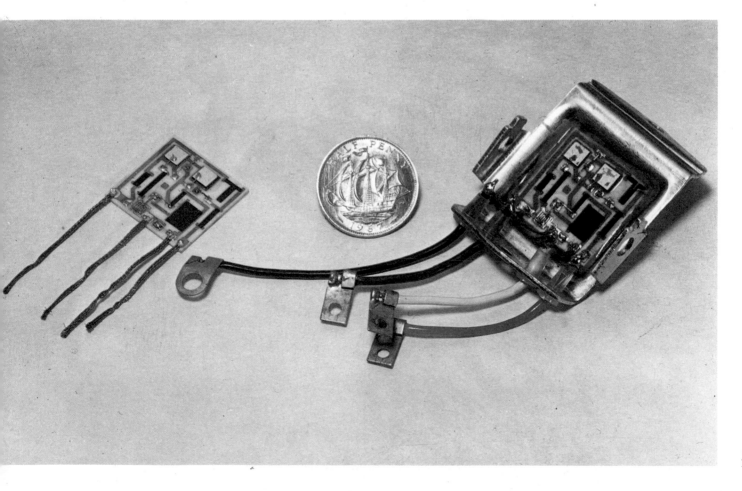

one direction and this feature makes a cut-out unnecessary. Therefore the only control required is a voltage regulator.

Some alternators have a version of the electro-mechanical regulator controlling the field supply but the trend is towards the electronic control because of its accuracy, reliability and its ability to handle larger currents more readily than the vibrating contact device.

The electronic control, which is now usually built in as part of the alternator, comprises a transistor which switches the field current and a control circuit.

The generated alternator voltage is fed to the control circuit which includes at least one more transistor, controlling the base current of the main field supply transistor, and a zener diode which only conducts when the voltage reaches a predetermined value. When this voltage is reached, the current which then flows in the diode causes the control transistor to conduct, so diverting the base current away from the field supply transistor, which in turn reduces the field current. The field current reduces until the load on the system balances at the voltage set by the zener diode breakdown voltage (the value at which it conducts).

This is the basic system, but to overcome excessive power loss in the field control transistor, extra circuitry is included to make the field control transistor switch on and off quickly, so that the average current is that required for load balance, and overheating of the transistor is prevented.

The starter A starter is a machine for rotating the crankshaft of an engine from rest to a speed at which the engine will commence to operate on its own. The starters used for internal combustion engines are usually battery operated, direct current electric motors, ranging in power from 0.5 hp on some motorcycle engines up to 15 hp on very large diesel engines.

The motors used are series wound and short time rated, that is, the windings of the rotor and stator are electrically connected in series, and the motor is designed to produce a high power output for a short period of time without exceeding a specified temperature. The series winding characteristics give the starter the large initial torque it requires to overcome the static inertia and friction of the engine, and

to accelerate it up to speed in the shortest possible time to avoid too heavy a drain on the battery.

The starter is a dead weight while the engine is running, and so it must be as light and small as possible. To achieve this the starters are short-time rated at two or three minutes: if a starter motor were required to deliver its maximum power over longer periods of time it would have to be bigger and heavier to avoid overheating.

The starter requires a heavy current to operate it. This is of the order of 150 amps on a medium sized car and 1000 amps on the very big commercial vehicles. The switching of this current is accomplished by means of a relay or solenoid operating a set of electrical contacts. The relay or solenoid in its turn is operated by a switch which is usually controlled by a key, and is placed in the driving cab of the vehicle.

Engagement with the engine is made through a pair of gears, the ratio of which is about 12 to 1, the larger gear being that on the engine. The smaller gear, known as the pinion, is positioned on the shaft of the starter, and the larger one is mounted on the housing of the clutch of the engine and is known as the ring gear. There are two methods by which this gear is engaged, the inertia method and the pre-engaged method.

The inertia starter uses the rapid acceleration of the starter armature, acting on the inertia of the pinion, to create a force which will drive the pinion up a helix on the shaft of the starter and hence into mesh with the ring gear. When the engine is running and the starter is switched off, the pinion is driven back down the helix and out of mesh with the ring gear.

A heavy spring known as a buffer spring is positioned on the shaft to absorb the force of the pinion as it is flung out of mesh, and a light spring is used to hold the pinion out of mesh while the engine is running. This type of starter is used on small and medium sized cars.

Below: an inertia starter. When the motor is switched on, the pinion is driven along the helix on the shaft so that it engages with the ring gear on the engine.

The pre-engaged starter is widely used on both petrol and diesel engines. The relay which operates the starter is replaced by a solenoid mounted on the starter, which is used to move the pinion up to and into mesh with the ring gear before switching on the current to the starter motor. In order to ensure entry when the teeth of the pinion and the teeth of the ring gear are not perfectly in line, some means of indexing the pinion gear must be provided. One such method is to arrange for the solenoid to compress a spring before it switches on the motor, so that on switching on, the pinion is rotated and the spring forces it into mesh.

The starter can now be held in mesh even after the engine is running, and to prevent damage to the starter an over-running device is fitted to the pinion. A roller clutch, which is a form of freewheel, is one such device. This consists of an outer race and an inner race, one of which is circular, the other having a series of taper steps so adjusted as to give a series of reductions in the gap between the two races. There is a spring-loaded roller bearing in each of these taper steps, the springs forcing the rollers into the reduced gaps. Rotating the drive in one direction will jam the rollers into the gaps and lock the two races together, so that torque is transmitted. Rotation in the other direction will cause the rollers to free, allowing the races to freewheel.

The pre-engaged system is a necessity for diesel engines which are inherently more difficult to start than petrol engines because of the high compression ratios used. In spite of being more expensive than the inertia system, the pre-engaged system is becoming more popular for a wider range of applications, since it is quieter and will operate better over a wider temperature range.

The speedometer The speedometer is the device on the dashboard of the car which indicates two things: the speed of the vehicle and total distance travelled. It may also have a 'trip' facility whereby the distance travelled on a journey may be shown.

The type of speedometer fitted to cars, motorcycles, and the majority of commercial vehicles since World War II is the magnetic speedometer, originally developed in the 1920s.

The speedometer is driven from a point on the vehicle transmission which is rotating at a speed directly proportional to road speed; there is often a specially provided point on the gearbox tail shaft. Drive transmission is by means of a flexible shaft of multi-strand wire rotating inside a flexible tube. This assembly is called the flexible drive, or more commonly the speedometer cable.

The flexible drive is connected to the main spindle of the speedometer, which carries a magnet. Close to this magnet, and pivoted on the same axis, is an aluminium disc or cup called the drag cup. This is connected directly to the indicator or pointer. On the other side of the drag cup from the magnet is a steel stator; when the vehicle moves, the magnet rotates, creating a magnetic field, and the stator is rotated. Although the aluminium drag cup is non-magnetic, it is conductive; the magnetic field causes the cup to try to follow the rotation of the magnet, but it is restrained by a hairspring. As speed increases, the torque on the drag cup also increases and overcomes the hairspring reaction, causing the pointer to move around the scale on the dial.

The most common type of speedometer uses a pointer on a circular or arc scale, but sometimes the design calls for a coloured line moving along a horizontal or vertical straight scale. This effect can be achieved in two ways with the mag-

105

netic speedometer. In one instance the drag cup is linked directly to a tube on which is printed a coloured helix. This is positioned behind a slot in the dial so that when it is turned by the drag cup the helix advances along the scale, giving the appearance of a moving strip of colour. An alternative means of providing a similar effect is the ribbon speedometer, which is more common in Britain. In this instrument the drag cup is linked by nylon cords to two vertically pivoted drums between which is wound a tape, printed half black and half red. In the static condition the red portion of the tape is wound around the left hand drum and held there by hairspring tension. As speed increases the drag cup winds the tape on to the right hand drum, so that the leading edge of the red portion appears in the slot on the dial.

The odometer is a counting device which acts as a distance recorder. It comprises a series of adjacent rotating drums or counters each numbered 0 to 9, positioned behind a slot in a dial so that only one number on each counter is showing at any one time. Hidden between the counters are tiny double-sided plastic transfer pinions, which are mounted eccentrically to the main counter axis on thin carrier plates, which in turn are anchored so that they cannot turn with the counters.

The transfer pinion has two sets of teeth engaging, one on each side, with the internal gearing on the counters. The internal gearing of the counter has twenty teeth on one side and just two 'knockover' teeth on the other. Each time a counter comes up to the '9' position, a knockover tooth engages with the transfer pinion to the right, and drives it far enough to rotate it one tenth of a turn, before disengaging.

Where a 'trip' facility is provided, the transfer pinions are mounted externally to the counters on a spring-loaded spindle, which allows them to disengage when the counters are reset to zero.

Drive to the counters can be provided by a system of worm-geared shafts driven from the main spindle of the speedometer, if the manufacturer does not wish to vary the ratio between distance travelled and turns of the speedometer cable. The ratio is usually 1000 turns to a mile. In some cases, however, car makers want to be able to alter the axle ratio or the tyre size without changing the pinion in the gearbox which drives the speedometer. To accommodate this need, the counters are driven through an eccentric spindle geared to the main spindle and carrying a pawl which engages with a ratchet wheel. By varying the number of teeth and the throw of the eccentric, variations in gear ratio can be provided.

Calibration of the speed indication part of the instrument to suit each vehicle manufacturer's requirements on gearing and accuracy is carried out by fully magnetizing the magnet and then demagnetizing it until the desired readings are obtained.

The tachometer The tachometer or revolution indicator is an instrument for measuring engine speed, and is calibrated to indicate the number of revolutions the engine crankshaft makes in any one minute. The number of revolutions per minute of the engine as a vehicle is shifted through the several gears is an indication of engine performance. The tachometer is useful to racing car drivers, drivers of large commercial vehicles which have many gear ratios available, and drivers of ordinary cars who try to get the best performance possible from the engine, or better petrol mileage.

Originally, this instrument was driven mechanically, using a magnetic movement similar to that of a speedometer. Later, however, with developments in electronic circuitry, it was possible to design electronic tachometers operated by pulses from the ignition system.

There are several variations of tachometer design and operation: only four designs are described here which will cover the main forms of triggering used for tachometers.

The coil ignition (or 'original impulse') tachometer is triggered by the current pulses produced in the low tension circuit by the contact breaker, which is operated by a cam on the distributor drive. The change of current in the low tension (LT) side of the coil generates the high tension (HT) voltage supplied through the distributor to the spark plugs. On any internal combustion engine this pulsing is directly proportional to engine speed and is therefore suitable for triggering the tachometer. This is done by the transformer principle of primary and secondary coils, the primary loop being formed from the LT lead. On a typical instrument, the loop is located on the rear of the instrument case by a metal strap which slots, either side, into the other half of the transformer core on which is wound the fine wire bobbin forming the secondary coil. This senses the induction pulse, which is amplified and fed to the triggering circuit designed into the circuit board. Since the pulse obtained from the contact breaker is of a particular shape, the trigger circuit is constructed to respond to this particular input signal. The circuitry interprets the frequency of the pulses as a voltage, which is fed to a moving coil voltmeter—this is the indicating dial of the instrument and is therefore calibrated in revolutions per minute rather than volts. The more

Left: a typical speedometer. The counting device is the odometer, or mileage counter; the numbers show through a slot in the dial.

Below left: a ribbon speedometer has a coloured line indicator instead of a pointer. This is in the form of a tape which is stored, like a typewriter ribbon, on the drums at each end of the device. As speed increases the instrument winds the tape on to the right hand drum against spring pressure.

Above: in car tests, an extra accurate 'fifth wheel' type of speedometer and odometer is used.

Right: the revolving speedometer cable, generally driven from the gearbox, turns a shaft, which has a short worm on it, operating the odometer by means of a ratchet. The internal teeth in the odometer are arranged so that one revolution of a counter turns the next counter one tenth of a revolution. A permanent magnet on the shaft pulls the drag cup and stator, and the pointer, which is linked to them, around against spring pressure by a variable amount dependent on the speed of spin.

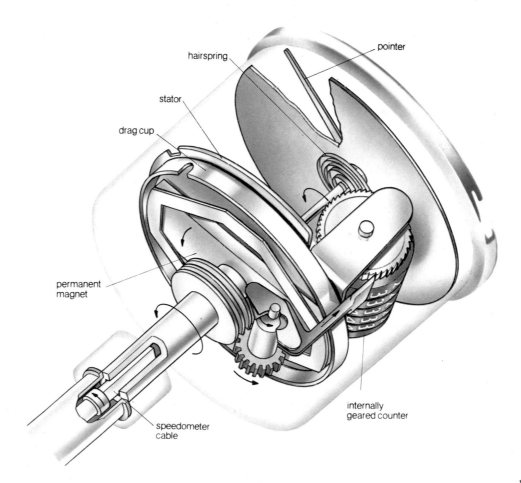

hairspring

pointer

stator

drag cup

permanent magnet

speedometer cable

internally geared counter

cylinders an engine has, the more pulses it generates per revolution, so tachometers have to be designed for engines with a certain number of cylinders.

The tachometer requires a power supply, which is obtained from the vehicle's battery via the ignition switch. Because the voltage fluctuates slightly, it is stabilized within the tachometer. Final calibration of the movement is completed by adjusting the resistance across the moving coil meter.

A later design, known as a blocking oscillator type, used by vehicle manufacturers fitting tachometers as original equipment, incorporates the primary loop within the tachometer case, which permits easier installation on production lines.

With the advent of transistorized and capacitor-discharge ignition systems to improve ignition characteristics and engine performance, the LT current was reduced to a few milliamps, thus changing the pulse shape, which made it ineffective for a current-triggered tachometer. This entailed a change to a different circuit design measuring the voltage pulse at the contact breaker terminal on the coil. The voltage triggered tachometer is now generally being used by vehicle manufacturers in preference to the current type.

The induction design was perfected for use on the diesel engine, which does not have an electric ignition system. It senses rotational or peripheral speed by means of a magnetic perception head. When a ferrous object moves in close proximity past the sensor there is a variation of the reluctance in the sensor's magnetic circuit. The resultant electromotive force in the form of pulses generated in the perception head coil is then transmitted via the two terminals on the sensor to the tachometer head. The instrument is also connected to the vehicle's 12 or 24 volt DC supply. The number of equi-spaced ferrous lobes permitted to pass the sensor per revolution varies depending on the ratio of the take-off shaft to crankshaft.

The self-generating type of tachometer was supplied to certain manufacturers for original equipment and has since been superseded. The installation used a generator which was connected directly to the instrument. The generator was mechanically driven from a suitable ratio take-off, producing an alternating current (AC) voltage proportional to the speed of rotation of generator shaft. By rectifying this voltage, a direct relationship between voltage and engine speed was obtained on the tachometer scale.

The high tension tachometer was specifically designed for marine engines and operates off the HT plug leads. It is connected to a 12 volt supply and senses the HT voltage via a screened trigger cable which is twisted around each plug lead. This enables the tachometer to operate effectively irrespective of the type of ignition system. To permit use on a wide range of engines with different numbers of cylinders, and thus pulses per revolution, a changeover switch is incorporated.

Electronic engine analysis A number of factors affect the performance of a car. When an engine misfires, it is a fairly simple matter to find out what is wrong. Improving the performance of a car which has no obvious faults, but where all systems may be running at reduced efficiency, involves much more subtle testing procedures since altering one factor, usually by trial and error, can have an effect on another.

Smooth running depends on such things as good carburation (the mixture of fuel and air before it is sparked off), a strong spark occurring at the right time for each cylinder stroke, and good compression, all operating at the correct engine temperature. The engine should burn the fuel efficiently, both for economy and anti-pollution reasons.

A complete diagnostic machine will test each of these simultaneously while the engine is running and display the results on meters, graphs or oscilloscopes. The machine is connected to the engine by leads or probes to the electrical system, and by flexible tubes to the exhaust system, the carburettor, or (to measure cylinder leakage) to one spark plug hole at a time.

One car manufacturer, Volkswagen, has wired the electrical test points to a 24-pin socket in the engine compartment, so that they can be easily and quickly connected to the diagnostic machine by means of a plug. The machine gives a printed result, showing how the readings obtained compare with the standard values for that particular model.

Analysis of the exhaust gases will give a good indication of the ratio of the air to fuel mixture, which must be correctly set to obtain maximum efficiency and economy. This is done by passing the gases over a heated filament, cooling it; the more hydrogen that is present, the greater is the cooling effect. As the filament cools its resistance changes, and this

change is easily measured on a meter. The change in resistance is proportional to the amount of hydrogen in the gas, and as this is in proportion to the air to fuel ratio, the meter can be calibrated in terms of this ratio.

Units for measuring the carbon monoxide content in exhaust gas (for anti-pollution purposes) use a heated filament which burns any combustible gases in the exhaust; the resultant temperature rise causes a change in the filament resistance which is detected by a meter calibrated to show the percentage of carbon monoxide present.

Simple measurements of battery and generator output voltages, checks for continuity in the vehicle wiring, and resistance tests on the distributor capacitor and ignition coil windings can be carried out using a multi-range meter which measures voltage, resistance, and if necessary, current. An instrument of this kind may have a kilovolt (thousands of volts) scale for measuring the very high voltages of the ignition system, or a separate kilovolt meter may be used.

Wear in the distributor cam or drive gear will be indicated by variations in the dwell time—the time in the ignition cycle during which the distributor contact points are closed. This is usually expressed in terms of the number of degrees through which the distributor cam turns during each operation of the points. The dwell meter and tachometer, both working from the ignition system, may be incorporated into one meter which is switched to give a reading of either engine speed or dwell angle.

To check on the efficient circulation of the engine coolant and to determine the oil temperature, a sensing head can be attached to various parts of the engine with a small magnetic clamp. The head contains a thermocouple, the electrical resistance of which changes with variations in temperature, these changes being read on a meter calibrated in degrees.

The suction produced in each cylinder can be measured by connecting a gauge to the inlet manifold via a tube

Above: an impulse tachometer used by mechanics and engineers, which is simply placed on any solid part of the engine and indicates its speed on a 'broken back' scale.

Left: a 'thick film' tachometer uses advanced solid state circuitry in its construction, making it far more accurate than the original mechanical type of tachometer, which used a spinning magnet like that of a speedometer.

Right: a blocking oscillator type of tachometer, with a primary loop fitted directly on to the instrument. This is the large white coil. This type of tachometer is fitted as original equipment by many car manufacturers.

attached to the servo tapping (a hole to which servo mechanisms are connected to take advantage of the vacuum in the manifold) or to a connector fitted to a hole drilled in the manifold. Variations in the readings indicate a fault such as damaged piston rings or leaking valves. The gauge can also be connected into the fuel or oil systems to measure fuel pump suction or oil pressure.

Unlike most of the other tests, cylinder leakage testing is not carried out with the engine running. The spark plug is removed from the cylinder to be tested, a threaded adapter is screwed into the hole, and with the piston at top dead centre compressed air at between 70 and 200 psi (5 and 14 bar) is fed in through the adapter. The quantity of compressed air required to maintain the pressure in the cylinder gives an indication of the rate of leakage caused by worn piston rings, excessive wear in the cylinder bore, badly seated valves or a faulty cylinder head gasket.

A visual display is exceptionally valuable for quick fault diagnoses, particularly when checking the ignition system. This is obtained with an oscilloscope, using either the normal round screen or a standard high definition monochrome TV screen. By linking the oscilloscope inputs to the ignition system, traces can be obtained which show the duration of the spark, the steadiness of the secondary voltage and its value during the spark, and any variations in dwell time.

A stroboscope with a high intensity xenon flash tube can be timed to operate in synchronism with the engine crankshaft, so that the timing marks on the pulleys appear to be stationary. This enables the ignition advance mechanism to be checked at different engine speeds.

A dynamometer is used to simulate road testing. The car is positioned with the driving wheels on rollers, which are spun by the wheels when the engine is running with the car

Above: a truck undergoing a brake test at an official vehicle testing station. The wheels rest on powered rollers turned against the force of the brakes.

Above right: testing a car for mechanical and electrical faults. This device will measure over 20 features of an engine's performance.

in gear. The rollers incorporate a hydraulic brake which is applied progressively, requiring increased effort from the car to drive them. In this way the ability of the car to rotate the braked rollers indicates the effective brake horsepower (bhp) of the engine which is available at the driving wheels. The dynamometer will also check the acceleration, gearbox and clutch operation and speedometer accuracy. There are usually two meters on the dynamometer console, one indicating 'road' speed and the other the brake horsepower. A small handset on a long lead enables the rollers to be controlled from the driving seat of the car.

The brake analyzer has rollers similar to a dynamometer, except that they are driven by electric motors instead of being driven by the car wheels. The motors only drive the rollers at about 3 mph (5 kph), and they are sufficiently powerful to enable the brakes to be tested to their limit. There are separate meters for each wheel, and the analyzer measures the power required from the motors to overcome the car brakes which, when applied, will tend to stop the rollers turning. The comparative braking efficiency of each wheel can be seen from the meter readings. Regular oscillation of the meter pointer could indicate an oval or damaged brake drum or a warped disc, while sudden movements are likely to be caused by hydraulic or mechanical faults.

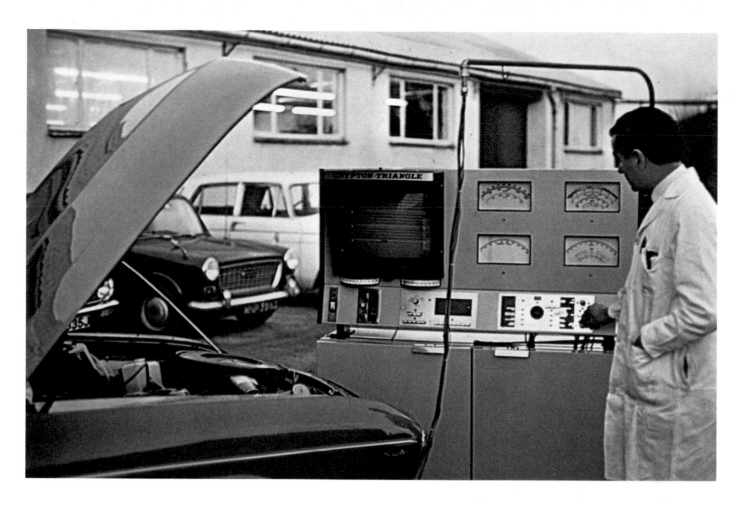

Below: Volkswagen pioneered the use of multi-purpose car
analysers which plugged straight into a multiple socket
in the car itself. They have been much copied.

Right: an environmental test. Using an infra-red gas analyser
to measure pollutants in the exhaust of a car.
The fan simulates normal air flow through the radiator.

Motor Sport

Racing Cars

The early motor car was a fragile, temperamental machine; they were built by men who were discovering design requirements as they went along. The first competitions were endurance contests rather than races, but beginning in 1895 motor racing became extremely popular and has been so ever since. Town-to-town races were the most common type; transcontinental races have been run, including one from Paris to Peking.

Racing has always been dangerous, and racing competitions on public roads, common in the early days, are now strictly limited. The worst accident in the history of racing happened in 1955 at the Le Mans sports car event; 83 spectators were killed, and for a while it was thought that the entire sport would be abandoned. The famous annual 500-mile event at Indianapolis, Indiana has averaged about one death a year, and is considered to be relatively safe.

There are several types of racing, each regulated by its own professional organization in various countries.

Grand Prix racing From the very beginning, racing contributed to the development of the automobile. An American newspaper publisher who was interested in this aspect of racing established the Gordon Bennett Cup, and six races were held from 1900 to 1906. The rule was that each country could enter three cars and that the cars had to be entirely constructed by the industry of the entering nation. In 1906, the French established the Grand Prix, which had no restriction on the number of cars which could be entered, and the Bennett Cup was abandoned. Since World War I, each European nation has held its own Grand Prix. Nations in North and South America also take part, and Japan and Australia are considering having their own Grand Prix.

A divergence in international racing took place before World War I when it became apparent that American racing was more for entertainment than engineering. Wooden board tracks were used for a while; the most famous American track is the Indianapolis Motor Speedway, a $2\frac{1}{2}$ mile (4 km) banked dirt track with identical corners which has been lapped at 200 miles an hour (331 kph) by the type of car bred for this type of racing. For some time the annual Indianapolis 500 race qualified as a Grand Prix in order to make the sport truly international, but now it no longer qualifies.

In Europe, Mercedes had competed sporadically; when Hitler came to power in 1933 he recognized the prestige in winning races and gave government support to Mercedes. At the same time the German Auto-Union was commissioned to build their own car. Mercedes, with its enormous engineering skill, was able to build a powerful (400 bhp) car within the rules, which then limited the weight of the car to 750 Kg (1650 lb). The battle between Mercedes' classic front-engined car and the Auto-Union revolutionary rear engine design resulted in a 'golden age' of racing from 1934 to 1939. The cars, despite high power and narrow tyres, were surprisingly safe, although Richard Seaman, the only Englishman to join the Mercedes team, was killed in the Belgian Grand Prix in 1939.

After World War II, the racing nations banded together to set rules and to make the sport international. There had been European Champions before, but now the international series of races became a series which resulted in a World Champion Driver on the basis of points. The first World Champion was the Italian Giuseppe Farina in 1950. Although attempts were made to build fully enclosed Grand Prix cars, the rules now effectively require that the cars be single-seaters with exposed wheels. Since the war, the Grand Prix car has been known as the Formula 1. At first the races were using left-overs cars from before the war, and superchargers on engines were common, but the rules formulated by the Federation Internationale de l'Automobile (FIA; founded in 1904) which specify engine displacements have nullified the advantage of supercharging; the last supercharged car to win a championship was the Italian Alfetta in 1951.

Mercedes built an exceptionally advanced car which driven by Juan Fangio of Argentina won almost every race for two years. The company pulled out of racing in 1955, and after that the competition was mainly between Italy and Britain. The BRM (British Racing Motor) and the Vanwall (a notably aerodynamic car built by bearing manufacturer Tony Vandervell) could sometimes beat the Italian cars, but British engineering superiority was established by a series of light cars powered by simple engines. Much of the weight saving came from adopting rear engine design, eliminating the heavy propeller shaft and enabling the driver to lie semi-supine, reducing frontal area and wind drag. The first such car to win a world championship was the Cooper, which enjoyed success during 1959-60, after which the lay-

Left: this surprisingly modern looking car is, in fact, an Auto Union of 1937. During the 1930s there was intense competition between Auto Union and Mercedes.

Above: a slightly earlier picture—1934—of one of Mercedes' main contenders, Luigi Fagioli, during practice.

Below: the layout of a Formula 1 single seater has been fairly similar for the past few years: mid mounted V8 or 12 engine, gearbox behind rear axle, etc. The 'radiator' here is an oil cooler; the water radiator is at the front. A mechanic is fitting on the large rear aerofoil which holds the car down at speed.

out was adopted by others.

The firm of Lotus was started by Colin Chapman, an engineer and businessman whose racing success built up demand for his sports cars. In order to reduce weight as the Grand Prix rules kept changing, Chapman introduced the monocoque chassis, using sheet metal to build the frame and outer skin of the car in one unit, in 1962. Another of his innovations was wider tyres, to enable as much power as possible to be transmitted to the ground. He was aided in this by tyre makers Goodyear and Firestone, who wanted to enter a field where Dunlop had had a virtual monopoly.

A modern racing tyre is tubeless and light in weight with comparatively low pressure, in order to avoid explosive blow-outs. It is purpose-built in different versions for wet and dry conditions, the 'dry' tyre having no treads in order to obtain maximum contact with the road. (Similar 'racing slicks' are also used on dragsters.)

Honda of Japan produced a complicated twelve-cylinder car which won the 1965 Mexican Grand Prix. This was the last of the 1½ litre (1500 cc) Formula 1; the rule was changed in 1966 to 3 litre (3000 cc), and the Japanese had further limited success before dropping out in 1968. (The figures refer to the total volume swept by the pistons in the cylinders.)

Races are held on closed circuits, three or four miles long, with the total length of a race varying from 150 to 400 miles. Since 1967 drivers' performances count in 9 out of 11 events; points are counted on the five best of the first six races of the season and the four best of the last five.

In technical respects there has been some stagnation in the design of Formula 1 cars since the 3 litre rule. They tend to be built by small specialist firms instead of major firms with unlimited research funds. Complaints are heard that they all look the same and even sound the same, since they usually use the 480 horsepower Cosworth V-8 engine, introduced in 1967 and developed with a major contribution by British Ford. But the fact that the cars are closely matched means that the result of a race depends on the skill of the driver, and the Grand Prix are not losing their popularity.

It is significant that in the Grand Prix the award goes to the driver, while in sports car racing it goes to the car maker.

A dramatic development since the war has been the adoption of aerofoil devices to improve the grip of the car on the track. It has been known ever since aircraft first flew that wings might be used to create reverse lift; the first car to make use of the idea was the Ferrari in 1967. The most effective place to mount them was found to be directly on the rear suspension, leading to the adoption of parasol-type wings high in the air above the car; a series of breakages led to hasty controls, and since 1969 their size and placement has been strictly limited. A good driver must decide how best to position the wings, balancing the improved cornering force against the wind drag on the straight.

Other formulae After World War II at the same time as Grand Prix racing went international, the fragmentation of racing formulae also began. Midget racing in the USA, with the cars limited to a wheelbase of 66 to 76 inches, got under way in the 1940s; in England, tiny cars with 500 cc motorcycle engines became popular because of their low cost and the close racing which they provided. The new formulae have become training grounds for young drivers.

In 1958 the Italians applied to have their national 'formula junior' recognized internationally. Ingenious British makers such as Lotus, Cooper (who built many of the English 500 cc machines mentioned above) and Brabham not only eclipsed the Italian cars but sent Formula 3 (as it has been called since 1965) into a cost spiral so that a fully-equipped Formula 3 car is out of the reach of many young drivers.

Consequently a variety of national promotional single-seat racing formulae have sprung up. The first of these was Formula Vee, introduced in 1961. Powered by a tuned Volkswagen 'Beetle' engine, a Vee has many other standard elements in its chassis, and has been useful for training drivers in Germany and the USA, as well as Brazil, where twice World Champion Emerson Fittipaldi raced them before coming to Europe.

More powerful new formulae are Britain's Formula Ford and France's Formule Renault. The essence of each is a tubular chassis carrying a mildly tuned 4-cylinder Ford or Renault pushrod engine. Narrow tyres of the road-going type are required and aerodynamic aids are forbidden. Formula Ford has been popular in Britain, Scandinavia and Austria, and has been 'exported' to the USA, Australia and parts of Latin America. Originally conceived as a £1000 ($2500) car, it now costs several times that. Formule Renault is a little faster, and popular in France, Belgium and Germany. It is heavily sponsored by French interests, and the successful Renault driver is virtually guaranteed a sponsored drive.

As a means of teaching racecraft to a driver, these formulae are ideal, being outwardly similar to Grand Prix cars and having a minimum of bodywork to be damaged and being easy to work on. For example, a Formula Ford has a gearbox with easily altered gear ratios, just like some of the Grand Prix cars.

New formulae have been introduced as an intermediate step above the promotional formulae. Formula Super-Vee, Formule Super-Renault and Formula Ford 2000 are some of them. It is increasingly difficult for a young driver to decide which class to enter. The next two expensive classes are the ones on which the aspiring driver fixes his sights: the Formula 5000, powered by highly tuned 5 litre American V-8 engines, and Formula 2, in which the most popular unit is the 4-cylinder BMW. The Formula 5000, with 500

Left: the Le Mans 24 hour race admits various classes of sports cars; here a Chevrolet Corvette (left), basically a production car, is about to be passed by a specially built Porsche 917 (right).

Below: typical Formula 1 'aerofoil' bodywork.

bhp, can be faster than a Grand Prix car, but its greater weight usually cancels the difference. A Formula 2, with 300 bhp, is nimbler than either. There are European championships for both, but the F5000 is mainly based in Britain; the F2 is more popular because it gives drivers a chance to race on more foreign circuits.

Sports car racing The sports car (or GT, Gran Turismo) is usually a two seater, sometimes four, designed for nimble handling rather than speed or power. It is, theoretically, a production car intended for private ownership, and must be 'homologated'—that is, a certain number must have been built. There are also special 'prototype' classes. Some builders of Grand Prix cars also make sports cars, such as Ferrari and Lotus. Some of the most famous car races are sports car events, such as the 24-hour Le Mans race, which is really an endurance contest; they are sometimes called Grand Prix events, which means that they are important national events rather than Formula 1 events, although some sports cars are not much different in terms of speed and power from Grand Prix cars.

Hot rod racing Several types of racing are peculiarly American, having arisen because of widespread car ownership in a large country without much public transport, and because of the availability of old cars. Hot rod racing is as much a hobby as a sport. The owner of a car usually does his own modifying of it, in order to compete with others against time or distance. The sport had bad publicity on account of illegal street racing, but is controlled in the USA by the National Hot Rod Association (NHRA). The cars may be ordinary street models, modified for performance, or they may be modified to an extent that makes them unsuitable for street use. For example, a high-performance camshaft may be intended for high-speed use, and may be damaged by stop-and-go city driving, which includes a lot of idling of the engine.

A recent Formula 1 car: the Ferrari 312 B3. The engine
has 12 cylinders, horizontally opposed, with two overhead
camshafts for each bank of six. There are four valves per
cylinder to improve gas flow. The cubic capacity is 2911
cc, giving a comfortable margin under the 3 litre limit
to allow for any future modifications. These are constantly
made, so that power output increases every year; in 1975,
the second year of development, it was 480 bhp at
12,000 rpm, but it is now well into the 500s. The car
has side mounted radiators (as does the Surtees on p 115)
to allow a more efficient aerodynamic shape at the nose.
Here the front aerofoil is a separate 'wing' rather than
an all in one fairing enclosing the front wheels. The
tyres shown are the treadless dry weather type; on a wet
track they are exchanged for tyres with a tread and a
different rubber compound.

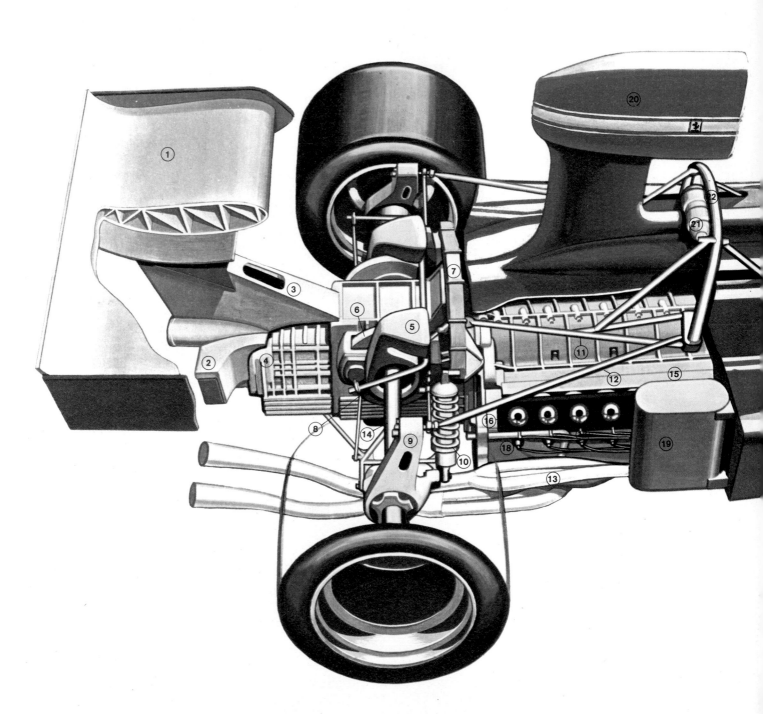

1 aerofoil
2 gearbox oil radiator
3 gearbox oil intake
4 gearbox
5 inboard brake cooling scoop
6 disc caliper
7 bulkhead
8 stabilizer
9 suspension upright
10 spring unit

11 engine support
12 radius arm
13 exhuast system
14 drive shaft
15 flat 12 cylinder engine
16 intake trumpets
17 injection nozzles
18 ignition plug
19 oil tank
20 air ram

21 extinguisher
22 roll-over bar
23 cockpit
24 water radiator
25 radiator vents
26 front spring unit
27 wishbone
28 steering link
29 front outboard disc
30 disc air scoop
31 front aerofoil

Stock car racing It is estimated that ten million people a year attend stock car racing in the USA. Cars which are not racing cars or sports cars are called stock cars or production cars; the car manufacturers sponsor cars and teams of drivers for the publicity. Stock car racing is said to have developed during the Prohibition era in the United States (1919-33). Bootleggers of illegal spirits tuned up and modified the engines of their cars so they could outrun the police.

There are several categories of stock car racing, depending on the type of car being raced and the degree of modification allowed. There are also demolition derbies, in which the drivers purposely damage each other's cars, while trying to avoid crippling damage to their own; the last car still able to move under its own power is the winner. In stock car racing, all glass is removed from the car, the drivers wear crash helmets and safety harnesses, and roll bars are installed inside the car to strengthen it in case it rolls over. Like virtually all American racing, stock car racing is done on oval-shaped dirt tracks. British stock car racing is done on a small scale; it is unsponsored and mostly

Formula Ford is an attempt to keep down the cost of racing by a rigid formula specifying standard Cortina GT (or Taunus) engines, normal road tyres, no 'wings' etc.

Below: much cheaper—a stock car, basically a wreck with glass removed and extra protection and strengthening.

old cars are used. British saloon car racing is analogous to stock car racing but on a normal circuit. (In Britain, a 'saloon' is a family car; the word is analogous to the obsolescent American word 'sedan'.)

Rallying Rallying is a sport in which privately owned sports cars or stock cars compete against the clock over ordinary roads. The object is to get from one control point to another; the driver takes a passenger with him to navigate and the ability to choose the best route between control points is as important as the skill of the driver. The object may be to travel at an average legal speed; in a stages rally there may even be penalties for completing a stage at too high an average speed. Safe, legal driving is the essence. In

other types of rallies the drivers are allowed to go as fast as they can. The Safari rally, held in East Africa, is an endurance contest over some of the worst roads in the world.
Drag racing A dragster is a specialized type of racing car which competes against a clock, or against another car on a parallel track, in a drag race. A drag race is essentially an acceleration test on a quarter-mile (400 m) track called a drag strip. Since World War II drag racing, an outgrowth of racing of modified cars by amateurs, has become a very popular spectator sport. A dragster starting from a standstill can cover the quarter-mile in as little as 6.5 seconds, reaching a speed of 200 miles an hour and requiring a parachute to help stop it.

American V-8 engines are popular for use in dragsters because of the high capacity, expressed in cubic inches, of their fuel combustion chambers. Ordinary automobile engines are built for durability and a certain minimum fuel consumption, factors which do not concern the drag racer, so the engines are completely disassembled and put back together with a great deal of balancing and polishing of the parts. The object is to make the engine lighter and capable of achieving the maximum revolutions per minute in the shortest possible time. The cooling system—radiator, hoses and water pump—is dispensed with, since the water in the engine's water jacket is sufficient for cooling during the quarter-mile run. (Dispensing with the water pump also restores power to the engine which is normally used in operating the pump by means of a belt off the crankshaft.) The rebuilt engine incorporates a supercharger and a fuel injection system; the fuel itself may be a nitro-methanol mixture which is highly combustible. The exhaust system consists of tuned pipes of exactly the right diameter to match the manifold on the engine for the right amount of back-pressure. Silencers [mufflers] are dispensed with, making drag strips very noisy places.

For a certain class of drag racing, a slightly modified engine may be mounted in an ordinary car body, but a true dragster is a glamorous construction completely unsuitable for driving on the street. It may be built from scratch of welded steel tubing, with an aluminium 'skin' covering it, and providing barely enough space for the driver. The tremendous accelerating power of a dragster tends to make the front end want to climb into the air, so it may be made as long as 30 ft, and the snout will be aerodynamically designed to keep it on the ground. The so-called 'slingshot' dragster has the frame extending well beyond the rear axle, and the driver's seat is located there, like the stone in a slingshot.

The rear axle halves themselves are often shortened to lessen the risk of snapping with the torque of acceleration. The wheels are 'mag' wheels made of magnesium alloy, combining light weight with high strength. ' Wrinkle-wall' tyres without any treads are used for maximum traction (the drag strip must be absolutely dry and clean). This type of tyre is called a slick, and is able to distort under acceleration without deflating. The mechanics sometimes pour bleach over the tyres just before take-off to make them grip better.

Drag racing, originally the province of amateurs, has become so costly that the dragsters are nowadays often sponsored by garages, auto supply shops and similar businesses.

Left and below: drag racing is simply an acceleration contest over a very short distance. The fastest and most specialized dragster is the 'slingshot' type, of which these are two examples. The lower one is supercharged by means of a Roots blower like that on p 57. Slingshots have all the weight concentrated at the rear to give grip to the huge 'slick' (treadless) tyres. The engine, almost always an American V8, has short, tuned exhaust stacks, but no cooling system: there is no time for it to overheat.

The Challenge to the Car Industry

Since 1973, world prices for crude oil have more than quadrupled, and the depletion of world petroleum resources threatens the future of all transportation. America, with its heavy cars and large engines, overnight came face to face with an urgent need to cut the fuel consumption of its cars.

In December, 1973, Russell E. Train, head of the US Environmental Protection Agency, suggested that the government should regulate the number of miles that passenger cars should get from a gallon of gasoline. In May, 1975, the Senate Commerce Committee proposed a bill to compel auto makers to boost fuel economy by 100 percent.

As listed by the EPA the 1975-model General Motors cars averaged 15.5 mpg; Ford's 15.9 mpg, Chrysler's 16.3 and American Motors' 21 mpg. That year Americans drove nearly 1 million million car-miles, and their cars consumed about 70 thousand million gallons of gasoline [petrol]. That's the equivalent of 14 percent of all energy consumed in the USA. Congress finally voted to set mileage standards in January, 1976. The bill became law on March 30, 1976.

Rules imposed under authority of the Energy Policy and Conservation Act set a minimum of 18 miles per US gallon for 1978 models and 20 mpg for 1980 models. There is a gradual increase to 22 mpg in 1981, 24 mpg in 1982, 26 mpg in 1983, 27 mpg in 1984 and 27.5 mpg in 1985.

The US Department of Transportation has also set fuel-economy standards for light trucks. The definition of a light truck is one whose gross weight, including a full load, is 6000 pounds or less. It starts with 17.2 mpg in 1979. At the same time, four-wheel-drive vehicles will be required to go 15.8 mpg.

The Environmental Protection Agency began publishing calculated fuel-consumption data for all cars tested for emissions in October, 1974. The figures are calculated on the basis of the federal emission test procedure, which is a simulated driving cycle. The test is run in a laboratory, not on the road, but on a dynamometer; thus, it ignores at least one vital factor: aerodynamic drag. The fundamental assumptions for calculating fuel economy on the basis of carbon balance are that the only source of carbon entering the engine comes in the form of fuel; that all of the carbon leaving the engine can be measured as HC, CO, or CO_2; and that no fuel or carbon leaks exist.

The minimum mpg requirements are defined as sales-weighted averages, which means that if a car maker has a range of models with fuel economy from 12 to 22 mpg, he has to sell more high-mileage than low-mileage cars to reach a 'fleet' average of 18 mpg. It is up to each manufacturer to maintain this balance, regardless of buyer preferences, which means that if one maker's least economical cars are more popular than his high-fuel-economy models, he has no choice but to curtail or suspend production of the cars that pull down his 'fleet' average.

This law is causing the greatest revolution in the American auto industry since the assembly line came along. Smaller and lighter cars must be developed, and more fuel-efficient power units designed and developed. New production methods must be developed. Factories must be retooled to manufacture four-cylinder engines instead of V-8s, and assembly plants reequipped to handle smaller vehicles with different components. It is estimated that the industry will invest at least 27 billion dollars over the 5-year period ending in 1981 in making these changes.

Above: the Volkswagen Rabbit's passive restraint system includes an automatic shoulder belt.

Speed limits In February 1974 the US Congress voted to impose a federal speed limit of 55 mph on all public highways in an effort to reduce energy consumption. Auto industry sources say that American cars run most economically at speeds between 37 and 47 mph (depending on design and engineering factors), and the Department of Transportation estimated that strict observance of the limit would save 200,000 barrels of oil every day, compared with fuel use under previous limits of 50-55 on ordinary highways and 70 to 80 mph on motorways. In December 1974 the nation-wide 55-mph speed-limit became permanent.

Most European countries had no speed limits outside built-up areas in the 1950s, but imposed them during the 1960s, for safety reasons, as traffic density increased everywhere. Sweden imposed strict limits in 1967, in connection with the changeover from left-hand to right-hand traffic. In the United Kingdom, a general 70-mph limit has been in force since 1967. Germany went to a 100-km/h general limit on ordinary roads in 1970.

In the aftermath of the 1973-74 'fuel crisis' France adopted limits of 130 km/h on multi-lane motorways, 110 km/h on dual carriageways, and 90 km/h on ordinary roads. Italy set similar limits, while German authorities merely recommended a maximum motorway speed of 130 km/h. No clear conclusions can be drawn about the benefits in terms of either energy saving or traffic safety as yet.

Aerodynamics Improving the shape of the car so as to slip through the air with less disturbance can give important energy savings. Aerodynamic drag is not proportional with speed, but increases in a geometrical progression. Speeding up from 60 to 75 mph will not bring a 25 percent increase in drag but a 100 percent increase in drag. For each car there comes a point where a 10 mph speed increase will double the air drag. Even at normal cruising speeds, air drag is the most important single influence on a car's performance and fuel economy.

At speeds of 100 km/h and up, more energy is used to overcome aerodynamic drag than is lost in any other way. Body shapes with lower air drag will raise the car's most economical speed, allow it to run more economically at any given speed, and reach a higher top speed. The basic problem is that the most efficient shape for practical space utilisation is difficult to combine with the requirements of smooth airflow.

Chrysler estimates that a 10 percent reduction in air drag translates into a gain of 0.7 mpg at 70 mph. What is the potential for reducing the air drag of a family car? Today's average car has an aerodynamic drag coefficient between .45 and .55. It can easily be brought below .40. For small (that is, short) cars the practical limit may lie around 0.35, but longer models can and have achieved values below 0.30. It can realistically be expected that air drag will be reduced by 22 to 27 percent whenever new models replace older ones.

The aerodynamic rules that apply to commercial vehicles

Above: a research safety vehicle on a Simca chassis.

are the same as for cars, but the problems are different. The main problem is peculiar to 'high-cube' semi-trailers hauled by highway tractors. The gap between the two units and the difference in height cause very high air drag. Such a combination displaces 18 tons of air per mile travelled, and requires over 100 hp merely to overcome the air drag at 55 mph. In the US there are over 400,000 such vehicles, each covering about 100,000 miles a year, which gives an idea of the scope for fuel savings by aerodynamic means. Experiments with fairings above the tractor cabs have shown that a 25 percent reduction in air drag is possible.

More diesel power More and more car makers are adding diesel-powered models, and the reason why is their superior fuel economy. The advantage is quite substantial. In the EPA fuel-economy list, the Oldsmobile diesel shows 37 percent higher fuel mileage than its gasoline-powered counterpart. In actual driving on Japanese roads, Nissan cars have shown improvements of 30 to 65 percent by going from gasoline to diesel power. In London, a major taxicab fleet switched from gasoline to diesel engines and found that the average fuel economy improved from 16 to 30 mpg. American car companies see the diesel car as the only way to keep large cars in production and still meet the required 'fleet' average.

The diesel engine has a dominant position in heavy commercial vehicles—about 90 percent in Europe and 50 percent in the US. Due to the difference in operating conditions, long-distance goods vehicles do not reap the same benefits from the diesel engine as cars. But the industry is working to maximize the economy potential of the diesel for heavy road vehicles.

This trend consists basically in reversing the torque curve which normally rises with increasing rpm, and making it rise as engine speed drops. This makes it possible to run engines for longer periods at lower rpm, which reduces fuel consumption.

The means that make this possible consist of a turbocharger and an intercooler. The turbocharger is a small unit that contains an exhaust-gas-driven turbine whose shaft turns a fresh air compressor. Thus, energy stored in the hot exhaust gas is utilized to force pressurized air into the engine. The intercooler is an air-to-air or air-to-water heat exchanger, which serves to cool the compressed air before it is admitted to the cylinders. By careful matching of the turbocharger to the engine, some manufacturers have developed engines with torque curves having their peak at 1,400 rpm, and falling towards their maximum speed of about 2,200 rpm.

The turbocharger permits a 40 to 65 percent boost in power from the same basic engine, without adding significantly to its weight, bulk, or cost. That provides an indirect fuel saving. Today, nearly all heavy commercial vehicle engines rated above 200 hp are turbocharged.

Above: a wind tunnel test for air flow pattern.

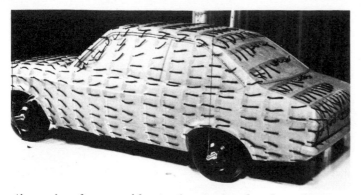

Above: the tufts are used for visual study of air flow. Lamp-black streaking is another visual method often used.

over-rich mixture and threaten to produce vapour-lock in the fuel lines, causing the engine to stall. But methanol sources are abundant. It can be extracted from coal. It can be produced from wood waste, agricultural waste in the form of plants, and even from domestic refuse. The cost of mass-producing methanol from these sources has not been firmly established, but it is certain that the initial investment would be enormous. Conoco estimates that it would take 400 million dollars to open a coal mine and build an adjacent methanol plant with capacity equivalent to a crude-oil refinery making 20,000 barrels of gasoline [petrol] a day.

The most promising fuel for the long term future is hydrogen. Liquid hydrogen is a potent fuel with chemical sign H_2, notable for extremely high mass energy density. It packs the most energy per pound of any known fuel. It is

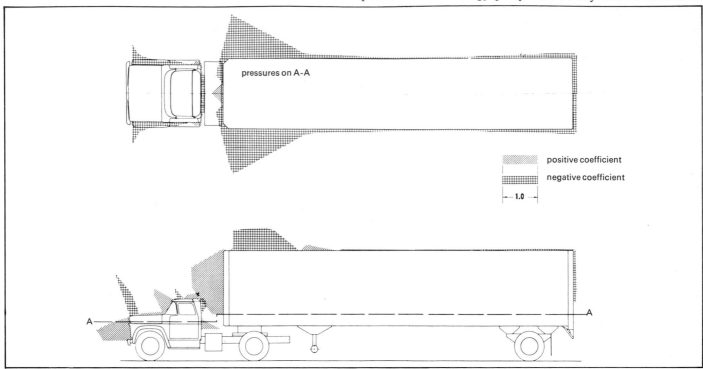

pressures on A-A

positive coefficient

negative coefficient

— 1.0 —

A ————————————————— A

The different types of air drag on a vehicle are carefully studied.

Alternative fuels What type of engines will be used in future cars depends above all on their compatability with the fuels that are available. The situation must be seen as a series of time frames—short term, middle term, and long term. Top priority for the short term is to find alternative fuels that are suitable for existing engines with a minimum of modification. In the long term, petroleum-based fuels will no longer exist, but technology may advance far and fast enough to provide new power systems for future sources of energy.

Methanol is a common name for methyl alcohol, which has the chemical sign CH_3OH. It is the most promising motor fuel for near and middle term use. It can be used as an additive to gasoline or as a single fuel for any heat engine. What methanol lacks is the concentrated energy content of gasoline. It has lower heat value, which means that the fuel tank must be $2\frac{1}{2}$ times larger to give the methanol-fueled car the same range. Methanol is corrosive, which means that the tank should probably be galvanized or made of plastic. It is also a strong solvent, which can cause carburettor problems. Cold starting is impossible in temperatures of $-20°F$ and lower, necessitating a special starting system using gasoline or ether, ammonia, or other synthetic fuel. In hot weather, the low vapourization point of methanol will tend to form an

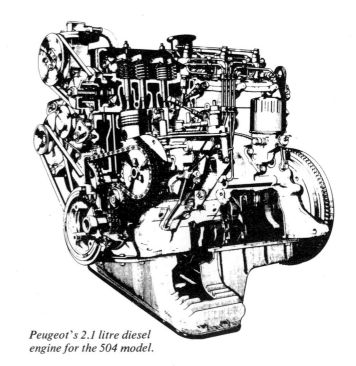

Peugeot's 2.1 litre diesel engine for the 504 model.

fully recyclable, and returns to water after combustion. It is abundant in nature. There will never be a shortage of hydrogen. It can be produced from coal by a steam reaction process. It can be produced from water by electrolysis. Hydrogen is also a by-product of the nuclear power station, generated from water by thermal dissociation. With increasing emphasis on atomic energy, the power industry will create a surplus of hydrogen.

In the short term, use of hydrogen in cars is restricted to such applications as hydrogen enrichment of gasoline-fuelled internal combustion engines, due to the problems of hydrogen storage and distribution. Hydrogen enrichment consists in adding small amounts of hydrogen to ultra-lean mixtures of air and gasoline to assure combustion. For this kind of blending, a hydrogen generator is needed. However, an onboard generator tends to waste energy, which upsets the overall fuel economy of the system. Control of the flow of produced gas to the engine during transient operation is another problem.

Spark-ignition car engines can be modified to run on pure hydrogen with relatively simple modifications. The major problems involve the hydrogen supply, onboard storage, and safety. Liquid hydrogen—separated—can only be stored cryogenically, which means using a bulky and expensive tank with its own refrigeration system. There is greater promise in chemical storage, in which hydrogen is combined with another substance, such as methanol, toluene, or a metal hydride.

Most current programmes take the metal hydride approach. Hydrogen can be combined with metal substances such as magnesium hydride or an iron-titanium alloy, which are relatively unstable chemically and can be split into their basic components at reasonably low temperatures.

Tests with hydrogen as a motor fuel have demonstrated several problems, such as rough combustion, low volumetric efficiency, high nitric-oxide formation, and a risk of back-flash in the induction manifold. Nonetheless, there are many reasons why hydrogen remains an attractive alternative fuel. For one thing, its wide air-fuel ratio tolerance will enable an engine to run on extremely lean mixtures under light-load

conditions. It has high knock resistance which will allow very high compression ratios to be used, with higher combustion efficiency.

Pollution Air pollution is not a general problem throughout the world, but a regional phenomenon depending on geographical and climatic conditions, industrial and population concentrations, and other factors, including motor traffic.

Until 1952, scientists had no data on the relationship between automotive emissions and smog formation, or their effect on the overall air quality. Then Dr. A. J. Haagen-Smit proved that the interaction between sunlight and nitrogen oxides from automotive exhaust gas causes the formation of photochemical smog, a local problem in the Los Angeles area of California.

Detroit began to work on emission controls in 1953 at the suggestion of the Director of the Los Angeles Air Pollution Control District. But no changes were made in production cars until California laws demanded positive crankcase ventilation in 1961.

On a completely uncontrolled car, the emission sources and their relative contribution were estimated as:

Open crankcase ventilation	20 percent
Exhaust emissions	62 percent
Evaporative emissions	18 percent

In 1963 the USA passed the landmark Clean Air Act (which was amended in 1966 and 1970). Its immediate result for cars was to force nation-wide installation of positive crankcase ventilation. The 1966 amendment added exhaust emission and evaporative emission standards. The limits were set as 275 parts-per-million of unburned hydrocarbons and 1.5 percent carbon monoxide, which meant a 43 percent reduction in CO and a 58 percent reduction in HC emissions, compared with estimates of what 'uncontrolled' cars were spewing out. These standards were met by simple means. Chrysler developed a system with recalibrated carburettors, retarded ignition timing, and revised camshafts that was good enough. GM and Ford went to air-injection in the exhaust ports, as a means of providing extra oxygen to assure after-burning of unburned hydrocarbons.

A Volkswagen taxi with a hybrid engine system.

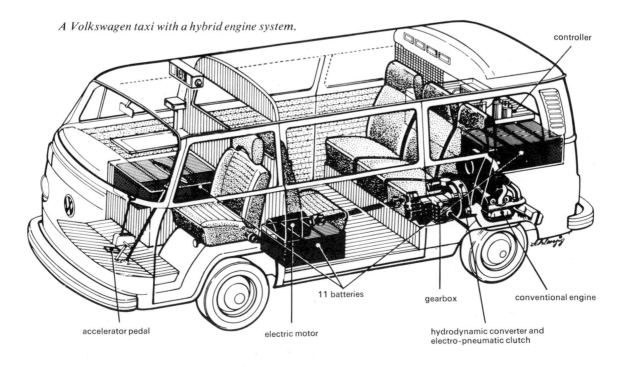

accelerator pedal

electric motor

11 batteries

gearbox

hydrodynamic converter and electro-pneumatic clutch

conventional engine

controller

Standards were tightened for 1970, and new test methods prescribed, with measurements to be made in grams per mile.

Cars are dynamometer-tested on a simulated driving cycle, and the exhaust gas measured by the CVS (constant volume sampler) method. The federal driving cycle is based on a 7.5-mile urban route in the Los Angeles area. It takes 1372 seconds, with an average speed of 19.6 mph and a maximum speed of 57 mph. It includes 18 acceleration-deceleration modes separated by idle periods of 0-39 seconds. The highest acceleration-deceleration rate reached is 3.3 mph per second.

It is estimated that the uncontrolled 1967 car had emission levels of 15-17 grams per mile of unburned hydrocarbons, 90-127 grams per mile of carbon monoxide, and 5-6 grams per mile of nitrogen oxides. The 1976-77 US federal standards gave a reduction in automobile exhaust emissions (from uncontrolled pre-1968 levels) of 97 percent for unburned hydrocarbons, 96 percent for carbon monoxide, and 93 percent for oxides of nitrogen. Thus, automobile exhaust emissions have been virtually eliminated as a source of air pollution in America. The government must now decide whether any further reduction in car exhaust emissions will produce any actual improvement in the overall air quality.

Commercial vehicles are also heavily regulated for emissions in the USA. This development started when the California Air Resources Board imposed limits on light-duty vehicles in 1965, and California has led the evolution.

Within the framework of an agreement adopted by the NATO Economic Commission for Europe at Geneva in March, 1968, a series of regulations on automotive emission control have been issued and ratified by the signatory nations.

The first emission control standards for the common market nations were in effect from 1971 to the end of September, 1975. The standards were known collectively as Regulation 15, with limits for hydrocarbon and carbon monoxide emissions from automobiles powered by spark-ignition engines, on a sliding scale according to the engine displacement and weight of the vehicle. Compared with American emission control standards, the ECE 15 limits are lenient.

Japan was only marginally behind the USA in enacting legislation covering automotive air pollution, and was the first in imposing limits, the first emission control standards going into effect in the autumn of 1966. It began with a limit on carbon monoxide to 3 percent of total exhaust volume, which was further reduced in 1969 to $2\frac{1}{2}$ percent when driving and 4.5 percent at idle. In April 1973, Japan adopted new standards, modified again two years later. The Society of Automotive Engineers (SAE) has observed that American cars meeting the 1977 California standards usually pass Japan's 1977 tests.

Emission-control methods Meeting the US federal standard for 1968 was relatively easy. Most engines received an air pump that delivered fresh air to the exhaust port areas, the oxygen assuring an afterburning of hydrocarbons. To meet the stricter standards of 1970 and 1972, further hardware and modifications were needed. Exhaust gas recirculation was adopted to lower the combustion temperatures and prevent nitrogen oxide formation. Compression ratios were lowered to enable engines to run on low-octane lead-free gasoline. Spark timing was retarded in accordance with load and speed, and dashpots were added to the throttle linkage to prevent sudden deceleration in rpms. Intake air was pre-heated for improved control of air/fuel ratios.

All of these modifications made the engines less efficient.

They became, in effect, less powerful. Displacement was increased, and fuel consumption soared. The emission control standards were blamed, but it was the industry that had chosen the means to meet the standards, and by 1973 a new generation of systems that would partly restore the fuel economy were developed. The catalytic converter was adopted for most 1975 American cars, and many imports.

Catalytic converters These are chemical reaction chambers, working as gas purifiers. A catalyst is a substance that initiates a chemical reaction or increases the rate of chemical reaction while remaining itself unchanged. Noble metals such as platinum and palladium trigger oxidation of carbon monoxide to harmless carbon dioxide and water vapour. Catalytic action starts when the engine reaches normal operating temperature, as the hot gas sweeps over the catalyst. The catalyst converters improved fuel economy by 7 to 15 percent, though most engines continued the various other devices adopted in the 1968-74 period (which had caused a fuel-economy loss of 12 to 28 percent). Cars equipped with the present systems can meet emission control standards through 1979. But their lack of fuel economy threatens the car maker's 'fleet average', and that's why the Detroit companies are developing more advanced emission control systems.

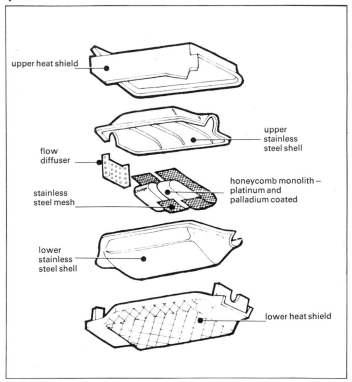

Above: the catalytic converter is used in the exhaust system to ensure emission reduction. The catalyst causes extra heat, hence additional heat shields are necessary, as is non-lead fuel.

Lean burn The term 'lean burn' is self-descriptive. The lean-burn approach to emission controls means using very lean mixtures (i.e. very high air/fuel ratios), so as to reduce the carbon intake and increase the air intake per engine cycle. Using less fuel per charge translates into a fuel saving.

Chrysler began using its lean-burn system on some engines in 1976, and have it on nearly all 1978 engines. The Chrysler lean-burn system consists of three groups of components; a specially calibrated lean-mix carburettor; electronic spark-timing computer, and the sensors for the computer, which measure inlet air temperature, manifold vacuum, coolant temperature, engine speed, and throttle position. With spark timing under continuous control, the engine can accept abnormally high air/fuel ratios, such as 18:1 compared with 13.4 to 16.5:1 for other engines. Tests with Chrysler cars show fuel economy improvements of 15 to 18 percent above former models with catalytic converters.

Ford of Britain has developed and tested a lean-burn engine capable of running reliably on air/fuel ratios as lean as 18:1. The key to its function lies in the turbulence generator which replaces the butterfly throttle valve. This turbulence generator takes the shape of a dart, working as a plunger in a convergent-divergent nozzle located in the intake manifold. Plunger movement is controlled to give sonic gas velocity, which sets up a shock wave downstream from the nozzle. The resulting turbulence helps promote combustion by intermixing burned and unburned gases at the flame front as it progresses across the combustion chamber. The engine brings a fuel saving of 12 to 16 percent, and an 80 percent drop in NO_x emissions, with a 17 percent reduction in HC emissions, and virtual elimination of CO emissions.

Fast burn A system developed by Nissan works with air/fuel ratios around 15.5:1 and high-volume exhaust-gas recirculation, plus two spark plugs per cylinder. This Z-system works by a 'fast-burn' process. It has a normal carburettor and does not include after-treatment of the exhaust gases (catalytic converters or thermal reactors). Instead, the concept relies on a closely controlled air/fuel ratio and a 'fast-burn' combustion process. Two flame fronts are started simultaneously by the two plugs, which are mounted on opposite sides. The flame fronts travel into the cylinder and converge as the piston goes down. There are no quench areas, and the end gas is concentrated in the center of the piston crown. Emission levels are lower than the limits set for 1978.

Its CO content fell within the 0.36-1.89 g/km band, with HC levels between 0.02 and 0.11 g/km, with NO_x levels as low as 0.11 to 0.20 grams per kilometer.

Closed loop The term closed loop simply means that the contents of the exhaust gas are continuously analyzed, and the results are utilized to monitor the mixture formation. In other words, what goes into the engine is based on what came out. The loop is closed, with control by feedback.

The best known closed loop system is the Lambda-sond which was developed by Volvo in collaboration with Robert Bosch and Engelhard Industries. It works with port-type fuel injection, exhaust gas recirculation, and a three-way catalytic converter. The term three-way means it handles all three regulated pollutants. Its action is only two-way, however, as a reducing catalyst for NO_x control, and as an oxidizing catalyst for CO control.

The Lambda-sond device is an oxygen sensor inserted into the exhaust manifold. Its signals are relayed to an electronic control unit, which commands an air/fuel ratio corrector linked to a special unit that functions as a combined air flow sensor and fuel distributor. Electronic control logic directs not only the air/fuel ratio of the incoming mixture, but also the ignition timing.

Tests of the Lambda-sond on Volvo cars show a 10 percent improvement in fuel mileage (over the 1977-model equipped for California) with emission levels that undercut those of the American research goals: 0.2 grams per mile of unburned hydrocarbons; 2.8 grams per mile of carbon monoxide; and 0.17 grams per mile of nitrogen oxides.

Stratified charge Various engines, experimental and production, have demonstrated the possibility of meeting future emission control standards without loss of fuel economy by charge stratification. It provides lower flame temperatures, improved cycle efficiency, reduced heat loss, less dissociation, and lower pumping losses.

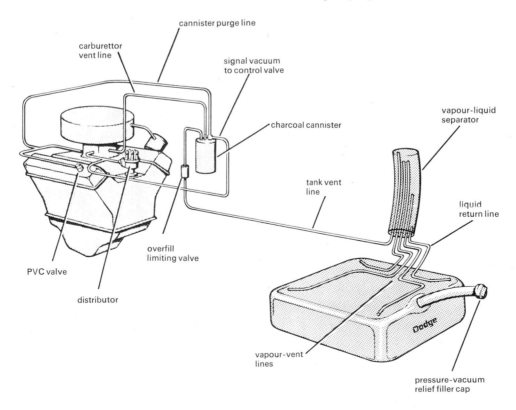

Above: another emission control device is a fuel-tank system which controls overflow and evaporation.

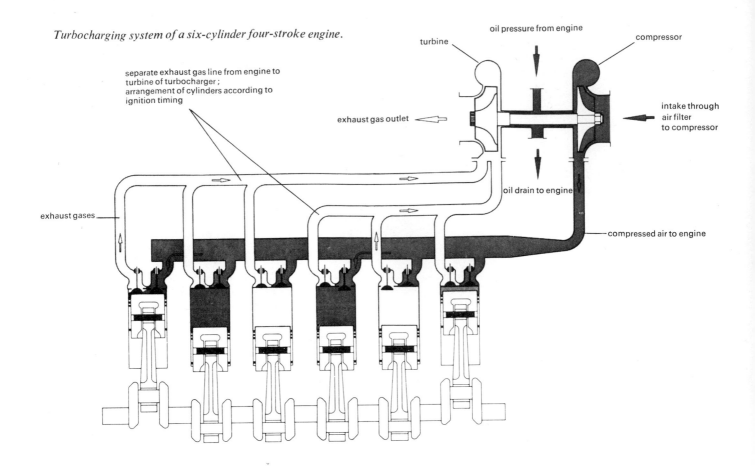

Turbocharging system of a six-cylinder four-stroke engine.

oil pressure from engine

turbine

compressor

separate exhaust gas line from engine to
turbine of turbocharger;
arrangement of cylinders according to
ignition timing

exhaust gas outlet

intake through
air filter
to compressor

oil drain to engine

exhaust gases

compressed air to engine

Of course, the air/fuel charge is not truly stratified. The gas does not arrange itself in well-defined layers of varying fuel density. There is no clear separation between each stage of rich and lean mixtures. It's a gradual pattern, with some overlap, from a rich-mixture core to a lean-mixture circumference. With a small combustion core, the engine can run and produce power with an extremely lean air/fuel ratio. Engineers are now looking at air/fuel ratios up to 30:1 for experimental stratified charge engines.

The best known stratified-charge car engine is the Honda CVCC (Compound Vortex Controlled Combustion) unit which uses a dual-body carburettor that prepares both a rich mixture and a lean mixture. The rich mixture is introduced into a small pre-chamber which contains the spark plug, while the lean mixture is admitted directly into the top of the cylinder. The gas flow is highly turbulent, with a compound vortex flow, which speeds up the flame front.

Systems developed by Texaco and the Southwest Research Institute use direct fuel injection (with the injector nozzle aimed into the combustion chamber, relying on its spray pattern and the induced turbulence to achieve stratification).

Ford's Proco (Programmed Combustion) engine belongs in the same family, but stands apart due to its deep piston crown recess and its use of throttled air intake. (See diagram at the bottom of page 44.)

Volkswagen and Porsche are developing a pre-chamber type of stratified charge engine with port-type fuel injection. One injector nozzle provides a rich mixture for the pre-chamber, while a low-pressure nozzle placed in the port area behind the intake valve delivers a lean mixture into the main combustion space.

Noise control Noise has been recognized as a health hazard as well as an annoyance. Interior noise is related to safety, in that loud noise aggravates driver fatigue.

In November, 1973, an addition was made to the USA Federal Motor Carrier Safety Regulations, establishing a maximum interior noise level of 90 dBA, measured during a stationary test. The reading was made with the engine turning at its maximum speed, and recording the noise with a sound meter held near the driver's right ear.

Control of exterior vehicle noise began in California in 1968, when a limit of 86 dBA during wide-open-throttle acceleration from 45 to 55 mph for passenger cars (measured at 50 feet) was established. From January, 1973, California limited car noise to 84 dBA and heavy vehicle noise to 86 dBA. Test conditions for heavy vehicles were set to reach maximum rated engine speed below 35 mph. At the start of 1975, the limits were lowered to 80 dBA for cars and 83 dBA for commercial vehicles. By 1978 the California standards lowered the limits to 75 dBA for cars and 80 dBA for heavy vehicles.

The USA Federal Noise Control Act went into effect in October, 1972. Under its authority, the Environmental Protection Agency was directed to develop noise criteria and promulgate noise regulation standards.

A typical diesel truck, made before the days of noise control, would have noise levels of 98 dBA from the (open) exhaust pipe, 88 dBA from the fan, 83 dBA from the engine, 75 dBA from the air cleaner and intake, and 75 dBA from other noises. Its total noise level comes to 98.4 dBA and is dominated by exhaust noise.

Tyre noise from heavy vehicles is a high-speed phenomenon, and the American tyre industry took its first steps towards reducing tyre noise in 1964. Truck tyre noise at 70 mph can reach 75 or 86 dBA (at 50 feet). At any speed, tyre noise varies greatly according to road surface, tread design, wear, and axle loading. In low-speed tests, tyre noise is completely masked by other sources of noise.

In October, 1975, the Environmental Protection Agency imposed noise limits on all vehicles used in interstate commerce, with gross weights exceeding 10,000 pounds:

	dBA
In zones with speed limits above 35 mph (at 50 feet)	90
In zones with speed limits below 35 mph (at 50 feet)	86
Idling (at 50 feet)	88

The test procedure was intended to show the worst noise a vehicle can make with any load at low speeds. The vehicle makes a full-throttle acceleration past a microphone placed 50 feet to the side of the vehicle's path, running in a gear low enough to reach maximum rpm before hitting 35 mph.

Early in 1977 the Environmental Protection Agency proposed limits on bus noise, to be staged in three steps over a seven-year period from 1979 through 1985. The noise level limits are:

	Exterior (at 50 ft)	Interior (noisiest seat)
1979	83 dBA	86 dBA
1983	80 dBA	83 dBA
1985	77 dBA	80 dBA

The EEC exterior noise standards still allow 86 dBA for vehicles with less than 200 hp and 98 dBA for those above 200 hp. Both European and Japanese laws aim at equally or more stringent value than the USA noise control regulations. The long-term goal is about 75 dBA under test conditions based on American standards.

New Safety Laws US legislators arbitrarily determined that frontal impacts posed the biggest danger, and that action in this area could save the most lives (15,600 per year, according to one report by the US Department of Transportation). European auto makers argued against setting crash performance standards on the grounds that there is no standard accident in the real world. The barrier crash, for instance, reflects conditions that can only be called exceptional. And in car-to-car frontal collisions, the vehicles rarely meet head-on, but in offset positions, and often at an oblique angle.

Most safety standards are not controversial. They merely specify dimensions of various safety items (mirrors, for instance) or set performance or strength levels (seat belts, door hinges, brake linings). Some standards are just endorsements of standardization moves by the industry, but a few have made valuable contributions. Standard 109 deals with tyres, specifying certain tests (plunger test for strength, drum test for endurance). Tyres that failed were either withdrawn from the market or improved to acceptable levels. Standard 121 deals with air brake systems for commercial vehicles. The rules were written to prevent skidding with locked wheels, especially for tractor-trailer combinations which may 'jackknife', and simultaneously shorten brake distances.

In a noise measurement test. the various sounds are picked up by microphones, monitored and analysed by electronic equipment in the van.

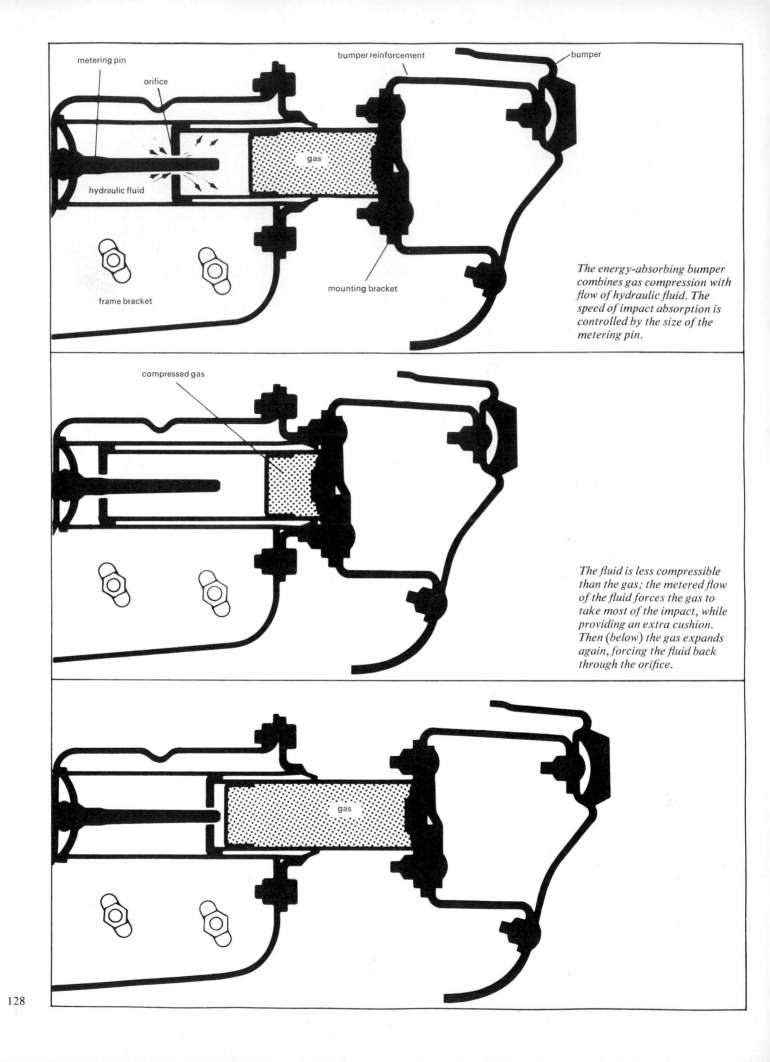

metering pin

orifice

bumper reinforcement

bumper

hydraulic fluid

gas

mounting bracket

frame bracket

The energy-absorbing bumper combines gas compression with flow of hydraulic fluid. The speed of impact absorption is controlled by the size of the metering pin.

compressed gas

The fluid is less compressible than the gas; the metered flow of the fluid forces the gas to take most of the impact, while providing an extra cushion. Then (below) the gas expands again, forcing the fluid back through the orifice.

gas

Above: the vehicle enters a curve at 30 mph; steering control must be retained when brakes are applied.

Standard 121 went into effect on January 1, 1975, for trailers and on March 1st, 1975, for other vehicles. The necessary equipment includes anti-lock warning systems and automatic antilock devices. Stopping distances, unloaded and with a full load, were specified for speeds from 20 to 55 mph. Standard 216 deals with bumpers, initially only at the level which involves damage to safety-oriented parts, such as lights, signals, fuel lines or exhaust systems.

Rules for energy-absorbing bumpers were written in 1970-71 and came into effect for the 1973 models. Cars had to pass tests including a 5 mph head-on barrier crash, and a $2\frac{1}{2}$ mph reversing barrier crash. For 1974 a pendulum test was added. The pendulum, equal to the weight of the car, exerted a force of up to 20,000 pounds on a big car. It swung five feet before hitting the bumper at 5 mph. Corner impacts at an angle were made at 3 mph.

On the 1979 models, the bumpers—front and rear—must prevent damage to any part of the vehicle in these tests, and for 1980, the bumper itself must be capable of withstanding the same impacts with no more than a $\frac{3}{4}$ inch flattening of the bumper face bar or a dent up to $\frac{5}{8}$ inch in depth.

The cost of safety Long before there was a fuel crisis, both the auto industry and the US government became concerned about the cost increases imputable to hardware designed to meet the safety standards. in 1971 President Nixon ordered the Office of Science and Technology to make a study of possible conflicts between regulatory action undertaken under authority of both the Clean Air Act and the Highway Safety Act, and the interests of the consumer.

This led to the RECAT report (Cumulative Regulatory Effects on the Cost of Automotive Transportation) which estimated that compliance with safety standards scheduled to go into effect in 1976 would add $755 per car, beyond safety features included on 1972 models. The administration began baulking the timetable for safety standards due to take effect, in the interest of the national economy. During the fuel crisis, the emphasis shifted to energy conservation, and the safety standards were proven to be the cause of substantial weight increases and a consequent loss of fuel economy.

Environmental Protection Agency administrator Russell E. Train said at the end of 1973: 'Studies have shown that every hundred pounds of car weight results in a fuel economy loss of one or two percent, and over the 12 model years from 1962 to 1973 the weight of most popular passenger cars has increased by about 800 pounds.'

Not all of this weight increase can be laid at the door of traffic safety legislation. Most of it was the result of a growth in car size, undertaken by the industry in what Detroit imagined was a response to the free market forces. But the safety standards played a prominent part.

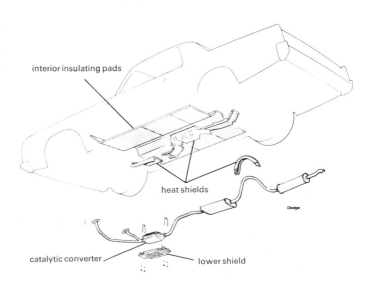

Above: the catalytic converter in the exhaust system.

The safety standards applicable to 1975 cars directly accounted for five to six percent of the total weight. The Chevrolet Vega weighed 2,400 pounds, with 133 pounds of safety equipment. The Pontiac Catalina weighed 4,400 pounds, with 223 pounds of safety equipment. Component changes undertaken to meet new safety and emission control standards between 1971 and 1975 added 243 pounds to the weight of the Ford Pinto. Because of these changes, the Pinto's fuel economy dropped 2.2 mpg (24.2 in 1971 to 22.0 in 1975, using the same test methods).

On a larger car, the penalty would be correspondingly heavier. Adding 1,000 pounds of safety equipment (with ancillary changes for their adaptation) to a 3,000-pound vehicle that normally had a fuel economy of 16 mpg would cause a 30 percent increase in fuel consumption, lowering the mileage to about 11 mpg.

According to General Motors, it would take an additional 600 to 1,000 pounds of energy absorbing material to provide occupant protection in a 45-50 mph impact, as foreseen in government standard proposals.

Given present technology, it is difficult to see how standards such as 215 and 208 can be met without adding a great deal of weight to the vehicle. There is a clear conflict between the pursuit of progress in traffic safety and the common energy-conservation objectives of the government and the public interest. Research programs that will help establish where compromises can or must be made are under way. The USA National Highway Traffic Safety Administration is sponsoring the construction of Research Safety Vehicles by three main contractors: Volkswagenwerk, Calspan (formerly Cornell Aeronautical Laboratory), and Minicars (a California corporation).

They are developing new technology, involving new uses and combinations of lightweight materials (flexible plastics and plastic foam). Tests will determine the advances made, and the findings will serve as guidelines for the formulation of future safety standards. It is also probable that future power systems will lead to standards for protective measures, according to fuel, energy storage and conversion processes. For instance, large-scale use of electric and hybrid-electric vehicles can be foreseen as leading to the adoption of a new set of safety standards for shock hazard, electrolyte spillage, battery explosion, violent battery movement, dangers due to slow acceleration, and uncontrolled energy release from flywheels or hydraulic storage systems.

Above: prototype electric city car, built in Japan.
Below: a new concept in public transport: the Steyr minibus.

The Car Factory: How Cars are Made

The production of cars is a process that takes many years and large amounts of money. Car makers employ thousands of people who do not actually put the cars together, from accountants and designers to the fellow who sweeps the floor in the factory. This chapter will attempt to describe some of the background to car production, with all its complexity.

Computers Computers play a role in car factories nowadays, as in almost everything else. The purchasing department is in charge of making sure that the glass, rubber, steel and everything else is on hand in the required quantities, and computers are used to keep track of it all. The computer schedules the construction of each car, and prints a sticker which goes on it, specifying trim, optional accessories, and even where the car is to be shipped when it is finished. There may be a computer terminal right on the assembly line.

Design The design of a new model begins years before any cars are actually built. Teams of draughtsmen must draw innumerable pictures of each part of the car, first for approval and then for the actual production. Production or engineering drawings must be done to scale and include all the dimensions of the finished parts.

Models are made of each part and especially of the body shell itself. This is partly to make sure that everything fits, as mistakes at this stage could be very expensive later on. Models of the car body, both to scale and full size, are used for example in wind tunnel tests: such important things as how rain water runs off the car in a high wind must be discovered long before any cars are built. The model making itself is a highly skilled and expensive business.

Design is complicated by several factors. Governments increasingly concern themselves with safety and air-pollution control; these regulations must be taken into account. A modern car engine, for example, may carry emmission control devices, as well as a compressor to operate the car's air conditioning; it can be a problem making sure that all this machinery fits in the engine compartment. In addition, car makers must concern themselves with the requirements of any foreign country where they hope to sell their product.

The concept of *ergonomics* is important in modern design. The word was coined in 1949 from Greek roots; it literally means combining work with natural laws. Centuries ago, when most people made their own tools, firearms, furniture and so forth, they designed these things so that they would be convenient and comfortable to use. Consequently the most practical design became a matter of tradition. A modern carpenter can look at ancient tools and tell immediately what they are. Nowadays, however, things are designed for us by other people, which means that designers have a profound effect on the quality of our lives.

Early cars were noisy, unreliable and subjected the driver and his passengers to a great deal of vibration and exposure to the elements. They were designed at the convenience of the builder; sometimes the brake lever was actually placed outside the driver's compartment, so that he had to reach out to set it. But early cars didn't go very fast, and there were not very many on the road. The car-owner's pleasure was partly derived from the novelty of it.

Ergonomics really got started during World War II. For example, men were flying at hundreds of miles an hour over long distances in circumstances of discomfort and extreme danger. Their seats had to be designed to provide as much comfort as possible in cramped circumstances; instruments had to be located so that they could be read at a glance, and so forth. In addition, the design of aircraft, ships and other weapons had to take into consideration ease of manufacture, availability of raw materials, and many other factors.

During the Second World War, the survival of a nation could depend upon the quality of its tools. Car design isn't quite that dramatic, but it has changed quite a bit since Henry Ford built his first gas buggy. A modern car is capable of moving under its own power at 100 mph or more; if the driver has to peek around the spokes of the steering wheel to find out how much fuel he has left, he might be in trouble before he looks back to the road again.

The designer must also consider the needs of his prospective customer. If the car is to be sold to a family, it must have storage space for luggage, baby bottles, dog baskets and all the other things a family might take along on holiday. A certain amount of owner maintenance must be provided for: the owner will be irritated if repairing burnt-out lights is too difficult. Another consideration is larger repairs; engine fitments must be replaceable by the dealer without the necessity for taking the engine out of the car. And finally the people on the assembly line have to be considered: when the car is being designed, the question of how it is to be assembled is already being examined.

Quality control Quality control in the factory begins with

Left: a computer terminal checking production at a Chrysler factory in Detroit. Mathematical techniques such as critical path analysis are used to speed up the production line.

Below: a hybrid computer system at British Ford. Computers are used to control stocks of materials, the flow of parts to the assembly lines, and much else. Next page: British Ford's Dunton drawing office. The production of a car starts on a drawing board.

specifications which fall into two categories. They may be official standards or legislation with respect to safety, pollution control and so forth, or they may be based on the standards of the manufacturer as embodied in product design, manufacturing techniques, testing procedures and cost analysis.

Some testing is done by subjecting the product to actual use. A machine part will be subjected to stress to see how much it will take before it wears or breaks; a car manufacturer will have a sample from the assembly line driven for thousands of miles on a rough test track, trying to duplicate years of ordinary wear in a few days. Then the car will be stripped by mechanics so that brakes, engine parts and so on can be examined. Most quality control, however, is part of the actual manufacturing process, and is also known as non-destructive testing (NDT).

Techniques range from the age-old ones using visual and tactile senses to the use of the most advanced modern instruments. For thousands of years craftsmen have visually inspected their work rejecting inferior materials and parts as they went along; today a painted piece of sheet metal is inspected visually for the quality of the finish, and the inspector will also slide his gloved hand across it, being able to feel ripples and bumps (in the sheet metal or in the paint) which are not immediately apparent visually.

Quality control is always moving towards objective, measurable standards rather than value judgements, and the technology of today demands the use of instruments. X-rays and gamma rays are widely used to determine the thickness of materials from paper to steel, of coatings such as zinc or tin on steel, and to measure the density of materials from slurries in pipes to bulk materials such as concrete. An important use of X-rays is to examine machine parts, castings and so forth for internal defects. The bonded surfaces of laminated products are inspected with sound; a device called an acoustic flaw detector is sensitive to the way the sound waves are reflected.

In the actual manufacturing process, quality control testing may be of single units, of batches, or of a continuous stream of units.

An example of single unit testing is the machining of a replacement part. The machine operator uses calipers, micrometers and other tools to check each stage of the work against the blueprint which tells him what is required. He

Above: model building is one of the important steps in car development which takes place long before actual production begins. Here British Ford technicians examine a mock-up Capri.

Models are built for a number of reasons, some of them full size and some smaller for such things as wind tunnel tests. The skills and costs involved in model building is one of the things which make new car development so terribly expensive, as well as time consuming.

Left: this set of pictures dramatically illustrate the factors involved in good design, which affect all manufactured goods, as well as motor vehicles. In the top picture, the tractor's controls are inconveniently placed, which results in stress and fatigue, to say nothing of the fact that the machine is not fully under control if it is moving while the controls are adjusted. By contrast, the combine harvester in the next picture is much better designed, with a comfortable seat, and controls that the driver can use without taking his eyes off the machinery. In the bottom picture, the fork truck has controls well placed, with diagrams on the tops of the knobs, so that even an illiterate driver can see what they are for. Visibility is as good as it can be on such a machine.

The micrometer is the most common of all precision measuring devices used in quality control.

Below, an inspector uses a three-to-four inch 'mike' to check the size of a piston for a diesel engine. At right is a cut-away diagram. The spindle has 40 threads to the inch (on an instrument which measures in inches) so that one turn moves the spindle exactly one-fortieth or 0.025 of an inch. The anvil and spindle face are ground parallel and lapped together to a tolerance of about three lightbands. (A lightband is the wavelength of sodium, a yellow colour: 0.000011 inch.) The machinist's micrometer at the bottom of the page, measuring zero to one inch, is open to .335 inch.

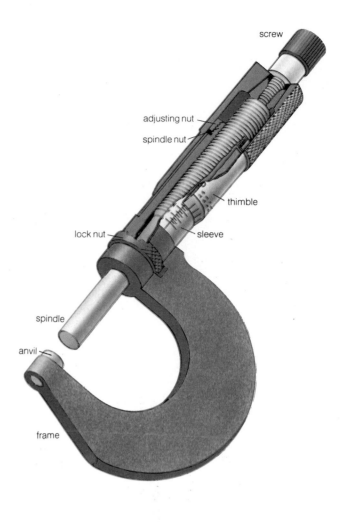

screw

adjusting nut

spindle nut

thimble

lock nut

sleeve

spindle

anvil

frame

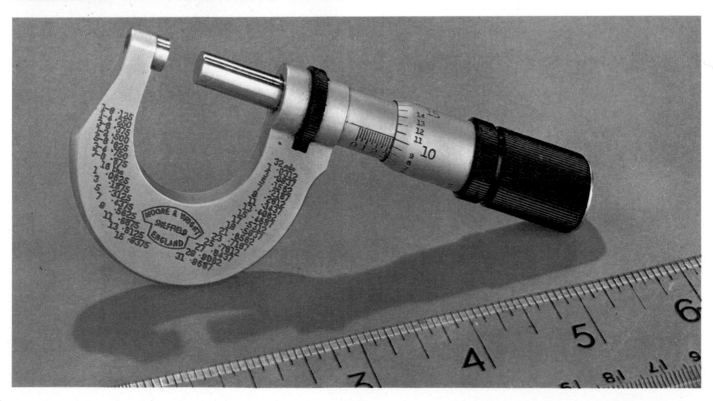

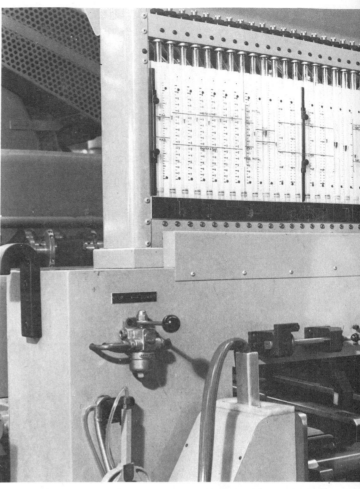

Above: electronic measurement of a machined surface. The output of a transducer varies according to the size of the piece in the guage, activating light-emitting diodes on the column. Similar devices use the resistance against compressed air to move an indicator on the column.

Above right: close control of machined surfaces of the Vauxhall Viva crankshaft is maintained by passing them through this master measuring machine on the production line.

Right: automatic guaging station for the Viva four-cylinder engine block. The block passes into the station and sensors are lowered into the bores, rotating slowly and checking bores at several points.

Far right: a British Leyland station for batch testing crankshaft measurements against master models.

does this not only to determine what remains to be done after each operation, such as how much metal remains to be removed after each cut on a motor shaft, but to prevent unnecessary work on a piece that has been spoiled by a mis-calculation.

In batch testing, the production machine operator may be provided with 'go/no-go' gauges, having holes or slots defining the tolerance of dimensions, to quickly test each piece as it comes out of the machine. An alternative procedure is patrol inspection, in which a mobile inspector is responsible for a number of workstations. He does not test all of the pieces in a batch, but uses a statistically controlled plan, based on the fact that measured quality is subject to variation as a result of random causes based on chance. Any deviation from the pattern of randomness expected can be detected by statistical techniques, using a chart with a curve which resembles a hospital patient's temperature chart. Simple random sampling techniques are also used, in accordance with statistical practice laid down in official schemes such as the British specification DEF-131-A ('Sampling Procedures and Tables for Inspection by Attributes') or the USA standard 414 ('Sampling Procedures for Inspection by Variables'). A sequential sampling and inspecting system has to satisfy a handicap of so many good articles before acceptance of a batch; a decision is reached regarding the disposition of a batch when the handicap is either reduced to zero or doubled.

An increasing amount of continuous testing uses an automatic closed-loop feedback control principle; the scanning of products by the previously mentioned ultrasonic and microwave techniques can be connected to the machinery, and automatic adjustments made to keep the measured quantity between tolerated limits. Such equipment is expensive to install; in the production of steel, for example, the scale of production justifies even small-scale improvements in overall efficiency. The thickness of sheet metal coming off the rolling machinery is monitored continuously by the absorption of X-rays or gamma rays in a radiation gauge and the mill rolls are adjusted automatically to keep the thickness within limits. Accuracies of about plus or minus $\frac{1}{2}\%$ can be achieved with error correction systems which compensate for variations in the output of the radiation source, the density and chemical composition of the steel, and so forth.

Besides the traditional measuring calipers, micrometers, and other mechanical inspection devices, there is a range of

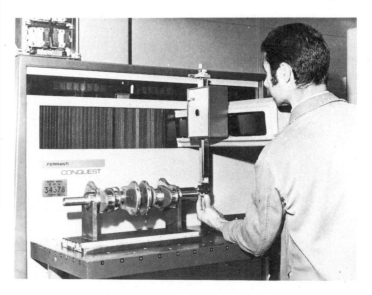

Above: machined castings and forgings are inspected for quality control on inspection tables with work surfaces which are extremely smooth and flat. Some such tables are made of marble slabs which are lapped against each other; the one in this picture is made of precision-ground cast steel. The article to be inspected is 'set up' on the table, and the various machined surfaces are compared with each other or with those on a master model, using precision instruments such as dial indicators, to see if they are within specified tolerances.

Above right: an MK III Cortina in British Ford's Dunton emission lab. Electronic instruments measure the amount of pollutants in the car's exhaust. The emission control devices must be efficient enough to confirm to the laws of any country where Ford hopes to sell the car.

Left: at the Mercedes-Benz plant near Stuttgart, two complete cars and two raw body shells are taken from the production lines each day for measuring on a huge 'micrometer'.

Right: at British Ford's Dagenham plant, every part of the car's electrical system is checked and the results registered by a computer.

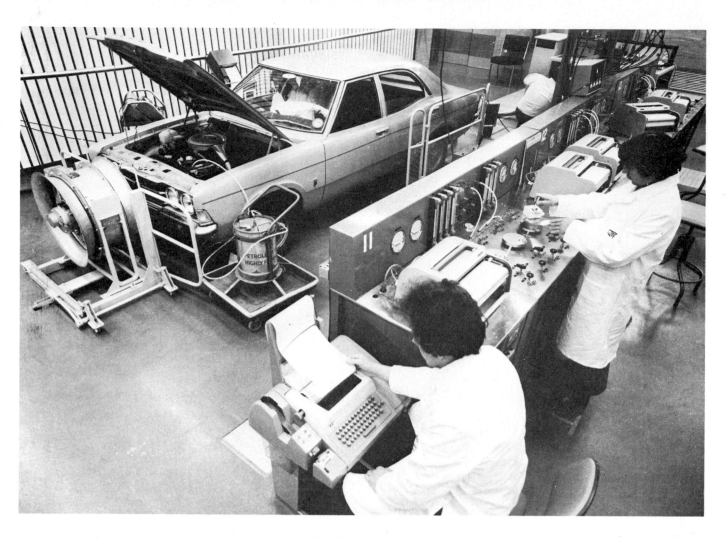

LUGGAGE COMP LIGHT   HAZARD WARNING   HEATER 1 SPEED
BONNET LIGHT   SIDE LIGHTS   HEATER 2 SPEED
LOWER BONNET   FOG LIGHT   REVERSING LIGHT
ALL SWITCHES OFF   IGNITION ON   HEATED BACKLIGHT
CIGAR LIGHTER
GLOVE BOX   HEADLIGHTS-MAIN BEAM   START
PARK LIGHT LEFT   HEADLIGHTS DIPPED
PARK LIGHT RIGHT   HEADLIGHTS-FLASHER   REV ENGINE
RADIO   HORN
INTERIOR LIGHT   LEFT TURN INDICATOR   END OF TEST
ADDITIONAL INTERIOR   RIGHT TURN INDICATOR
LEFT DOOR FRONT   BRAKE LIGHT   PROGRAM READY
LEFT DOOR REAR   HANDBRAKE WARNING   READ IN CARD
RIGHT DOOR FRONT   WIPER-FOOT SWITCH   FAILED
RIGHT DOOR REAR   WIPER 1 SPEED
MAP READ LIGHT   WIPER 2 SPEED

Above: a Ford Granada undergoing noise tests in an anechoic chamber, which absorbs sound, making possible testing under controlled circumstances.

devices which is becoming more complex.

Quality control potentiometers are employed to indicate variations in material composition and heat-treatment of ferrous metals, using the principle of variation of magnetic properties.

Microjets and an ultra-high-magnification pneumatic gauging unit are employed in the control of roller bearing manufacture to detect roundness errors of as small as 0.0001 mm, about 1/600 of the thickness of a human hair.

Profile projectors, or shadowgraphs, can nowadays be mounted directly on production machinery so that work in progress may be observed to an accuracy of 0.0025 mm (0.0635 inch) and recorded on Polaroid film.

The previously mentioned industrial X-ray units operating at 320 kV and 14 mA with a focal spot of 3.6 mm × 3.6 mm (0.14 in × 0.14 in) and a penetrating power of 10 cm (about 4 inches) of steel are used in the non-destructive testing of welds, sheet, plate, tubing, casting and forging. The spectroscope finds application in the analysis of steels and nonferrous metals in steel mills and scrap yards.

Steel, the Press Room and the Car Body

The steel industry is one of the effective barometers of the economy. If orders for steel are falling off, it's a sure sign that the economy is in trouble. The car industry is one of the biggest users of steel, and the largest car companies may make their own steel, as well as glass and other materials.

Steel is difficult to define because it can be made in many different varieties, each with its own particular characteristics. It can be defined broadly, however, as an alloy of iron and carbon, the carbon content being not more than 1.7% and usually only about 0.2 to 0.3%. The carbon means that the steel can be hardened. Other elements can be added to produce specific properties such as ease of machining, toughness, or the ability to resist wear or attack by heat, corrosion or chemicals.

Steel is made from cast iron, which contains up to 3 or 4% of carbon and much smaller percentages of other elements, especially sulphur, phosphorus, silicon and

Below left: the doors of an open-hearth furnace. The shallow furnace hearth is charged with scrap and limestone, then molten iron, then the flames from a gas or oil burner are blown over the surface of the charge. Oxygen is blown in by a water cooled lance to speed the process.

Below centre: the top of a basic oxygen converter. This process evolved from the Bessemer process, and it uses a water cooled lance to blow oxygen on to the surface of the metal, instead of blowing air up through it. This is now the major method of steelmaking.

Below right: an electric arc furnace. The furnace is charged with cold scrap metal and fluxes, then the roof is closed and the three electrodes are lowered. The power is turned on and an arc is created which produces the intense heat needed to make the steel.

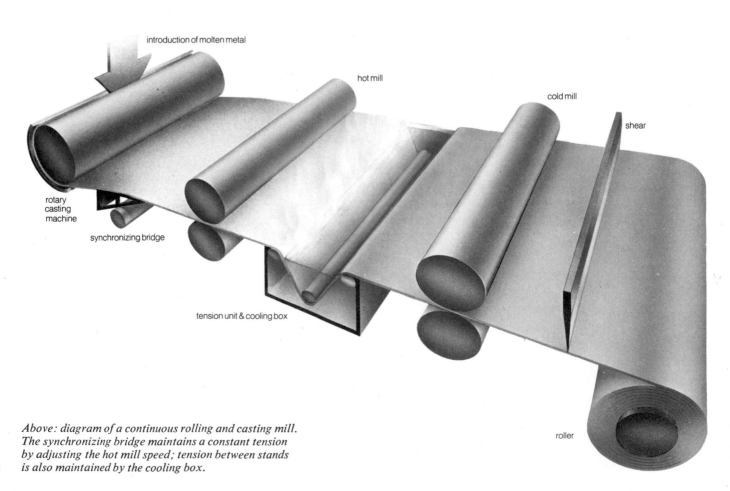

introduction of molten metal

hot mill

cold mill

shear

rotary
casting
machine

synchronizing bridge

tension unit & cooling box

roller

Above: diagram of a continuous rolling and casting mill.
The synchronizing bridge maintains a constant tension
by adjusting the hot mill speed; tension between stands
is also maintained by the cooling box.

142

Left: a section mill at Lockerbie in Scotland, producing I-beam girders. A variety of complex shapes can be rolled, including seamless tubing, but not shapes with re-entrant angles.

Right: a model of a cold strip mill with hydraulic loading and guage control. One way of reducing the rolling forces involved in metal rolling is to use rolls of smaller diameter, which reduces the contact surface, giving an increase in applied pressure.

manganese. Carbon is not wanted in steel in anything like this amount, so a major function of the steelmaking process is to reduce the carbon content to the percentage required. In practice this is done by removing the carbon completely and adding the exact amount needed when the steel is molten. The other elements are not usually required in the steel but they can be controlled to some extent during the ironmaking process. Such small amounts as remain can be removed by the addition of fluxes, such as limestone, while the steel is being made.

To remove the carbon, a simple chemical reaction is used. if molten cast iron is brought into contact with oxygen, the carbon and the oxygen unite as carbon monoxide gas, which passes out of the metal.

Casting   Casting is a process in which a molten metal is poured into a mould and allowed to solidify so as to take the shape of the cavity within the mould. The commercial production of high quality, often intricately shaped castings required by industry, such as components for pumps and engine blocks, demands expertise of a high order. Cast products that are not intended to be greatly altered in shape by any later process are known as castings, and they also may be produced from metal moulds, although other mould materials based on, for example, sand, refractory (able to withstand high temperatures) cements or ceramics are probably more important. Castings are generally named according to the mould material or casting process used, for example a sand casting is made in a compacted sand mould, and a centrifugal casting is produced in a rotating mould.

Apart from semi-permanent ceramic or graphite moulds which may be used several times, moulds made from non-metallic materials are destroyed when the casting is removed, so a new mould must be made for each casting operation. It is therefore necessary to use a pattern to make the mould cavity. The pattern is not usually an exact replica of the desired casting because it must incorporate various devices to facilitate the manufacturing process. Pattern-making is a highly skilled trade.

Casting is a versatile metal shaping process because it enables intricate three-dimensional shapes to be made in one operation. The more complex the shape, however, the more difficult it is to produce the mould; one of the problems that has to be dealt with is the presence of *undercuts*. An undercut is a re-entrant hollow or region that projects in relief, which, if no provision were made, would prevent the pattern from being withdrawn from the mould. There are several ways of dealing with this problem—by using an expendable pattern for example—but the result is always a more complicated process and greater expense, so the design of

castings has to take account of the manufacturing process to be employed.

Sandcasting is the most versatile of the casting processes: it may be used to produce castings in almost all materials in sizes varying from a few grammes to several hundred tons.

The pattern, made of wood or metal, is placed in a box and the moulding sand is compacted around it either by hand or, more commonly these days, by machine. The pattern is then withdrawn to leave a cavity of the required shape. To facilitate withdrawal the pattern must be tapered and its dimensions must allow for contraction when the metal cools. The simplest type of mould has an open top but more generally the cavity is completely enclosed by sand (apart, of course, from the small openings through which the molten metal flows into the cavity): the mould must therefore be made in two or more parts which are separated to enable the pattern to be withdrawn.

Investment casting is an important method of producing very precise shapes, generally in jointless moulds, by the use of an expendable pattern. It is also known as the *cire perdue*, or lost wax, process and was first used by the early Egyptians. It is widely used by artists today to manufacture metal sculpture and statuary. The Flying Silver Lady mascot adorning the Rolls Royce car is cast by this technique. In industry it is used for the manufacture of precision parts in all branches of engineering, including the gas turbine and aerospace fields.

The expendable patterns are commonly made of wax or plastic by injection into a master die and are removed when solid; frozen mercury may be used in the same way. Precision castings are often quite small so several patterns may be attached to a common runner to make an assembly

Above: a selection of items which can be diecast using low pressure methods, including car wheels, casings for pumps and gearboxes, and many consumer goods.

Left: a plate mill, showing the rotary shears and the control room mounted over the production line. In this instance, the plate being fed to the shears is in the cold finished state.

Below: centrifugal casting is a modern method of making hollow cylindrical shapes. The mould is being rotated rapidly and centrifugal force distributes the metal evenly until it solidifies.

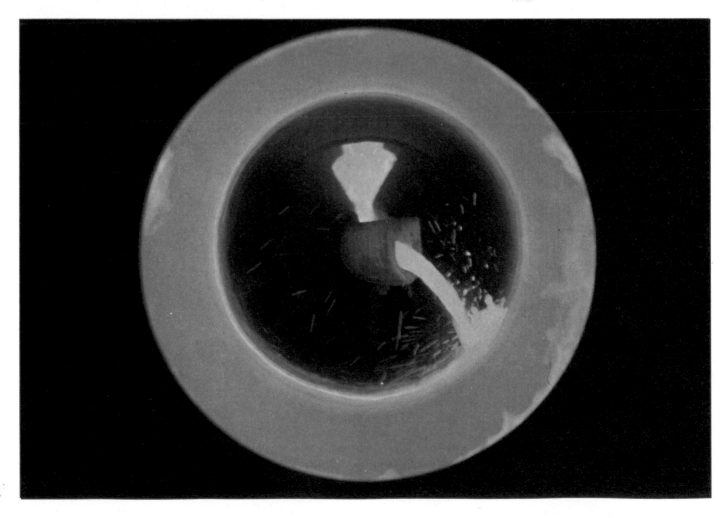

known as a 'tree'. This is then dipped into a refractory slurry of very fine silica and ethyl silicate to form a precoat which may then be thickened by the addition of sand and a binder in a fluidized bed (ceramic shell process). Alternatively, it may be directly invested into a suitable sand by inserting it into a container and surrounding it with the moulding mixture (block mould process). The pattern is melted out during firing of the mould which is then ready for casting. For high precision, investment casting is rivalled only by pressure diecasting. The surface finish is excellent and final machining almost unnecessary; there is a virtually complete freedom of component design.

Permanent moulds are used for diecasting, the molten metal being simply poured into the mould, in which case the process is known as permanent mould casting in the USA, and gravity diecasting in Britain. The metal can also be injected into the mould under pressure, in which case it is known as pressure diecasting. Many aluminium, zinc and magnesium alloy components are made by diecasting.

Gravity diecasting is used for producing large numbers of fairly small simple castings and in principle is similar to sand casting. It is not suitable for castings of very complex shape because, being hand-operated, the withdrawal of large numbers of metal cores is beyond the capacity of the operator. In contrast, pressure diecasting is used for the production of highly intricate, thin section castings, such as automobile carburettors and mechanical parts for consumer durables.

Casting is naturally dependent on the melting point of the metal and the higher this becomes the greater the problems. For example the melting points of lead and tin, 327°C and 232°C respectively, are so low that these metals can be melted easily over a simple gas ring. At the other extreme, the refractory metals such as niobium and tantalum, with melting points in excess of 2000°C, are so difficult to melt that shaped parts are normally produced the powder metallurgy way, which does not involve melting at all. Instead, the powdered metal is poured into a die and compressed at a high temperature (but below its melting point) which causes the grains of metal to bind together. Sometimes the heating process is carried out separately. In the intermediate range, the temperature required to melt bronze (about 950°C) is low enough for casting to have been practiced from very early times, unlike castings made from iron, which has a melting point of 1539°C, beyond the reach of most primitive peoples.

Forging Forging is the shaping of metal objects by means of hammers or presses. The metal to be forged has been heated to a temperature at which it attains a plastic state; that is, a state in which the metal can be shaped by hammering it. The blacksmith, who heated and bent a bar of metal and shaped it into a horseshoe by beating it with his hammer on an anvil, called his furnace and then his shop a forge. In modern industrial plants, the blacksmith's forge has been replaced by more efficient furnaces, and his hammer has been replaced by machines capable of exerting many tons of pressure.

The advantage of forging over other ways of shaping metal is that the grain pattern and therefore the strength of the metal is rearranged in the direction appropriate to the withstanding of stresses by the finished product. Gear blanks, connecting rods and other forged parts are therefore stronger than they would be if they were machined from cold stock.

There are several types of forging processes, according to the type of object to be forged. Drop forging includes hammer and die forging, and other methods are called press forging, a slow squeeze; upset forging, for shapes like the heads on bolts and screws; and roll forging, for cylindrical shapes.

Hammer forging is the method most directly analogous to the blacksmith's shop. The process is used for forging relatively flat, simple shapes, which must sometimes be machined by conventional methods to their final dimensions. Only flat dies are used. The anvil is the lower part of the machine on which the piece to be forged is placed; the hammer or ram is raised and dropped between vertical guides by steam, air or mechanical methods. Steam or pneumatic installations can be designed so that the steam or air can be diverted and used as a cushion to control the force of the blow. The size of the hammer is about 50 lb per cross sectional inch (3.5 kg/cm²); the total weight of the hammer can be from 200 lb (91 kg) to 50 tons.

The largest of these machines must have strong foundations, sometimes separate from the rest of the machine. Sometimes the foundation is built in an excavation in the ground; some excavations have been made all the way down to bedrock. At the other end of the scale, the smaller machines may be fitted with springs to make the blow 'elastic'.

Die forging is similar to hammer forging except that the hot billet is shaped by dies as it is struck. The machinery is therefore necessarily more precise; for example, means must be provided for adjustment of the guides to compensate for wear in order to ensure the accurate meeting of upper and lower dies.

The dies are blocks of alloy steel which are machined square. The shape of the object to be forged is laid out on the die faces and the impressions are carefully machined. The dies are heat-treated for a combination of hardness and long wear and finished to size by grinding and polishing. A single die may include several areas for working of the piece: a swedger or edger for the breakdown, or preliminary shaping; a blocker for developing the shape; and a finisher for final shaping, which includes a gutter for accommodation of flash or excess metal, which may be trimmed off while the piece is still hot or later after it cools. The die may also have a relief cut on the edge for accommodation of tongs so that the operator can hold the piece while it is being forged and move it from one area of the die to another between blows.

A great range of objects can be drop forged, weighing from several grammes to several tons. Almost any object can be die forged as long as it can be removed from the die. One of the most common forged parts is the connecting rod for car engines. This part takes a lot of stress in the operation of the engine; hot forging it means that the particular arrangement of the metal will result in the greatest possible endurance of these stresses.

In drop forging the machine is operated by means of push buttons or a foot treadle. The operator (or *hammersmith*) is responsible for controlling the number of blows as well as their force in order to shape the piece with the least possible amount of wear on the dies. The blank or billet must be of exactly the right size and shape for efficient forming while avoiding undue work for the machine, and must be heated to the correct state of plasticity (above 920°C for steel alloys). Forging machines for smaller parts in mass production operations can make as many as 300 blows a minute; the pressure of the blow in drop forging can be from 500 to 50,000 pounds per square inch.

Left: one stand in a six-stand finishing mill. Each stand consists of a set of rollers and all the stands together are called a 'mill train'.

Right: a forged crankshaft being removed from the dies. Note the exposed upper die. Any object can be forged so long as its shape allows it to be removed from the die.

Below: the continuous casting of steel is one of the newer techniques. The steel strip emerges endlessly from a vertical moulding tank and is carried to the horizontal while still soft to be cut into lengths.

Rolling steel Rolling is possibly the most important of the major mechanical working processes. In principle it is exceedingly simple: a pair of cylindrical rollers made of iron or steel rotate in opposite directions with a gap between them which is smaller than the cross-section of the piece which is to be rolled. The workpiece is entered into the gap and as it passes between the rolls it is squeezed, its cross-section being progressively reduced. Since the working volume remains constant, the result of one pass through the rolls is a lengthening of the workpiece and a precise reduction and shaping of the cross-section. The reduction accomplished in one pass is commonly within the range 10 to 30%, so a great many passes are normally required.

Despite its basic simplicity, the modern rolling mill with all its control gear and equipment for manipulating the stock is an immensely complex piece of engineering. The forces involved are enormous. As the workpiece passes through the roll-gap it exerts forces on the rolls which causes them to bend and spring apart: in a large mill these forces could easily attain several hundred tons. The rolls must therefore be mounted in massive steel housings capable of minimizing the deflections that necessarily occur (excessive deflections would, of course, spoil the shape and dimensions of the emergent workpiece).

A set of rolls mounted in a pair of housings is called a stand. Single-stand mills are common but quite often two or more stands are used together to make a mill train. Several arrangements are possible: for example, a looping train has several stands placed side by side with adjacent stands necessarily operating in different directions, whereas a tandem train has two or more stands following each other in a straight line. Often, all the stands in a train operate simultaneously on the same workpiece. Powerful electric motors are used to drive the rolls and, in some types of mill, must be capable of periodical reversal to change the direction of rotation of the rolls.

All rolls are based on a cylindrical shape but the exact form depends upon the nature of the product. There are three main classes of product: first, rods and bars and sections of more complex shape such as rails, angles, channels and so on; second, flat products, such as plate, sheet and strip, and third, hollow shells for working into seamless tubes.

For rolling plates, sheet and strip, each roll amounts to a plain cylinder (the diameter is often increased slightly at the centre to compensate for roll bending) and different reductions are accomplished by varying the separation of the rolls. Products vary from plates as thick as 300 mm (approximately one foot), for use in heavy engineering, to strip only a few microns thick (1 micron is 0.0000393 inch), for the electronics industry. In terms of productivity, the most highly developed example of flat rolling is the continuous production, in mult-stand tandem mills, of the steel base for tinplate.

The metal may emerge from the final stand at speeds exceeding 60 mph (96 km/h) therefore the engineering of ancillary equipment such as coilers and flying shears represents a considerable achievement. The forces sustained by the rolling mill can be reduced if the rolls are made smaller in diameter. Unfortunately, this also makes them weaker for the same width of product, so to prevent excessive deflections and possible breakage they must be supported by relatively massive back-up rolls. A mill with a single pair of rolls is known as a '2-high' mill and is most likely to be employed in the early stages of reduction. A '4-high' mill has one pair of work rolls and one pair of backing rolls. Mills with six or more rolls are termed cluster mills and are used for the production of very thin strip in hard materials. For example, one mill used in the United States for producing computer tape in alloy steel to thicknesses as little as two or three microns has a total of 20 rolls, and the work rolls are no larger than knitting needles.

Rolling may be carried out either hot or cold. Some products are never cold-rolled at all, but it is rare for rolled products not to be hot-rolled, at least in the early stages, and black bar, for example, may be sold in the as-hot-rolled condition. Hot rolling is employed because it is the most effective method for breaking down the as-cast structure of the ingot—rolling forces are smaller and certain casting defects are more easily eliminated when the metal is hot. Hot rolling is carried out at temperatures above $0.7T_m$ (where T_m is the melting point of the metal concerned on the Kelvin scale), that is, at about 1000°C for mild steel and 450°C for aluminium. Cold rolling is carried out at room temperature and has the effect of hardening the metal, which must therefore be periodically softened by heat treatment (annealing). Some sheet or strip may be sold in the annealed condition or strengthened by the hardening produced in the final rolling operation.

The sheet metal produced in the rolling process then goes to the press room.

The presses The power press is also used in minting coins, making gramophone records and many other industrial processes. The press has tools called dies installed in it, the material to be shaped is placed in the machine between the dies, and the machine closes, forming the material.

In many cases the press is powered by hydraulic cylinders or by steam pressure. For ordinary sheet metal forming, however, the machine is often a simple mechanical press.

The lower part of the press is a table called the bolster plate, on which the lower die, or female, is installed. The upper part of the machine, which goes up and down between

Above: diemakers finishing a 25-ton die for drawing floor pans for cars. Final grinding and polishing are done after some test pieces have been drawn.

Below left: Volkswagon roofs being finished in a Brazilian plant. Tiny dents and dimples must be removed using polishing wheels; the work is hot and dirty.

guides installed in the frame, is called the ram. The punch or male die is installed on the ram. In a mechanical press, the ram is connected by means of one or more connecting rods to a crankshaft, which turns in bearings installed, like the guides, in the frame of the machine, one on each side. On the side of the machine a clutch, a brake and a flywheel are connected to the end of the crankshaft. An electric motor drives the flywheel, either by means of several rubber V-belts running in grooves around its perimeter, or by means of gear teeth, in which case the flywheel is in effect a large gear, with teeth around its perimeter. When the operators push all the buttons, the clutch is activated, the crankshaft makes one revolution, and the ram makes one trip down toward the bolster plate and back up again. The upper die strikes the piece of metal placed on the lower die, forming it by means of the pressure or impact. The pressure provided by the various types of presses varies from less than one ton to more than 5000 tons. (Some hydraulic forging presses have up to 50,000 tons capacity.)

Some presses have a geared flywheel on each side, and intermediate geared shafts, pulleys or gearwheels between the motor and the flywheel. There are also presses with eccentric shafts instead of crankshafts; an offset section of the shaft functions like a cam. Some presses have large gearwheels enclosed in the top of the machine which are not flywheels but are connected to the top of the ram by means of rods attached to eccentric pivots.

Cutting out a shape from a piece of sheet metal upon which other operations are then performed is called *blanking*. Punching a hole in the metal is called *piercing* or *punching*. Certain presses whose only function is to cut sheet metal with long horizontal blades instead of dies are called *shears*.

Often more than one function is carried out simultaneously during one stroke of the machine; in the forming of a car door, for example, the door may be formed between the dies, blanked out so that a narrow strip of scrap is separated from the perimeter of the door, and a hole punched out for the door handle. This is accomplished in a double-acting or triple-acting press; the double-acting press has one ram inside the other, and the triple-acting press has an additional ram below which comes up instead of down. The upper, outside ram is operated by means of a lever or toggle instead of by the crankshaft; such a machine is sometimes called a toggle press.

Below centre: floor pans are clamped in jigs with other parts at the beginning of the spotwelding sequence which results in a car body made entirely of sheet metal.

Below: the press room in a car factory. The presses may be making separate parts or performing various functions on the same part, connected by conveyers.

Above: the inside door panel removed from the press at British Ford's Dagenham plant by a suction device. It will be placed inside an outer panel, the edges of which will be crimped around it by another press.

Presses which make large sheet metal parts, such as for cars, are called straight-sided presses and are as large as small houses. They are constructed simply by stacking one part of the machine on top of another, and held together by huge vertical bolts which, at the lower end, may extend through the floor with the nut tightened on from underneath. Installing the dies in such machines requires large purpose-built fork lift trucks and electric travelling overhead cranes. For these reasons, the press room in a large factory is often specially constructed.

By contrast, the open-back inclinable is a common type of press for the manufacture of smaller parts. Its frame is in the shape of a letter C and is open at the back so that the finished pieces or the scrap may be ejected through it and into storage tubs, often by means of compressed air. It can be inclined on its base for convenience of operation. Such a machine may be only about eight feet (about 2.4 metres) high and four feet (1.2 m) wide. For extremely fast production of small parts such as washers, a dieing press may be used; the punch is pulled down rather than pushed, and it may make several hundred strokes a minute, with mechanical attachments feeding a strip of sheet metal past the lower die.

Large presses are often automated nowadays. A common form of automation in the production of large sheet metal parts comprises conveyers made of wide rubber belts operated by electric motors and long steel arms with suction cups on the ends which reach into the press and remove the blanked piece, dropping it on the conveyer which takes it to the next operation. The reaching arms travel on a rack-and-gear device which is operated by electrical limit switches; the suction cups can be aided by pneumatic cylinders.

The installation of dies in presses can be a complicated operation taking several working shifts to accomplish. Shims (spacers) can be installed behind the dies, and the connecting rods are made of two or more threaded parts so that they are adjustable for length. The clearance between the dies is carefully calculated; a mistake of a fraction of an inch in the wrong direction will result in serious, expensive damage, such as a broken crankshaft or damage to the dies. Springs and pneumatic cushions are used behind dies and parts of dies to adjust the amount of impact during operation of the press.

Safety in the press room is of great importance. The operators of large presses must have both hands on control buttons before the machine will operate, to prevent careless hands from being crushed when the ram comes down. On smaller presses, the operator may have a tough leather strap or wire cable attached to his gloves; the other end of the strap is connected, through tubing, to the top of the ram, so that if the operator is careless his fingers are jerked away from the danger area by the operation of the machine. Smaller automated presses have guards which can be raised and lowered, and must be in the down position before the machine will operate.

Maintenance of the presses is important for safety as well as other reasons. The clutch and the brake must be properly adjusted so that the stroke of the ram begins and ends in the right position. Pound for pound, other machine tools can cost more than a press, which is a less complicated machine, but an accident with a press can be more expensive, because a damaged die or a broken crankshaft costs far more to repair or replace than a broken tool in a lathe or a milling machine. It is also interesting to note that whereas the load on a machine tool is usually continuous, the load on the bearings on a press crankshaft is concentrated at one point in its revolution, namely the point at which the ram is making contact with the lower die. For these reasons the inspection, adjustment and proper lubrication of the press is quite important, especially since a great deal of machine failure is due to improper or inadequate lubrication to begin with.

The blade on a continuously operated shear must be lubricated about once an hour by means of painting it with a soap solution. Otherwise the blade quickly becomes dull, meaning more work for the machine and jagged edges on the sheet metal being cut, increasing the chances of injury to the hands of the people handling the stock.

Dies are made of expensive, high-quality steel blocks. A large die may be cast to the approximate pattern required before being finished; when the die cavity extends all the way through the block it may be roughed out by a flame-cutting process or on a jig saw.

After the block has been roughed out, most diesinking is done on automatic machinery. End mill cutters of appropriate profile are used in vertical milling machines, with the die block bolted to the table. A pantograph may be used to follow a pattern made of plastic or sheet metal. A tracer attachment to the milling machine may follow, by means of a stylus, a model of the die made of wood or some other soft material. The surface of the die is finished to size and to a high degree of polish by means of hand scrapers, grinding wheels, polishing cloth and similar tools. Die hobbing is the use of a hardened and polished male plug, pushing it into a soft steel block by means of hydraulic pressure. Dies produced in this way are for limited production of simple parts, or for production in soft materials such as plastic.

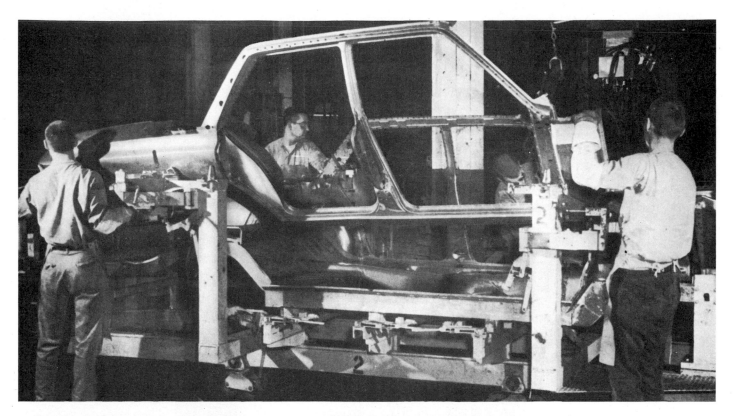

American Motors, smallest of the four US car companies, has been building smaller, less expensive cars than its competitors for many years. The company was also the first to mass-produce cars using the unit-body principle. This picture was taken during the winter of 1962-63, when the Rambler was Motor Trend magazine's 'car of the year'. The 'Uniside' spotwelded sub-assembly is being fitted into the framing buck, near the beginning of the body line.

Left: in spot welding, a metal seam is clamped between electrodes. The electrical resistance is least in the area under pressure, so that most of the current is confined to the area of the electrodes. For sheet metal this is the fastest and most economical method of fastening where mechanical strength is the only consideration. The strength depends on the number of spots.

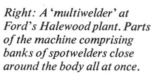

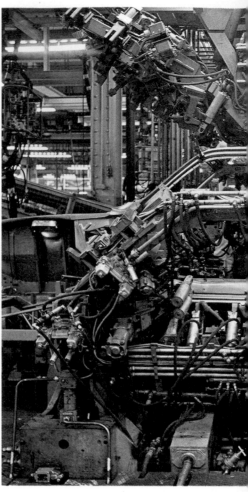

Above: a framing buck at British Ford's Dagenham plant. The parts are all held in place by clamps while spotwelding takes place.

Right: A 'multiwelder' at Ford's Halewood plant. Parts of the machine comprising banks of spotwelders close around the body all at once.

Sheet metal parts for cars are complicated to produce nowadays because designers want the finished product to have a 'sculptured' look. This often means that a single piece of metal must be bent or stretched in several directions, and that the forming must be done in several steps. The quality and composition of the metal and the degree of forming which can take place at each step is carefully calculated; the sharper the bend in the finished piece, the less bending can be done at each step. The clearance between a punch and a die, or the rake on the working edges of a blanking die, is also calculated. The thinner the sheet, the less clearance is necessary. The size of the clearance affects the smoothness of the fracture when piercing metal; with less clearance the fracture will be neater but more pressure is required from the machine.

Nearly all sheet metal forming requires lubrication, so that the parts do not stick to the dies and so that the dies last longer. A wide range of soaps, oils and other materials are used, depending on the material being formed and the speed of production. Lard or sperm whale oil is used for punching copper, iron or steel. For drawing brass or copper sheet, soap dissolved in hot water is applied. Paraffin [kerosene] can be used on aluminium; aluminium can never be formed without some kind of lubrication, but on the other hand metals with a 'greasy' composition, such as tinplate, can be worked with no lubrication at all. Lubrication is applied automatically by felt rollers or manually by pads, brushes or rags. Sheet metal parts must usually be washed before they can be painted or finished.

The body division The large sheet metal parts of the cars, such as the roof, door panels, floor pan and so forth, now go to the body division on conveyers, which are usually hooks connected to chains which are pulled along the ceiling by electric motors. (There are many miles of such conveyers in car factories, and they carry everything from sheet metal parts to engines to the cars themselves on the assembly line.)

In the body division, sub-assemblies of the floor and the sides of the car are made by placing the sheet metal parts in *framing bucks*, where they are held in place by clamps while they are spot-welded together. Spot-welding is a resistance welding process. The welding instrument looks like a large G-clamp with copper tips; it is water-cooled inside. When the operator presses the button, the clamp closes and a surge of electrically produced heat flows through the two layers of sheet metal, welding them together. A finished car will have thousands of spot-welds in it. Sparks fly in every direction; safety goggles are absolutely necessary. People who do such work learn not to carry matches in their shirt pockets.

The sub-assemblies are then installed in a larger framing device with clamps sticking out all over it. These framing bucks are then pulled by a conveyer down the first of the assembly lines, called the body line. The roof and the rear wings [called fenders in the USA] are all spot-welded onto the car, along with various framing parts. The front fenders are often screwed on for ease of replacement in case of damage. Sometimes the sub-assemblies of the doors, the bonnet [hood] and boot-lid [trunk-lid] are also added at this point; or sometimes they are painted separately and added later.

Above: not all the welding is spotwelding. On this Chevrolet Camaro a console support is welded into place with an electric arc.

Below: a completely automated assembly line at a Fiat plant in Turin. There are 18 of the robot welders, which can do 500 welds without supervision.

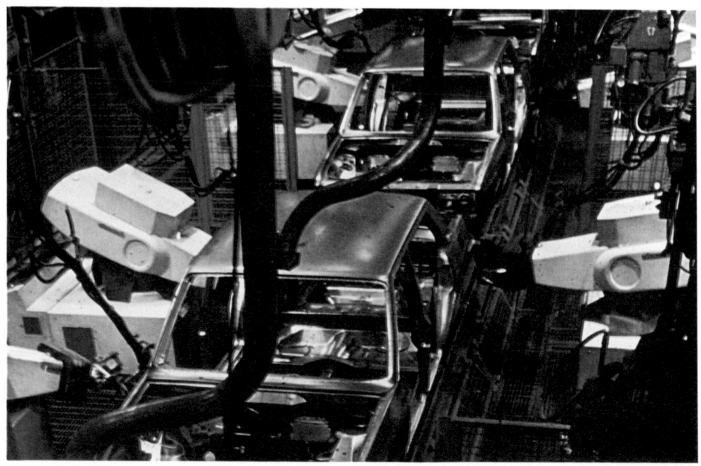

The car as described is of *unit body* construction. Nowadays most cars are built this way, but a few cars (and all cars in former times) have separate frames, made of heavier steel, to which the completed car body is bolted, using rubber grommets to prevent squeaking in the finished product.

When the body is complete it goes into a tank full of special paint which rust-proofs it. The paint is sometimes applied electrostatically; that is, the tank contains paint and water, and the steel is electrically charged so that the particles of paint are attracted to it.

When the rust-proofing primer is dry, the car is spray-painted in the specified colour. The various coats of paint are often dried by passing the body through a drying oven, but a recent development is radiation curing, in which a specially formulated paint is 'set' almost instantly by infra-red or ultra-violet radiation.

Above left: Pontiac bodies being inspected for paint quality between baking operations, at a Fisher Body Plant in Pontiac, Michigan.

Left: this body shell is immersed in water containing an anti-rust paint, after a phosphate treatment to clean it. The body is connected to a positive terminal and the walls of the tank to a negative terminal, creating a magnetic field, so that the particles of paint are attracted to all parts of the body, depositing a uniformly thick layer of paint.

Below: spraying a Ford with acrylic enamel paint.

Metalworking in the Car Factory

The machine tools which perform all the drilling and shaping operations on engine blocks, crankshafts and so forth have not changed in their basic principles since they were defined by the brilliant engineering of Henry Maudslay (1771-1831) in England. Their versatility, however, has made enormous strides since then. The principles of machines being used to repair other machines and to make new machines goes to the heart of modern industrial technology, and the machine tool industry of today is an even more fundamental barometer of the economy than steel: the orders for machine tools fall off several years before the economy itself actually suffers, and indicates a lack of will on the part of industry to invest in new equipment.

Ordinary machine tools such as Maudslay built in his workshop, but larger and more sophisticated, are used in the maintenance division of the car factory to repair the production machinery.

The maintenance division The machinery which makes the parts of the car must be maintained and repaired when it breaks down. In addition there is a lot of work to be done on the electric wiring, the plumbing and the heating in the kinds of buildings large enough to house car factories.

These tasks are the job of the maintenance division.

The toolmakers are the highly skilled people who make jigs and fixtures for the assembly lines, and the dies which stamp out the sheet metal parts for the cars. In many car factories, the machine repairmen will work out of the same area and belong to the same union as the toolmakers, because they have many of the same skills.

When a production machine breaks down or needs adjustment, the foreman in that part of the plant reports it to the maintenance division. If the adjustment is routine, it may be done on a late shift or a weekend when the machine is not in use. If this is the case, the foreman sends a complaint slip to the person in charge of scheduling the work; the foreman may be able to say what's wrong with the machine, or he may not know. In that case someone is usually sent to find out what needs to be done. Depending on the problem, it may be necessary to have electricians and other skilled men on the scene as well.

If the machine is vital and the breakdown threatens to stop production, a repairman dismantles it immediately if necessary. He has a padlock which he uses to 'lock out' the switchbox so that no one can accidentally start up the

155

machine while he works on it.

He may be able to perform an adjustment or a makeshift repair which keeps the machine running; here the question of safety is important, and also the danger of further damage to the machine. Some spare parts are kept on hand for the production machinery, but often the repairman will have to make a new part himself, to replace something which is broken or worn out. In this case, he goes to a 'cut-off' room and obtains a piece of metal cut off to the right length. He has to know which type of metal he needs; there will be several different kinds of steel alone to choose from, depending on the service required of the new part, whether or not it will be heat-treated, and so forth.

Suppose the repairman has to make a new rotor shaft for an electric motor. He will require a piece of cold-rolled steel, perhaps three inches (about 7.5 cm) in diameter and twelve inches (30 cm) long. He puts it in a lathe and 'faces

Above right: a selection of chucks. Top left: a four-jawed chuck with reversible jaws; top right and lower right: self-centering three-jawed chucks with interchangeable jaws, for internal or external gripping; lower left: a drill chuck with a Morse tapered shank, often used in the tailstock.
All jaws are hardened.
Right: the back end of the headstock with cover removed.
Below: the lathe, with diagrams of cutting operations. The blue arrow shows direction of rotation; small arrows show direction of feed. 1 straight cutting with a centre in the tail stock; 2 tool holder with sharpened tool bit; 3 in thread cutting, speed and feed are geared together; 4 facing off; 5 boring; 6 cutting off is done with slow feed and plenty of cutting oil.

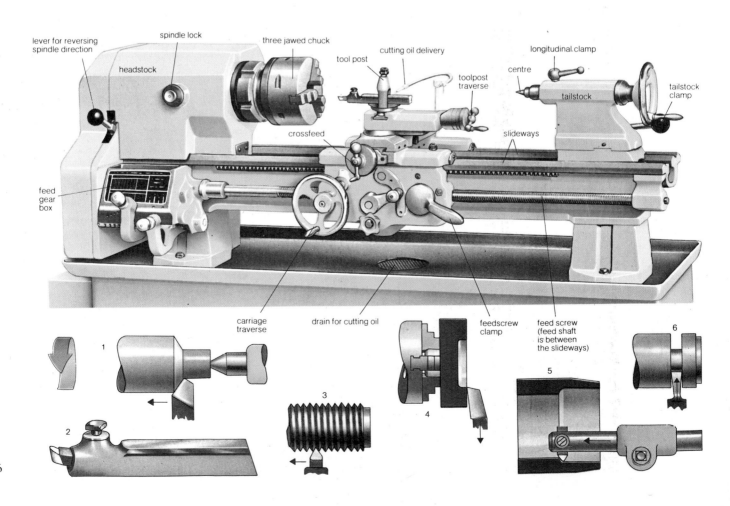

Below: a sleeve being machined in a three-jawed chuck, using a multiple tool-post.

Right: a horizontal milling machine. The work-piece is being held between centres and the dividing head is geared to the lead screw of the table, so that it turns at the right speed as the table moves past the cutter. The result is helical flutes on the piece. Note coolant tubing above the cutter.

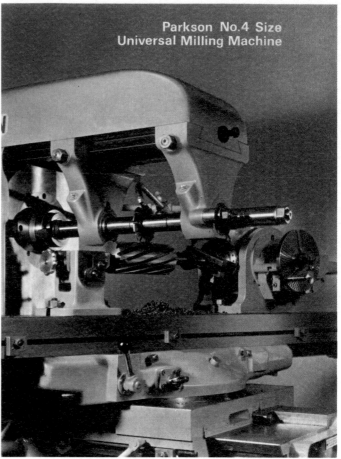

Parkson No.4 Size
Universal Milling Machine

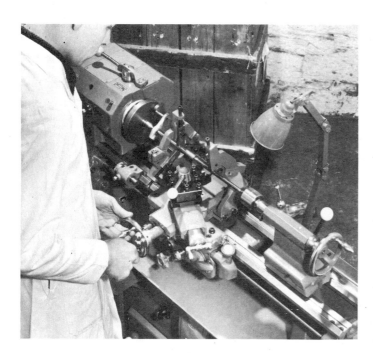

Above: thread cutting. The piece is held being held between centres, using a dragger (lathe dog) on the chuck plate and steady-rests. The spindle speed is slow, but the feed is relatively fast. The tool is specially ground and carefully mounted; the operator makes very small increments with each pass.

Right: a vertical mill. A machine body casting is being finished; cast iron can be machined without coolant.

157

off' the ends so they are square with the diameter; then he cuts a centre-hole in each end of the shaft. The centre holes will be the reference points for the rest of the work to be done on the piece. Then he 'sets up' the work in the lathe between centres. The piece is turned down almost to its major finish diameter, which in this case is the press-fit onto which the rotor will be pushed when the motor is re-assembled. Then the repairman cuts a bearing surface on each end of the shaft, leaving a few thousandths of an inch for the grinding machine after heat treatment. The last lathe operation is cutting a thread on each end of the shaft for the nuts that hold the assembly together. All the edges may be broken with a file while the piece is turning, or *chamferred*, so that none of them are sharp.

Next the shaft is heat-treated. This means heating it in a furnace to a certain temperature; depending on the type of steel being treated, it may be allowed to cool in the air, or it may be *quenched* in a bath of oil or water. Tool steel will be hardened all the way through by heating it to a very high temperature and quenching it in oil. A temperature of several hundred degrees centigrade will cause its molecular structure to change; the quench cools it fast enough so that the change is not reversed. Cold-rolled steel may only be hardened on the outside, which is then called the *case*.

Then the rotor shaft goes to a grinding machine operator,

who puts it between centres again and grinds the finish surfaces to their precise sizes. The shaft is now finished and the motor can be re-assembled.

The repairmen and toolmakers use several different kinds of machine tools in the course of their duties. The lathe, already mentioned, is for cylindrical work. Shapers and planers are for machining flat surfaces, and they are reciprocating machines; that is, the cycle of operation commences with a cutting stroke, followed by a return stroke during which no cutting takes place. The return stroke is speeded up to save time.

In the shaper, a ram advances across the work, which is held in a clamping device or bolted to the work table. The planer is for larger pieces: the work is bolted to a table, which reciprocates under a stationary toolholder.

Unlike these machines, which use a single-point cutting tool, the milling machine uses the rotation and travel of a multi-toothed cutter. The teeth on the cutter do not cut steadily but intermittently, on the side of the cutter being fed into the work. There are two types of milling machines: horizontal and vertical. The horizontal mill uses a flat, round cutter resembling a circular saw blade; the vertical mill uses an end mill, which resembles a twist drill, except that it more teeth, it is flat on the end rather than pointed, and it is more precisely made out of higher quality steel. Both types of machines can be fitted with other types of tools, by means of special collets and chucks. Both types can have automatic table traverse and cross feed; the vertical machine can also have automatic feed up-and-down. Another feature of some machines is an off-set head, which can turn the spindle in an arc as it rotates the tool, allowing eliptical holes and other unusual shapes to be generated.

The use of a dividing head with either type of milling

Below: the shaper. This is a reciprocating machine, which means that cutting takes place only on the forward stroke; the return stroke is speeded up to save time. The planer is a larger machine with a similar action. except that in the planer the tool is stationery and the work table reciprocates. Such machines are used, for example, to rough out blocks of steel from which dies will be made.

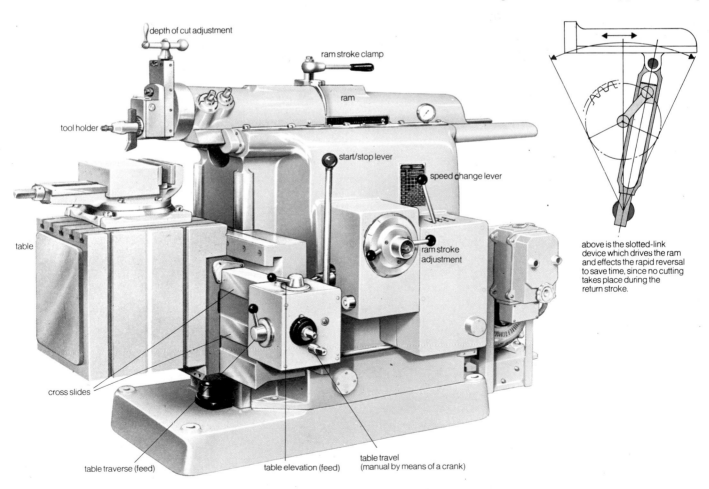

above is the slotted-link device which drives the ram and effects the rapid reversal to save time, since no cutting takes place during the return stroke.

machine renders it more versatile. The dividing head is mounted on the table and has a chucking device which holds the work. It has an indexing crank with a pin which fits into a hole in a plate; the plate has a geometrical arrangement of holes which allows the work to be turned the required number of degrees. There may be several interchangeable plates. If the dividing head is geared to the feed screw of the table, so that the work can be turned as it is fed past the cutter, helical work can be done, such as twist drills or helical gears.

The most elaborate milling machines are used by toolmakers and diesinkers to make the dies that stamp out the big sheet metal parts for the cars. Contoured surfaces can be generated using modified cutters. Jig bores, mill bores, and boring mills are essentially large milling machines, some of them as large as rooms.

Production machinery These machine tools are adapted and automated for the machining of engine blocks, pistons, axles, crankshafts and other solid parts of the cars.

For all the tons of swarf (metal chips) made by metal cutting, more than 90% are from drilling operations. This can be seen from the large number of holes in pieces such as cylinder blocks for internal combustion engines. Where high production is needed, the indexing automatic transfer system may be used, where the component is moved automatically from one machine station to the next. At each station a *unit head* is arranged as required in a vertical, horizontal or angular attitude to the work piece. Each unit head is driven by its own electric motor, and is provided with 'pick-off' gears for the feeding motion instead of an elaborate gearbox. The actual feed may be hydraulic, pneumatic or cam operated, but simplicity of construction keeps repairs to a minimum.

A unit head can be designed and equipped to perform more than one cutting operation. Each head advances at its station and retracts when its cutting job is complete; when all heads have retracted and tripped their respective limit switches, the machine automatically indexes to the next work station. Many such machines are of radial design: the stations are arranged in a circle; the operator stands in one place; each time the machine indexes, the operator removes a finished piece from a fixture and inserts a fresh one.

For greater mass production, the in-line transfer system is used. A typical installation for machining cylinder blocks for Austin cars is 65 feet (20 m) long and has fourteen stations. Its operation commences with a casting picked up by an air-operated carriage which places it on a transfer bar conveyer. The piece is located at the first station. The tools advance, carry out their machining operation, and retire. The piece is then advanced to the next station, located, machined and so on until it reaches the end of the line. Meanwhile other castings are following it. A finished block comes off the end of the line about every four minutes. Such an installation may perform drilling, reaming, tapping, boring, honing and milling operations with only two operators, one to put the casting on the line and one to take off the finished block.

In the meantime, other parts are also being prepared. The pistons are turned in automatic lathes, and are graded according to their precise diameters in steps of perhaps 1/10,000 of an inch.

The connecting rods for the engine have their internal diameters machined and are then cut in half by a power saw, resulting in the rod and its cap, which will fit around the bearing surface on the throw of the crankshaft. These

Two types of surface grinders are shown on this page. On the machine above, the table reciprocates under the grinding wheel. Normally the grinding takes place only during the pass against the direction of the wheel's rotation. The machine does not have automatic feed, but the operator cranks the work toward the wheel in small increments with each pass. Small jobs like this can be carefully done without cooling. The table on the machine below revolves under the wheel; a water soluble coolant is used. Both types have magnetic tables to hold the work.

Left: a grinding machine for cylindrical work. The work turns relativly slowly in the direction opposite to that of the wheel's rotation. Such machines are automated for the generation of bearing surfaces on crankshafts and other mass production.

Below: a transfer bar machine for the automated machining of engine blocks. Machining cast iron results in a gritty powder which gets all over everything, despite the fact that most of it is taken away by the coolant, which is filtered and recycled. Keeping such a place reasonably clean is a big job.

Bottom: Oldsmobile V-8 engine blocks coming off the end of the transfer bar. They are still wet with the water-soluble coolant. There may be as many as 119 machining units on this line; the hydraulic valves and tubing which operate the machinery can be seen on each side.

Below: the hole in the piston is for the gudgeon pin (called 'wrist pin' in the USA) which holds the small end of the connecting rod. Here the operator is air-guaging the bore and grading the pistons in steps of 0.00025 inch.

Bottom: crankshafts picked up by automatic transfer equipment and moved from one conveyer to another.

Right: Leyland engine assembly.

Right centre: an automatic machine with 8 stations for machining Vauxhall Viva connecting rods. Each rod is weighed by the machine and the correct amount of metal is automatically removed from the counter-balance bosses, for final balance in the engine.

Right below: engine assembly at Dagenham.

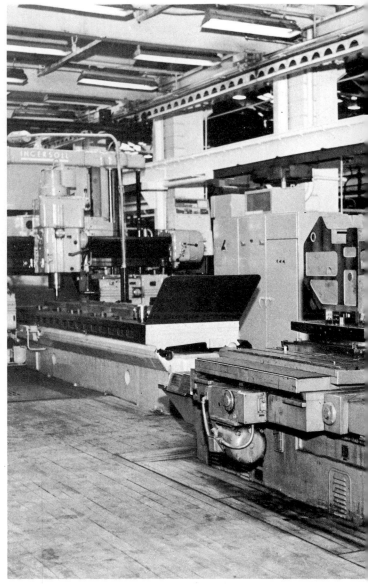

two pieces are a matched set and will stay together through the rest of the machining.

The rear axles are tempered by an automatic electric machine which heats them to a prescribed temperature and quenches them with cold water.

The forged or cast crankshafts have their bearing surfaces ground on automatic machinery: steel fingers reach into the rough grinder, lift the crankshaft out and transfer it to the finish grinder. As the machines run, the grinding wheels wear down. The wheels are automatically 'dressed' by a diamond tool and automatic compensation is made by the machine for their subsequent smaller size.

The crankshaft is turned relatively slowly between centres while the edge of the grinding wheel, which turns in the opposite direction at several thousand of revolutions per minute, is carefully brought to bear. Coolant fluid must be continuously used during heavier grinding operations. Inherent in grinding is the production of heat because of friction; if the surface being ground is allowed to expand because of heat, the wheel will 'dig in', ruining the work and probably causing an accident.

Conditions of careful manufacture, handling and storage of grinding wheels must be adhered to. The wheels are very brittle, and the strength of the bond is limited by the necessity for tiny pieces of the abrasive material to come

loose in the grinding process. The turning speed of the wheel is specified by the manufacturer, and must not be exceeded: tremendous centrifugal force is generated by the high speed, and a disintegrating grinding wheel will cause grave damage to operator and equipment.

The machinery which cuts the gears for the differential is among the most precisely and ingeniously designed equipment in the entire factory. The machine which cuts the crown gear has two cutters; the rough cutter generates the teeth in the gear blank, which must then be precisely indexed for the finish cut; otherwise the cutter teeth will be sheared off like popcorn, a disastrously expensive accident.

In order to cut helical teeth, the chuck which holds the gear blank is indexed for each tooth, and the revolving cutter moves in and out. Not only is the cutter revolving, but the spindle turning the cutter is itself turning slowly in an arc. This amounts to a spindle revolving eccentrically within a larger, hollow spindle. The mathematics for the set-up of such a machine are so complicated that when a new differential is designed, the manufacturer of the machines may use computers to advise the car factory on the set-up.

Machine tool automation Digital readout devices for machine tools are now becoming common. On a lathe, the digital readout screen will have two lines; the inward travel

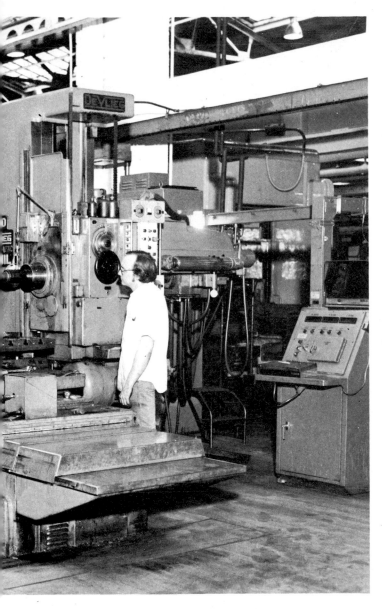

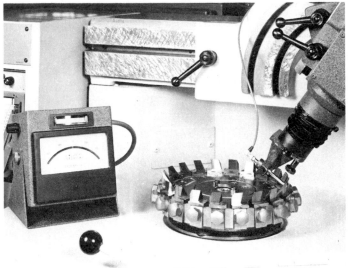

The pictures on this page describe the Gleason gearcutting machinery, built in Rochester, New York, which makes the pinion and crown gears for a car's differential, as described in the text. This type of machinery is among the most complex, precise and best-maintained machinery in the entire factory. A tiny mark anywhere on the gear train inside the machine can result in chatter marks on the finished product, which would mean a noisy differential; repairmen may use a stethoscope to listen to the machine while it is running in order to find such defects.
At top left is a hypoid pinion production centre. The machine automatically processes the pinion from the blank casting to the finish cut.
Lower left: the testing machine, in which the finished gears are run together.
Centre: a vertical milling machine in use at the Gleason works: machines making more machines.
Above: the proximity gauging device for inspecting blades on the cutter itself.

of the tool and the lengthwise travel of the carriage causes transducers to transmit dimensions to the readout device. The operator stops the machine when the required size is reached.

For grinding machines, automatic work sizing is accomplished by a Microtonic feed whereby the wheel head is actuated by an electric stepping motor, controlled by digital information programmed on the control panel. The system uses solid state electronics with printed circuits; the stepping motor can advance the wheel in increments as small as .000025 inch (.006 mm) as finish size is approached.

In plugboard control, the board comprises a grid pattern of holes, each horizontal row representing a machine function. Insertion of plugs completes circuits when scanning by an indexing uniselector, and actuates air cylinders connected to slideways.

Numerical control is economic if used with large machining units in mass production, and if checking, inspection, adjustment and so forth can be kept to a minimum. NC is also used to perform the maximum number of machining operations on a large, complicated work piece. Numerically controlled co-ordinate settings are recorded as a set of 'numbers' on punched tape, which may be paper, film or magnetic tape. The information is 'read' by the machine and transferred into movement of machine heads.

In the 'point to point' system, used for drilling or straight milling, the tool must be at 'A' and perform some operation, then get to point 'B' and so forth. The path of travel between points is not important because no cutting is taking place. In the 'continuous path' the path is important and so is the speed of travel, because this is the actual feed rate, dictated by the type of tool, material being worked and other considerations. A typical tape one inch (25 mm) wide may have eight channels for instructions; the TAB code is a spacer between instructions and EOB means End Of Block, telling the 'reader' to stop the tape and act on instructions up to that point.

Unit heads are in use which can change their own broken or worn-out tools, or change tools in spindles for alternate operations, and machinery is under development which repairs itself. In addition, non-machining processes are in use for certain applications, such as ultrasonic grinding, laser and electrochemical metal removal.

The Final Assembly

The assembly line is the basis of modern mass production methods, enabling large quantities of goods to be produced at relatively low cost. In the automobile industry, the mass production techniques first used by Henry Ford have brought car ownership within the reach of millions of people. One of the earliest examples of mass production was in 16th century Venice, where a reserve fleet of 100 galleys was stored in prefabricated sections ready for assembly when needed. But true mass production did not really develop until the 19th century when it was used by Eli Whitney and Samuel Colt for the manufacture of guns.

The basis of the assembly line is repetitive work. Each worker does the same simple task over and over again as the work moves past on some sort of conveyer. Time-study analysis is important here; the various jobs must be as efficient and economical as possible, and many things must be taken into consideration. For example, it may seem obvious that the worker who installs the headlamp on one side of the car has enough time to install the other one as well, but the time it takes to cross in front of each car and back again has to be taken into consideration.

In one case, a time study expert decided that both headlamps could be installed by one person. He neglected to take into consideration that at that point on the final assembly line there was a pit underneath the car where other people were working. The employee involved would have had to jump back and forth across the pit all day.

Time study, or work study, was the brainchild of F W Taylor, an American who was a friend and associate of Henry Ford. Like many idealists, his faith in human nature was touching, his knowledge of it somewhat inadequate. He treated the human body as though it possessed no consciousness, assuming that the average worker was not very bright, yet expected the worker to share in the increased profits accruing from more efficient work. The dehumanizing effect of repetitive work is only now being dealt with by means of experiments in work sharing, team work and so forth. And the natural tendency of many early industrialists was to keep all the profits for themselves. One of the most important functions of the labour union is the organization of the workers so that a balance of power can be maintained, yet for many years such unions were not even legal. In any case, there can be no doubt that Taylor and Ford between

Left: a multi-spindle radial drilling machine, drilling holes in brake linings. Each spindle has its own electric motor; travel of the spindle is controlled by an electric limit switch.

them invented a technique which has resulted in an outpouring of consumer goods and a material standard of living unique in history.

Sub-assembly A car factory contains a large number of assembly points; the body line, as we have seen, is one of them. Each car factory has its own method of building cars; for example, the trim line may be part of the body division or it may be the initial part of the final assembly line. In either case, the 'trim' can be loosely defined as those parts of the car which are not part of the drive train.

The trim can be fitted as soon as the paint on the body is dry. It includes any chrome strips or name plates fastened to the outside of the body, which are usually attached by means of clips through holes in the sheet metal. It includes all of the interior upholstery: carpets or rubber mats on the floor, seats, padding on the instrument panel, door panels, headliner and so forth. Window glass, door handles and their associated mechanical linkage, the fuel tank and many other parts may be installed on the trim line.

The steel part of the instrument panel may be part of the body, with padding, instruments and so forth added later, or the entire instrument panel may be pre-assembled and added on the final assembly line.

The car as it reaches the final assembly line may be regarded as a sub-assembly itself.

Engines are usually assembled on a fixture which can be turned for the convenience and efficiency of the assemblers.

In order to assemble a particularly quiet differential, the

Left: a multiple exposure of an automatic machine tool in operation. Up to 24 different tools are stored on the drum in the required sequence of use; the rotating arm selects them one at a time and brings them to bear on the work.

Right top: automatic boring of bearing components.

Right centre: a rotary transfer machine. The operator stands in the foreground, removing finished pieces from the fixtures and inserting fresh ones. The table indexes one station each time and the four work-heads all perform their function at once.

Right below: automatic production of pistons for diesel engines, using a diamond cutting tool. The electric motor on the machine drives the lathe spindle through a friction clutch, and also drives the bar on which the cutting tool is mounted by means of a drum with channels on it. The channels act like cams on a peg which is connected to the bar.

165

Above: the Mercedes-Benz 200 to 280 E series is assembled at Sindelfingen, near Stuttgart.

Left: Italian workers in the Innocenti factory, Milan, assembling British Austin A40 cars. Preparing for entry into the Common Market, the British Motor Corporation established a sales and service office in Geneva and began shipping car components to Italy. The car industry today, like nearly all industries, is an international one; but a combination of economic, social and political problems have been crippling Britain's ability to sell its products abroad. A Ford door assembly line in England makes many fewer units a day than an identical line across the channel in Belgium; yet the problem cannot simply be blamed on the workers.

Above right: paint inspection at Vauxhall Motors in Luton, England.

Right: a Cadillac is tested under simulated conditions on a dynamometer. It is 'driven' up to 70 mph (112 km/h).

Above: in the 'pit' on an American Motors assembly line.

Right: American Motors' Kenosha, Wisconsin plant is one of the biggest in the world, because nearly all the company's output is under one roof. Here the engine and rear axle assembly are trundled around the roller conveyer to go up into the car in one smooth operation.

pinion and crown gears are lapped together in a lapping machine which duplicates the operating conditions of the completed differential. After lapping, the two gears are kept together as a set. They are inspected together in a machine in a quiet room which determines the exact thickness of shims (sheet metal discs used to ensure a close fit) required in the assembly to ensure quiet operation; then they go to the differential assembly line. All the gears in the system are installed against roller bearings, the proper shimming is installed; then the unit is test-run, filled with a heavy oil and sealed. Quiet operation of the differential is essential in a vehicle with unit-body construction, as opposed to a separate body bolted to a frame, because noise from the differential will be transmitted by the body itself.

Final assembly   The final assembly line is the culmination of the whole process. Here all of the sub-assemblies come together, nowadays often directed by computer, and the cars drive away from the end of the line under their own power. A single assembly line may produce 1500 cars a week, taking anywhere up to 90 minutes travel on the line for each car, depending on how much trim remains to be added at this stage. If the final assembly line includes virtually all of the trim, it can be nearly a mile long. Parts and small sub-assemblies from all over the factory are delivered by conveyer to the final assembly department, carefully timed to arrive at the right time, or they may be delivered in steel tubs or on wooden or steel pallets by fork lift trucks. Many parts of the car are not made by the car factory at all, but are bought from outside suppliers, which may or may not be partially owned by the car factory. These items vary from one manufacturer to another, but can include the instruments, steering column, lights, radiators, gearboxes, and the *harness*, which is the assembly

of wires and is usually mounted on the firewall behind the engine. Part of the assembly process is the connecting of the wires to terminals for lights and instruments all over the car.

The underside of the car is fitted out by the workers in the pit, including the silencer [muffler], tubing for fuel and brake fluid and so on.

The most dramatic part of the final assembly line is where the engine joins the rest of the car. Again, each manufacturer has his own way of doing it. One typically convenient way of doing it is as follows: the rear axle assembly complete with differential, the drive shaft and the engine arrive separately at a small sub-assembly area next to the main line, where they are bolted together. (The gearbox is already bolted on to the back end of the engine.) Then they are dragged around a curving section of a conveyer, on rollers, which steeply rises as the assembly mates with the underside of the car. Assembly-line workers are standing ready to fit nuts, washers and other parts on to downward protruding bolts as the heavy steel plate on to which the engine is mounted fits over them.

In one car factory some years ago, a group of employees tried to obtain a car loaded with every conceivable optional

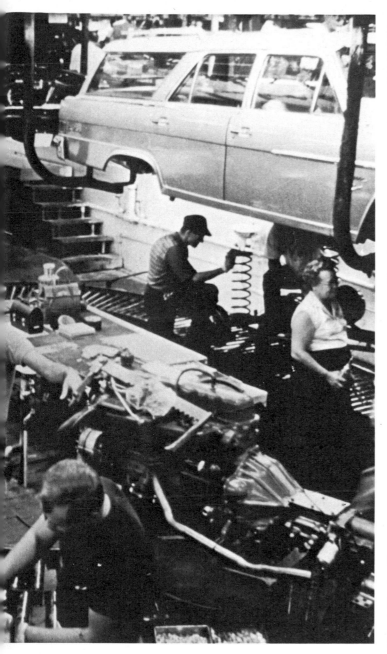

Right top: an AMC Pacer near the end of the line. Soon it will be driven away under its own power.

Right centre: a British Leyland car is lowered onto its engine. Note the cross-engine layout.

Right below: the Chevrolet Camaro has a separate frame with the engine mounted on it; the body and the frame come together on the assembly line for the first time. This method of assembly leaves the bumper and grille until later. Insulation is used between body and frame to prevent squeaks.

Next page: a French Renault final assembly line.

extra at a stripped-down price, and with an employee discount at that. The computer-printed broadcast sheet attached to the bumper of the car gave no hint of what was going on; the plan required the cooperation of a great many people up and down the line. It was only foiled because the 'souped-up' engine wouldn't fit into the car at that point in the assembly, causing a great deal of confusion. In the end, several people lost their jobs.

169

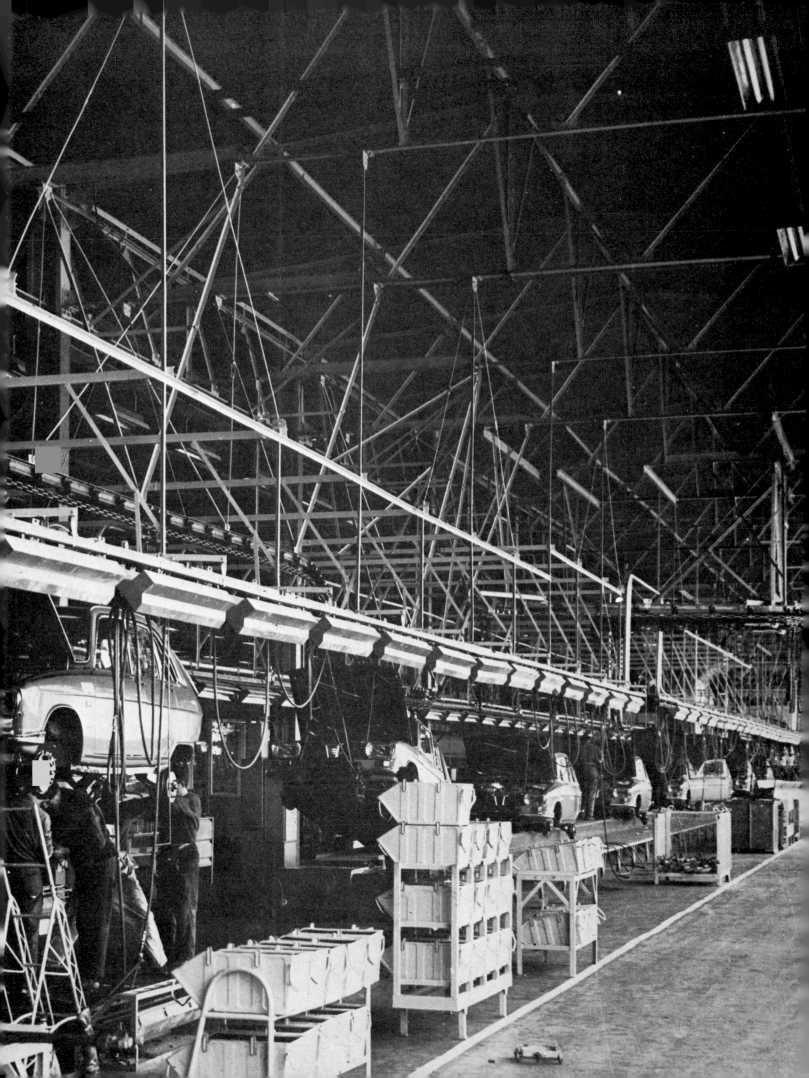

The sequence of pictures on these six pages describe the production of a brand-new car, the Chevrolet Vega 2300, which is built at Lordstown, Ohio.

The unitized body starts here, where the floor pan and other sheet metal parts are placed in fixtures for welding.

Automatic welding equipment, similar to that in the picture on page 153, places 95 per cent of the 3900 welds on each Vega body.

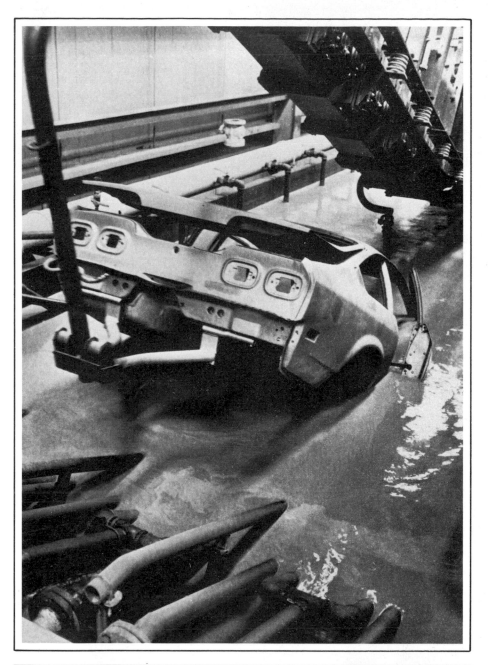

The body is dipped in a tank containing 65,000 gallons (US) and the electrically charged particles of paint reach all the bare metal surfaces.

Each body undergoes a four-minute deluge to check the tightness of body seals.

The Vega's engine has an aluminium block. The engine and rear axle assembly are lifted hydraulically by a 'dolly' which travels along at the same speed as the body: about 30 feet (9m) per minute.

Hydraulic machinery is used extensively in the car factory, for example to operate the transfer bar machines in the machining division (see the pictures on page 170). Hydraulic power depends upon the fact that liquids are relatively incompressible. Electric motors drive pumps which supply the pressure of the fluid; valves operated by electronic solenoid switches distribute the pressure to the rams or pistons, which are connected to the machinery to be moved. The hydraulic fluid is an oil of high quality which must be kept clean, because the valves are precision instruments and both valve actuators and rams are surrounded by neoprene piston rings to keep the oil from leaking past; grit in the oil would quickly cause these to need replacement. The oil is a light mineral or castor based oil which has a low freezing point and also acts as a lubricant. The pressures vary from 1000 to 5000 psi.

The air-operated wrench is similar to that used at Leyland (see page 169).

The grill is made of plastic, attached by a small air wrench.

The car touches the floor for the first time. The next installation is the bumper and valance.

Hatchbacks up and doors open, the cars receive their seats and carpeting. The plastic sheet on the fender protects the paint from scratches while the car is finished.

Straddled by giant vents to remove exhaust, the car is test-run on a road simulator which duplicates any normal driving condition.

The Vega heads for another inspection area under its own power.

Ready for shipment, each car has passed about 50 inspections and five different functional tests as a completed unit.

A new shipping technique called Vert-A-Pac stows 30 cars nose-down in a completely enclosed railway carriage.

Above: Ford products leaving Wayne County, Michigan. Car haulage is a lucrative sideline to the industry.

Next page: retirement village in the Arizona desert.

Above: a Pontiac body lowered onto its separate frame.

Below: wheel nuts tightened up.

Bottom: each manufacturer has a method of anti-corrosion treatment in addition to the paint undercoat. Here the box structure of the car is being injected with a wax containing anti-rust additives.

If the assembly line has to stop for any reason during working hours, a light goes on in the offices of the higher-ups, who immediately want to know what the problem is. For 'down time' results in thousands of people standing around doing nothing, and getting paid for it. This is one reason why the arrival at the assembly point of the right parts at the right time is one of the most important functions in the car factory.

Long before any assembly begins, an order commissioning the car has been printed by the computer, and the colour, trim specifications and other information about the finished car are already known. Cars for export may have left-hand or right-hand drive; they may have specially-built engines for countries where high-octane fuel is not available. The combinations of specifications to which a car can be built are almost without limit.

All up and down the line, power tools, operated usually by compressed air, are used to tighten up nuts and bolts. Each tool is adjustable to provide the right amount of torque. If the tool is a large and heavy one, it is suspended from the ceiling on a pulley, and counter-balanced (this is true of the spot-welding device in the body division as well).

As the car reaches the end of the assembly line, the wheels are put on and the nuts tightened with a power tool, probably operated by compressed air; the radiator is filled with year-round coolant and sealed; and some fuel is pumped into the tank. (This last operation is carried out in a strictly no-smoking area.) Then, if all goes well, the car starts.

The car is given a check-out on a dynamometer, which in this case consists of rollers built into the floor so that the car can be 'driven' without going anywhere. The brakes and brakelights are tested here, as well as the gearchanges.

The headlamps are adjusted, all the lights are checked, the steering alignment is set up, and the engine fitments are adjusted on the 'tune-up' line. If there is anything seriously wrong, the car goes to a final repair department; otherwise it is driven to a company parking lot to await shipment to a dealer. Transport charges within the country of origin are usually the same within a wide area, so that customers who happen to live far away from the factory are not unduly penalized. Some car companies will allow a customer to pick up his own car, thus avoiding transport charges altogether.

Pictures supplied by
Endpapers: Camera Press; Opposite title page (making pig iron) Ford UK; Pages 2–3 Camera Press; 4–5 American Motors Corp. USA; 6–7 Popperfoto; 8 Ford UK; 9 Scala; 10–11 TL&C/National Motor Museum TR/Tecnisches Museum; 15 T/General Motors C/Fiat; 16 Science Museum; 17 Rover; 18–19 Jan P. Norbye; 20–21 TL/Radio Times Hulton Picture Library C/Ford UK BL/GES Germany BC/Hart Associates BR/Enfield Automotive; 22 Staatsbibliotek Berlin; 24 T/National Motor Museum B/Staatsbibliotek Berlin; 25 Ford UK; 26 Camera Press; 27 T/Ford UK CR/Shell Research—photo: Paul Brierley; 28 T/Rolls-Royce B/Colour Library International; 29 Radio Times Hulton Picture Library B/Bettman Archive; 30 T/Triplex Safety Glass B/Jan P. Norbye; 31 Daily Telegraph Magazine; 32–33 BC&BR/Camera Press CR/Wilmot Breedon; 34–35 (Fiat emissions lab) Jan P. Norbye; 36–37 General Motors; 37 T/Ford USA; 38–39 TL&TC&TR/Leyland C/Rolls-Royce; 41 BL/Central Press Photos Inc. CR/Model and Allied Publications Ltd. BR/Leyland; 45 Ford UK; 46 T/National Motor Museum B/General Motors USA; 48 SU Carburettors; 50–51 Joseph Lucas Ltd.—photo: Mike St Maur Sheil; 51 T/Porsche; 52 Hart Associates C/Porsche; 54 TL&TR/Esso CR/Tecalemit; 55 Grundy—photo: Mike St Maur Sheil; 56–57 Rolls-Royce; 57 T/Motor Magazine; 58 Perkins; 59 Cummins; 62 Picturepoint; 64 Paul Brierley; 65 Automotive Products Ltd.; 66 T/Morse ® Borg-Warner; 67 Ford UK; 70–71 Borg-Warner; 71 Science Museum—photo: Chris Barker; 75 Hart Associates; 77 T/ Centrax Gears Ltd. B/Photri; 78 Radio Times Hulton Picture Library; 80 Ferodo Ltd.; 82 Automotive Products Ltd.; 83 TL/Science Museum —photo: Michael Holford TR/Spectrum; 84 Vauxhall; 88–89 TL&C/ Michael Holford BL/Hart Associates TR/Ford UK; 91 T/Goodyear Ohio B/Dunlop; 92–93 Goodyear Ohio; 95 AC Delco; 97 AC Delco— photo: Michael Newton; 99 C/Champion R/Bosch Ltd.; 100 Science Museum—photo: Chris Barker; 103 Joseph Lucas Ltd.; 104 Hart Associates; 105 AC Delco; 106 Smiths Industries; 107 'Motor'; 108 Smiths Industries; 109 C/John Watney B/Smiths Industries; 110 Crypton; 111 T&BR/Crypton BL/Volkswagen; 113 TL&TR/Staatsbibliotek Berlin B/Colour Sport; 114 Mike Cornwell; 115 Daymark; 118 T/Mike Cornwell B/Anastasios White; 119 LC/Photo Library of Australia B/Susan Griggs Agency—photo: Mike Holland; 120–130 Jan P. Norbye; 132 T/Barnaby's B/Ford UK; 133 Ford UK; 134 TL,C&BL/Council of Industrial Design; 135 Ford UK LC/Spectrum B/Hart Associates; 136–37 TL/Paul Brierley TC&BC/Vauxhall BR/Leyland; 138 T/Leyland B/Erik Johnson; 139 Ford UK; 140–41 TL/Ford UK BL&C/British Steel R/ASEA; 142 British Steel; 143 Quay Dynamics Ltd.; 144 TL&B/British Steel TR/ Alumasc; 146 British Steel; 147 GKN Forgings Ltd.; 148–49 TL,C&R/ Vauxhall BL/ZEFA/Pictor; 150 Ford UK; 151 T/American Motors Corp. USA B/Ford UK; 152–53 TL&C/Ford UK TR/General Motors USA BR/Fiat; 154 TL&C/General Motors USA CL/Wolff, Laing & Christie B/Ford UK; 155 BNFMRA—photo: Paul Brierley; 156 Boxford Machine Tools Ltd.; 157 TL/ C M Dixon TR/T Parkinson & Son Ltd. BL/Boxford Machine Tools Ltd. BR/Cincinnati Milacron; 159 T/C M Dixon B/ Herbert Machine Tools Ltd.; 160 TL/Cincinnati Milacron CR/Leyland B/Ford UK; 161 TR/Leyland CL&CR/Vauxhall BL&BR/Ford UK; 162–63 Gleason Works Rochester NY; 164–65 L/Cincinnati Milacron C/J Allan Cash TR/Bardon Co. CR/Herbert Machine Tools Ltd. BR/ Sunday Telegraph; 166 T/Erik Johnson B/Camera Press; 167 T/Vauxhall B/General Motors USA; 168–9 T/American Motors Corp. USA CR/ Leyland BR/General Motors USA; 170–71 Camera Press; 172–77 General Motors USA; 178 TL/General Motors USA TR/Ford USA CL/Broom-wade Ltd. BL/Wolff, Laing & Christie; 179 Bavaria Verlag

Art works
Pages 12–14 (across bottom) Typographics; 12–14 Ben Manchipp; 22–23 Ken Lewis; 43–44 Tom McArthur; 45 Eric Jewell Assoc.; 47 Tom McArthur; 49, 53 & 55 Allard Graphic Arts; 57 Frank Kennard; 60 John Bishop; 63 Frank Kennard; 66 Tom McArthur; 68 John Bishop; 72, 75T & 76 Tom McArthur; 75B Frank Kennard; 79–80 Tom McArthur; 81 Frank Kennard/Girling; 83 Frank Kennard; 85 Tom McArthur; 86–95 Osborne/Marks; 96 Allard Graphic Arts; 98 Osborne/Marks; 100 Eric Jewell Assoc.; 101 Tom McArthur; 102 Osborne/Marks; 107 Tom McArthur; 116–17 John Bishop; 135 Allard Graphic Arts; 142 Thomson Santer; 156 & 158 Frank Kennard